TOWARD A FEDERATED NATION:

IMPLEMENTING NATIONAL CIVICS STANDARDS

By

Robert Gutierrez, Ed. D.

Gravitas/Civics Books

This is a non-fiction work for instructional purposes and to inform a general audience of educational issues.

Published by

Robert Gutierrez

Tallahassee, FL

Ebook ISBN: 978-1-7345813-0-0

Print ISBN: 978-1-7345813-1-7

Cover photo of Florida Capitol by Robert Gutierrez

Dedicated to my wife,

Cinda Huntzinger Gutierrez

About the Author

Robert Gutierrez is a former educator who retired from Florida State University where he was an assistant professor in the School of Education. In his career he taught students at every level from seventh graders to doctoral students. He performed educational tasks from hall duty to supervising dissertations. He also worked nearly three years at the City of Miami in its youth programs during the late 1970s. He is the author of various professional journal articles including the following:

"Our Federalist Roots: A Neglected Past?" *Theory and Research in Social Education,*

"Moral Code for the Current Secular State of Affairs." *Education,*

"The Predisposition of High School Students to Engage in Collective Strategies of Problem-Solving." *Theory and Research in Social Education,*

"The Prevailing Construct in Civic[s] Education and Its Problems." *Action in Teacher Education,*

"Rekindling Concerns over Moral Politics in the Classroom." *The Social Studies,*

"What Can Happen to Auspicious Beginnings: Historical Barriers to Ideal Citizenship." *The Social Studies.*

Acknowledgements:

The writer of this account owes a great deal to a good number of people. The timeline regarding these relationships stretches back to his high school days when he was taught by Christian Brothers, at LaSalle High School in Miami, Florida. Then he was fortunate to encounter very influential professors at Florida State University. The latter group includes the late Charles H. Adair, who introduced this writer to the importance of abstract thinking.

Also having a profound effect were the professors of his doctoral program at Florida International University, including Judith S. Slater and Stephen M. Fain. Their instruction in Curricular Studies helped shape the pedagogical content of this book. In terms of the book's political content, this writer wants to express his gratitude to the late Daniel J. Elazar – considered "Mister Federalism" during his day – and to Donald S. Lutz, who served on this writer's doctoral committee.

Dr. Lutz was instrumental in making this writer question and critique political science's bias supporting behavioral studies. He also influenced this writer to consider a more historical approach to the study of politics as legitimate. This influenced not only how this writer sees the study of politics but also how he perceives morality.

Of special note is the help the writer's long-standing friend, Steven H. Woolard, provided. He has been not only a partner in many a political conversation through the years but also served as a reader of this manuscript. His comments and suggestions were given full attention. He had a career not only in education but also ran an agricultural dealership for years. A special note of gratitude needs to be extended to Sarah Drake Brown of Ball State University who initially suggested the path this book took.

But naturally, none of these mentors, teachers, or friends are in any way responsible for any shortcomings the reader might ascribe to this work. And a last note, but of prime importance to this author, is the patience, input, and proofreading his wife has rendered this account. Cinda H. Gutierrez is owed a great deal of credit not only in the production of this book, but in allowing the author the time and other necessary resources such an effort demands.

TABLE OF CONTENTS

INTRODUCTION   13

1. C3 FRAMEWORK OF STANDARDS   27

2. APPLYING FEDERATION THEORY   59

3. A LOCAL POLITICAL CHALLENGE,
     THE OPIOID CRISIS   104

4. A NATIONAL POLITICAL CHALLENGE,
     TORT LAW   138

5. AN INTERNATIONAL ISSUE,
     FOREIGN TRADE   180

6. CONCLUSION   221

BIBLIOGRAPHY   243

Preface

The overall goal of this book, *Toward a Federated Nation*, is to apply a political mental construct to the study of civics, both in the courses entitled civics and American government. School systems offer civics mostly to middle school students and American government to high schoolers. In either case, the involved educators are charged with the responsibility of encouraging good citizenship by advocating it and imparting to their young students the knowledge necessary to become good citizens throughout their lives.

To understand the claims of this book, the reader needs to understand the function of a mental construct. A people need a central view of governance and politics to establish and maintain a political system. That view is a mental construct, a man-made model that basically describes and explains what governments are and why they exist. Not everyone agrees with how these concerns should be considered and, therefore, they do not all share the same mental construct.

This book claims that the origins and maintenance of the American system were based on a political mental construct known as federalism – a view based on the formulation of a polity through either a covenant or a compact. This book will explain what that means, but for the purposes of this Preface, the reader should simply see the formulation of this instrument – the government – as the product of a people coming together – directly or through representation – and writing out an associational agreement that sets up a partnership.

To the extent that the populace lives by the agreement, it is a federated people exhibiting the attributes of a grand partnership. A partnership honestly felt presupposes quite a few social qualities. They include a true sense of communal bonds, a value orientation toward advancing the common good, a respect for the legitimate interests of its members, and a general understanding that each member's long-term interests are indelibly tied to the survival and advancement of the partnership: what the late eminent political scientist, Daniel J. Elazar, called, federalism's processes.

The book further argues that for most of the nation's history, Americans held federalism as the dominant construct – that they saw governance and politics through federalist lenses. This changed after World War II. In years after that great war, Americans have drifted away from that sense of partnership toward an ever more expansive adoption of another construct. That is the natural rights view. This latter view heightens individualism and places a form of liberty – defined self-centeredly – at the forefront of its political leanings.

What is a civics teacher to do? This book attempts to begin – some might argue, continue – the effort to regenerate a more viable civic outlook among Americans. If this is worthwhile, then one needs to seriously ask: what is possible? What can educators, civics teachers, realistically set out to do? One mistake would be to think "the good old days" can be resurrected. They cannot be and should not be.

The older version of federalist thinking has had its day and it cannot be seriously considered viable by present day educators. For one thing, that vision was highly parochial and unjustly excluded various ethnic and racial groups from the partnership – at least in terms of the partnership's benefits. Traditional/parochial federalism needs to be left in the past. Instead, a newer version can be defined and implemented for current civic conditions; the nation's schools, parents, other citizens, groups, and organizations can opt for what this book calls liberated federalism.

Liberated federalism, as a mental construct, can guide the nation's civics curriculum. And current educational developments in civics provide an opportunity. That is, the National Council for the Social Studies' civics standards (C3 Framework) have been issued in recent years. The effort here first critiques the standards; second, it reviews how the proposed construct – mostly referred to as federation theory – can guide the implementation of that framework.

To further advance application of the construct, three "unit" chapters follow in which the construct is further explained, and lesson ideas are shared. Each unit highlights an issue that challenges federalist values: the opioid crisis, tort law, and foreign trade and its effects on job availability. The book concludes with a further overview of the construct and a review of the instructional advice that the book promotes.

Prime audiences for this book are civics teachers, social studies teachers, and college students in social studies' teacher preparation programs. In addition, school administrators (especially those in charge of curriculum), state and federal administrators, concerned parents, and concerned community advocates are also targeted by what the book offers. While academics in the social studies are not considered as this book's primary or even secondary audience, they might find its ideas worthy of consideration as they define for themselves what their field should strive to accomplish.

This author feels the book should be incorporated in teacher preparation course work, especially those courses that instruct students concerning curricular matters and, to a lesser degree, instructional matters. The strengths of this presentation are:
- a focus on the content of secondary civics courses (with some attention to instructional strategies),
- a utilization of current political/economic/social concerns and problems that engaged citizens can address through political action, and

- an incorporation of the NCSS standards (that were developed through the federal government Common Core project).

These goals encompass various skill areas: analyzing relevant historical knowledge, developing verbal interaction skills in discussions, arguments, and debates, and familiarizing and improving oneself in political engagement activities. This book addresses each of these skill sets.

Hopefully, the reader will find these areas of involvement as not only interesting but also worthy of a level of excitement that politics has engendered among so many fellow citizens. There's a serious playground out there that deals in efforts to improve the partnership and, by doing so, to improve the nation.

Note: At various points in the text of this book, the terms footnote(s) and endnote(s) are used to refer to citations. The paperback version of the book uses footnotes and the ebook version uses endnotes.

INTRODUCTION

Teaching at any level is a complex endeavor. That is particularly true when one considers professional teaching. Most books, articles, and other literature dedicated to teaching usually emphasize the processes of teaching. That literature often reflects a basic division between those who advocate traditional, didactic methodologies (based on strategies that present information) and those who advocate inquiry approaches (based on strategies that have students discover information).

This book comments on these approaches as they relate to civics education, but the thrust of this account is not instructional processes but rather instructional content. Its writer believes that the problems of civics – which are reviewed below – have to do with what schools are teaching students, not about how the lessons are being taught. Therefore, to begin this account, a word about how teachers, school administrators, state and national officials, and academics view the content is offered.

A simple general notion is that to teach something, one needs to have an overall view of what that something is. To teach physics, for example, a teacher needs a view of what physics is in terms of how the subject is structured, the processes its practitioners use, the function the subject serves (mostly discovering the principles, generalizations, and information constituting its studied content), and the context in which it exists.

Such concerns are usually encapsulated within a theory – the theory that high school physics uses is known as Newtonian physics. A theory is a mental construct – invented by the human mind. A theory has significant evidence to support it as being a viable explanation of the subject matter. Having stated that, one should not forget that a theory or its elements can be disproven or found to be not sufficiently comprehensive of the subject matter (hence, for professional physicists, Einsteinian physics is more encompassing of physical reality than Newtonian physics).

A general explanation that is logical and has evidence to support it, but not to the degree a theory has, is known as a model. The social sciences, as opposed to the natural sciences, usually are dependent on models (human behavior, it turns out, is more difficult to predict). Despite this technical distinction, the term theory will be used in this account – it's more in common use – to indicate a social model or two.

This account's basic claim is that the current dominant construct, the natural rights theory, is deficient for instructional purposes in the field of civics education and should be replaced by federation theory. The origin of federation theory can be found well entrenched in the nation's history – more on this below.

One should not underestimate the challenge this change represents. It not only involves changing one's mind about some common concerns, but also includes changing entire perceptions, emotions, values, and other strongly held beliefs. Civics education is important; the nation's democracy depends on a viable, civics education program. Its governing construct, therefore, should be given serious thought even under ideal conditions.

But civics is in bad shape. Of late, to illustrate, the *CBS Sunday Morning Show* cited statistics indicating the American public is lacking in governmental knowledge and is exhibiting low levels of civil behavior – this reflects poorly on civics educational efforts.[1] This account reviews various indicators of this claim including low levels of political knowledge, participation, and other factors including the upsurge of mass killings.

---

[1] To see an introductory news account of this state of affairs, see "Why It Matters," *CBS Sunday Morning Show.*

An extensive review of these civic indicators can be found online. There, the reader can find an "online Appendix" to this book that reviews various indicators supporting this overall evaluation.[2] The nation's political environment provides ample evidence to support this general observation.

To name one observation, some justifiably cite that the nation's politics is becoming tribalistic[3] and this, in turn, suggests that civics needs transformative change if one holds, as an ideal, that the nation should have a citizenry being federated within itself.

Yet among educators, journalists, and other commentators there is a lack of ability to identify, much less elaborate on what civics educators need to do to actuate effective reform. That commentary lacks the following: knowledge as to why the problem exists; a realization that what is needed goes beyond teaching methods to how civics' content is perceived; and an appreciation that the problems of civics education are tied to societal conditions that are often accepted as "that's just the way things are."

But there is a source of hope, i.e., the National Council for the Social Studies (NCSS), the professional organization of social studies educators, has issued a set of standards that, under its call for civic virtue, promotes a view of governance and politics one can associate with being more collaborative,

---

[2] An overall report of the state of civics education can be found online. That report is entitled "How Effective Is Civics Education?" This account makes references to this report at various points in its text. To gain access to the report, which is considered an Appendix to this book, the reader can use the following URL: http://gravitascivics.blogspot.com/. It directs the reader to all online cited readings author offers to augment the content of this book. The site is to the author's blog, *Gravitas: A Voice for Civics*, and the reader needs to access that blog's posting for October 23, 2021. That posting is entitled "A Digression."

[3] Jonah Goldberg, *Suicide of the West*.

communal, and federated. Referred to here as the C3 Framework[4] – a shortened title – it is part of the US Department of Education's Common Core project.

It can also be judged as a recognition by civics educators that the state of that curriculum is in bad shape.[5] Again, for further evidence of this unhealthy state of civics, see the online Appendix – "How Effective Is Civics Education?" – of this book. That is a comprehensive and extended report that one can find online.[6]

One should consider that unlike other school subjects, the results of civics education are readily observable. One need only look around and see how well the nation's citizenry acts. While many factors can affect this observation – such as the state of the contemporary economy – overall, one can gauge how readily the citizenry exhibits good citizenship. For example, does one see or hear knowledgeable political discourse or observe general civility?

One, in the course of daily life, usually has the pleasure of encountering pleasant and good-hearted people, and the claim here is not otherwise. What this account is saying, in relation to the nation's body politic, is that there are ample examples of fellow citizens who are lacking good citizenship qualities and ultimately that negatively affects the quality of American politics.

Of late, one can experience too many instances of dysfunctional civic behavior. Worse, too many people have counterproductive views of what should characterize good, public servants.[7] The online Appendix, looking at indicators of good

---

[4] National Council for the Social Studies, *Preparing Students for College, Career, and Civic* Life, *C3*.
[5] Of note, this effort is being initiated when fewer than ten states call for civics being part of their state testing program. See "Civics Education Testing only Required in 9 States for High School Graduation: CIRCLE Study," *Huff Post*.
[6] Reminder: this report can be found at an online site with the following URL: http://gravitascivics.blogspot.com/ , October 23, 2021.

citizenship, reports, for example, that only about 40% of the electorate vote in mid-term elections. Given how undemanding voting is, such findings reflect poorly on civics education.

But by way of context, unfortunately, civics does not stand alone in this regrettable state. This judgement of civics can be readily lost in practically an onslaught of negative reports concerning schools.[8] This account will not expend a lot of space to make this more general claim, but it should be cited and kept in mind as one considers civics education.

In addition, civics does not seem to garner the sense of importance other subjects enjoy. For example, one hears about a general acceptance that schools need to improve their STEM (science, technology, engineering, and mathematics) offerings. The general public seems to be accepting that pursuit, at least according to media reports. To date, there has not been a comparable call among the citizenry for improvements in civics.[9]

There are other factors at play – for example, there is not one educational system, but fifty state systems. These factors complicate any efforts at reform. This book's charge is to address the civics' portion of this problem and below, this Introduction offers an overview of how this account will attempt to do so; but before that, this writer wishes to emphasize that real reform cannot be accomplished unless civics educators adopt a different view of the subject. The view currently dominant – the natural rights view – stands in the way of what needs to be done.

---

[7] For example, see Dvorak, "The Epic Fail of the American Electorate," *The Washington Post*.

[8] While different reports vary somewhat, the US ranks about seventeenth in its schools' success rates when compared to other national systems. For example, see Wilde, "Global Grade: How Do U.S. Students Compare?" *Great Schools*.

[9] To be accurate, some prominent citizens – e.g., former Senator Bob Graham and former Supreme Court Justice Sandra Day O'Connor – have become active in promoting improvements in the nation's civics offerings. But this list does not indicate an extensive number of people being so involved.

By calling upon civics educators to adopt another perspective, this book asks educators to accept an alternative view of governance and politics. This other view aligns with the nation's history but provides an updated version to address its earlier shortcomings and to meet current realities. This other view can be called liberated federalism. In this book, the more encompassing term, federation theory, is used to denote this construct.

Listing of This Account's Content

Chapter 1 describes the prescriptions of the C3 Framework and critically reviews its provisions and how it can advance the scope of federation theory and the process of an inquiry approach. Chapter 2, by describing federation theory as a view of governance and politics suitable to guide civics instruction, will begin that effort by pointing out how it can promote the NCSS's effort to improve civics in American classrooms.

Hopefully, this Introduction encourages the reader to consider that transformative change is needed in civics education. But before this account advances any further, a point needs to be made. These cited deficiencies are not the blame of any one segment of the educational establishment – and that includes the teacher corps. These problems reflect systemic and cultural problems. These problems demand transformative change (changes in attitudes and values) and that is never easily or quickly accomplished.

As a matter of fact, the approach that is described and explained within these pages will probably need to be worked on over years for it to be fully implemented. For example, part of the approach calls for a reverse order by which the content of government and civics is generally presented. As it is now arranged, most secondary courses emphasize a national approach while federation theory calls for a local emphasis.

The federated approach, presented here, starts with the local civic issues and progresses to national and then to international issues. Since this meaningfully changes the order of content for about every American civics course of study, this would need to be approved by either a school or a district administration. This will not be done automatically.

But that does not preclude adopting portions of what is being proposed here. With the C3 Framework, a nationally prescribed effort, there seems to be a new appreciation for a more experiential approach to civics instruction and that would be bolstered by a local emphasis.

And one cannot be satisfied with the nation's efforts in civics until one can detect improvements among the citizenry by the following indicators, i.e., the levels of political knowledge, political engagement, political skills, civility, and law-abiding behavior. To a meaningful degree, this writer cannot visualize such improvement without a meaningful revision of how the bulk of the citizenry views governance and politics.

In terms of the book's progression, beyond Chapter 2, the book will present three strategy or "unit" chapters. The first will describe and explain how a civics course can address a local political problem. In doing so, the chapter will utilize – as it will with the subsequent chapters – content choices guided by federation theory. This theory will be introduced in Chapters 1 and 2 and more fully developed through the rest of the chapters. Each chapter will target that portion of the theory that most readily relates to the issue each chapter addresses.

Those portions of the book will provide, among other things, a short explanation that distinguishes federation theory from the natural rights construct. The aim here is for educators to see civics content through a different "lens." So, what is this different lens; what is, in general terms, federation theory?

Here is a rudimentary review of what both a theory is and

what federation theory is. A theory is a general explanation of some reality or notion of reality. It is composed of a set of interrelated generalizations and principles. Depending on the nature of a given theory, it can rely on purely empirical evidence (observed or hypothesized) and/or normative evaluations (statements as to what should be – an element primarily relating to social theories and models).

As such, choices in selecting theories, models, explanations, or constructs[10] are important in determining the nature of a given curriculum, since any curriculum needs to reflect a given view of what is being taught. Where there is little to no debate among the scholars of a given field of knowledge, usually in math and the sciences, the choice of a basic theory engenders among the general public little to no controversy. [11]

On the other hand, in subject matter that depends on a social science – civics being one of them – the content can elicit, among interested parties in the general population, a great deal of controversy. That is, this book proposes a fundamental change in the theoretical basis for civics – that being toward federation theory. This means that this book is calling for what might very well be a controversial policy.

The theory proposed here takes on both functions or roles identified above – both empirical and normative. Federation theory, while not new to Americans, is at odds with fundamental, basic beliefs *and* values that are prominent today. Americans predominately held federalist values through most of their history. That earlier version of this view can be called

---

[10] These terms, as used here, are synonymous. If the reader is not so familiar or wants to see how they are treated here, he/she is directed to a posting on the blog, *Gravitas: A Voice for Civics*. See Gutierrez, "How to Define and Evaluate Theories," *Gravitas: A Voice for Civics*.
[11] This is not to say that other subject areas are completely immune from vying theories. For example, there are educators who ascribe to the more contentious construct, critical theory, and whose fields are either math or science.

parochial/traditional federalism and was dominant up until World War II.[12]

So, this book proposes the use of federation theory – more specifically a newer version, liberated federalism. This specific version has been developed not for political science research purposes, but for the teaching of governance and politics in American schools. As such, it should not be evaluated in terms of how it can guide research, but on how it can guide civics instruction.

A more viable way to judge this version's usefulness to civics education is to appreciate the relevant evolving politics of the nation. At the origins of this polity – back during the colonial times – a previous version, parochial/traditional version – defined legitimate political inclusion to those who were acceptable participants.

As will be described in this book, defined inclusion was extended to the descendants of those who came before. Yes, for practical purposes – given the varied populations that arrived in ever bigger numbers – inclusion expanded, but there were limitations. Also complicating matters, there was institutionalized slavery. So, while the basic agreement that set up the polity – actually, a series of agreements starting with the *Mayflower Compact* – it was theoretically inclusive, but operationally it was not.

Before dismissing parochial/traditional federalism as being illegitimate, though, this Introduction will make some points about its role in the development of the nation. Elsewhere,

---

[12] If the reader wants to view an expression of this value system, he/she is invited to view Turner Classic Movies and watch pre-1945 films and analyze what was considered the "right way" to see what was happening or what should have happened in the plots. By and large, one will see and hear a federalist biased theme. Today, such plot lines are considered unrealistic or too idealistic. As one watches these films, one should remember these films were projects made to make a profit; that is, they needed to fall within what an audience would accept – they needed to fall within certain normative parameters.

this writer has made the case that this earlier form had a profound effect on forming this nation's constitutional principles.[13] Some writers refer to it – or some version of it – as classical republicanism.[14]

This book is not the place to review this entire history or this entire theory. The reader is encouraged to read two sources by the late political scientist, Daniel J. Elazar. They are: *American Federalism: A View from the States*[15] and *Exploring Federalism.*[16] And another writer who adds insight into the earlier role that federalism played is Donald S. Lutz.[17] By reading their works, the reader can garner a rich understanding for federalism and its role in the development of the American democratic/republican system of governance.

Those works do not emphasize the structural elements of federalism – essential elements to be sure – but rather the political values supporting those elements; what Elazar calls federalism's processes.[18] Here, this account emphasizes these processes and counts on the reader to see that what existing civics and government courses teach, limited to mostly structural elements such as describing the three branches of government, is deficient.

The reader, in Chapter 1, is introduced to some federalist attributes and their related values as that chapter makes the case for interpreting the C3 Framework (again, a set of national standards) as encouraging and directing civics instruction to

---

[13] Gutierrez, "Our Federalist Roots: A Neglected Past?" *Theory and Research in Social Education*, 218-242.

[14] For example, Guelzo, *The American Mind*.

[15] Elazar, *American Federalism: A View from the States*.

[16] Elazar, *Exploring Federalism*.

[17] Lutz, "The Mayflower Compact, 1620," 17-23, "The Fundamental Orders of Connecticut, 1639," 24-35, "The Declaration of Independence, 1776," 138-145, "The Virginia Declaration of Rights and Constitution, 1776," 150-165, "The Articles of Confederation, 1781," 227-248 a series of essays in *Roots of the Republic: American Founding Documents Interpreted*.

[18] Elazar, *Exploring Federalism*.

impart a communal, collaborative mode of governance and politics, i.e., more in line with federalist processes.

Chapter 4 provides a fuller listing of related federalist values. A civics curriculum that adopts a federalist foundation, seeks to communicate, and encourage the promotion of those values. To address those aims, this account will answer a set of questions. They are, in general terms: What is the history of federalism in the US? What is the moral view of federation theory? What is the federalist view of governance and politics? The aim is to show how this theory can help an educator present relevant civic material.

Progressions in Political Landscapes

In terms of how this presentation sees the subject, portions of early chapters (1 and 2) give a *cursory* presentation of what constitutes federation theory. Subsequent chapters further that presentation by describing and explaining other portions of that view as it relates to the respective issues or problems those chapters highlight.

As alluded to above, federation theory emphasizes local or grass roots politics. In that vein, the book follows a progression. Chapters 3, 4, and 5 progress from highlighting a local issue (opioid crisis), to a national one (tort law), and then an international one (loss of jobs to cheap labor nations). But this plan reveals a challenge; as one wanders farther from a students' immediate surroundings, the subject becomes more remote and seen as less relevant to their concerns and, therefore, such material will be defined as less relatable to their interests.

Therefore, it becomes imperative to find a local angle to faraway governmental/political issues - if possible, by identifying some of their local elements. The individual units that compose a civics course can build upon one another and, hopefully provide the appropriate instruction for preparing students to be able to handle more expansive political landscapes. But this progression needs a local emphasis and federation theory, by its very nature, provides such an emphasis.

Helpful, Chapters 2 through 6 present portions of federation theory as it pertains to the topics of each of those chapters. By doing so and while having students utilize historical information, the chapters seek to describe how students can take on more efficacious roles. The application of federation theory calls for such engagement – and, in turn, encourages students to become viable and responsible citizens.

The object is two-fold: to impart an accurate view of reality *and* to impart an understanding of an ideal of what that reality should be or should become.[19] Each view provides insightful mental imagery that is relevant to what the use of federation theory aims to have. This construct does this by targeting relevant mental images, emotions, and recognitions of physical/biological factors.

A challenge – especially a political challenge – engenders varying mental images, emotional forces, and physiological drives or needs that usually compete to gain dominance in one's thinking. When so confronted, a person forms a holistic imagery; it is that imagery that tells the person what is, how one can deal with what is, and how one evaluates the situation. Instruction aimed at social realities, including governmental/political challenges, needs to address each of these aspects.

So, the presentation here definitely aims to impart through instruction the realities of designated political landscapes and, in addition, asks what those landscapes should be. Elazar argues that political theory needs to address both political realities and their relative normative concerns.[20]

---

[19] Argyris and Shon, "Evaluating Theories in Action," in *The Planning of Change, Fourth Edition*, 108-117. This source uses the terms theories-in-action (for the holistic image of a challenge), theories-in-use (for the perceived factual elements of the challenge), and espoused theory (for the relative normative elements of the challenge).

While instruction emanating from this book's lessons questions students' imagery of their and others' roles, it is equally – if not more – concerned with students' evaluations of those images, i.e., it questions what ideals students bring to the political challenge or confrontation under discussion.

While people don't always live up to their ideals, they do after all "sin," they can aspire to act in line with what they judge their behaviors should be.   In this spirit, federation theory promotes citizens behaving in moral ways that emanate from applications of federalist values (listed in Chapter 4).   They are more likely to do so if they actively formulate and harbor morally sound, espoused ideals.

The Practical Turn

And now a word about instruction – the process of a curriculum. This book sets out to inform and convince the reader of various claims.   A list of them has already been stated; for example, the need for transformative change.   To implement that change in terms of instruction, a certain approach should be utilized.   That approach, the historical dialogue-to-action (HD-to-A), is a discovery mode of instruction that would satisfy the C3 Framework's bias for inquiry (see Chapter 1).

Chapter 2 describes HD-to-A model and its main elements.   Through its implementation, the derived instruction imparts and has students practice dialogue skills mainly concerning historical information.   The skills are logical discussion, arguments, and debates.   The bulk of this book presents three "unit" chapters in which HD-to-A is applied to political confrontations or challenges by, in part, having students learn and practice these dialogue skills.

These chapters make practical the theoretical aspects of this book by sharing ideas about how federation theory can be

---

[20] Elazar, *Exploring Federalism.* He uses other language to express this need.

implemented in the classroom. Each chapter first introduces the issue or problem highlighted, including how it relates to federalist values; then the chapter presents a short history of the issue/problem; it concludes by providing a succession of described lessons for a suggested unit of study. Within each lesson, examples of relevant factoids, insights or, in Chapter 4 on tort law, information about prior judicial cases is included.

With those concerns identified, this account can begin to demonstrate how federation theory can be a viable guide in the pursuit of a responsible study of civics by promoting community, collaboration, and a sense that a citizenry should strive to be federated among themselves.

Of note: This book has various references to online sites. Each has its own URL. To assist the reader in gaining access to these different sites, there is another site that has links to the cited sites within the book. To gain access, go online, http://gravitascivics.blogspot.com/ , October 23, 2021.

CHAPTER 1: C3 FRAMEWORK OF STANDARDS

The body of this book begins with an assumption that the reader believes that American efforts in teaching the next generation to be good citizens need serious revision. If this judgement on the part of the reader is in doubt, then it might be useful to read the online Appendix.[21]   That appendix addresses the state of American civic knowledge, attitudes, and behaviors.

Short of that, he/she is invited to look around his/her immediate environs and ask: how much do his/her fellow citizens demonstrate functional levels of civic literacy, civic engagement, civility, and law-abiding behavior? As indicated by the research cited in the online Appendix, those levels are dysfunctional and deserve to be addressed.

One might ask: what standard should they use to measure that functionality?   This account treats functionality as demonstrated by how civic behaviors reflect or promote democratic and republican beliefs and attitudes within the nation's citizenry. Currently, as the evidence demonstrates, those behaviors rank low. The educational establishment has reacted to this deficiency and, in part, this chapter looks at one such reaction.

Establishment's Reaction

The Introduction calls for transformative change. Transformative change is difficult. It calls for those involved to change their attitudes and/or values. Usually, attitudes and values are held for a reason(s); they can represent the way one was introduced to whatever is in question or the product of previous conversions and/or experiences. Regardless, people who have beliefs and

---

[21] Again, see http://gravitascivics.blogspot.com/ , October 23, 2021.

feelings hold on to them because they are comfortable, seen as prudent, and/or held in a sacred fashion.

When those beliefs and/or feelings have to do with professional responsibilities or job-related protocols, more is at stake. Beyond the conscious or subconscious commitments, people *reluctantly* go about changing things when a paycheck is involved. This is real and should not be dismissed. Therefore, people should not consider transformative change lightly or readily, especially when it relates to how they earn a living.

Such change should be considered only when one perceives sufficient evidence that it is needed or demanded. Unfortunately, that is the case with civics education. If a civics educator agrees with that evaluation, then he/she is called upon to, one, become aware of the challenge; two, become informed of alternatives; and three, adopt called-upon changes in how one does his/her job.

This book further assumes that the reader is someone involved in civics education (usually as a teacher but can also be an administrator or a parent) and is disposed to meet this challenge despite the effort, costs, and time it promises to consume – meeting the challenge can promise to be slow and extend over many years of gradual steps.

Such an educator or parent, as a potential initial step, can become aware of how those in authority see the problem area and consider what their voiced concerns and solutions are. This chapter is dedicated to informing such parties – educators and parents – what one national effort is and what it calls on civics teachers to do.

Within the US, civics educators – along with all social studies educators – generally adhere to one of two theoretical perspectives concerning the content of their subject matter: one is the establishment's view (summarily called in this book, the natural rights view) and the other is the view which the academic community supports (summarily called the critical theory view). Unfortunately, this chasm exists between these two factions and it divides the civics field because there is a lack of a coherent voice among the field's professional educators and concerned non-educators.

Generally, the establishment consists primarily of educators who work within the public-school-systems – both at the state and school district levels – and officials within the federal government, mostly in the US Department of Education. The academic contingent is mostly the professors at the nation's colleges and universities (particularly those institutions that dedicate their efforts to producing published material in peer-reviewed journals).

One can readily identify what those theoretical allegiances are. The former is basically guided in its dealing with civics' curricular matters – particularly its content – by the natural rights construct; the latter is guided by the critical theory construct. Between the two there is palpable discord in what social studies policy – including civics education – should be.

---

[22] The term, natural rights, is used advisedly. As it is used here, it is in the mode used by John Winthrop. He, as the first governor of Massachusetts Bay Colony, makes a distinction between natural liberty – those rights enjoyed by wild animals – and federal liberty – a liberty derived from covenantal agreements. Chapter 3 will make this distinction clearer. (See "The First 'On Liberty,'" Intercollegiate Studies Institute: Educating for Liberty") Of further note, the problem is that in the 1700s, Scottish, common sense philosophers, such as Thomas Reid and Francis Hutcheson, argued that compact-al agreements need to be based on the natural faculty that humans share; i.e., a moral sense. Such a use of the term suggests a definite communal bent to the meaning of natural rights. As Gary Wills points out, this communal use stands in counter-distinction to John Locke's sense of rights. See Wills, *Inventing America: Jefferson's Declaration of Independence*. Current use sides with Locke but exceeds his sense of individualism.

[23] The only exception occurs when educators at the school site promote values that support cooperative behavior that uphold a school's administrative rules.

Summarily, the natural rights construct promotes a laissez-faire approach that abandons any meaningful effort toward promoting a values-based content. The reason for this is that, being based on a natural rights view,[22] the intent is to promote liberty – specifically, a natural rights liberty as currently defined. As such, students are considered free agents and they are free to determine their moral beliefs and their social demeanor.[23] Resulting views tend to be individualistic and oriented toward market processes.

As a result, those who are in the position to determine the elements of typical civics curricula are left to present descriptive content describing structural matters – the structure of government. If they decide to dabble in values issues, they limit such attempts to popularly determined topics – i.e., what dominates the news of the day and is considered "controversial," such as gun control. This is a market orientation, and it centers on what currently "sells."

In turn, market biases are no more than the accumulation of individual choices. Therefore, the approach furthers an individualism that tends to ignore communal concerns. There is no or little thought about how the instruction responds to communal interests or asks what constitutes the general good or the commonwealth's health and well-being.

On the other side, there is academia guided, as stated above, by the critical theory construct. With academia, there is a viable and well-thought-out value commitment. That is, those who adhere to this construct see this nation's – or, for that matter, the Western world's – social/economic/political arrangement as being in the grip of an economic, exploitive class.

In turn, that class, through institutional mechanisms, determines the substance, processes, and functions of establishment policies. That includes school policies. And as for curricular content, critical theorists view establishment efforts as advancing those exploitive relationships. Consequently, these academics claim that such course work as in social studies directs instruction toward justifying these relationships or ignoring them. These academics support inclusion of content that describes and explains this exploitive regime.[24]

This other view is a compilation of theoretical/ideological substantive material,[25] but the one tradition it favors is a Marxian perspective of societal conditions and developments. To varying degrees, critical theorists rely on Marx's view of how society is and has been organized through the course of human history.

In terms of public perceptions, including that of teachers, regarding this "debate," they are usually subject to published material issued by the establishment. Through overarching, professional organizations, the field does produce certain, written products. These products usually focus on curricular issues by attempting to tell teachers what they should do. Usually, those publications follow the establishment's bias for a natural rights perspective.[26]

In 2013, with a supplement added in 2017, the national professional organization of social studies – the National Council for the Social Studies (NCSS) – issued such a document. It is entitled *College, Career, and Civic Life (C3) Framework for Social Studies State Standards*. This account will refer to it as the C3 Framework and this chapter offers an analysis of its content.

C3 Framework's Purpose

---

[24] For a reader friendly – i.e., not overly antagonistic – description of this perceived reality, the reader can read Paulo Freire's account: Freire, *Pedagogy of the Oppressed*.

[25] Cherryholmes, "Critical Pedagogy and Social Education," in *Handbook on Teaching Social Issues: NCSS Bulletin* 93, 75-80.

[26] There are meaningful exceptions to this general observation. For example, the source cited above, *Handbook on Teaching Social Issues: NCSS Bulletin* 93, contains articles that generally apply critical theory positions.

This account, in the upcoming pages, provides a critical review of the C3 Framework. It does so by recognizing that that published statement is issued by the establishment and by asking: does this publication offer a direction to implement the needed transformative change that civics education needs? Upon reviewing the C3's initial paragraphs, one finds it difficult to pin down, in operational terms, its purpose.

In its stated purpose, the developers of the publication employ language that does not exude much hope that it varies significantly away from a natural rights view of governance and politics. As one reviews not only its purpose but its identified principles, [27] one walks away with vague and undeterminable aims as to what the document is offering.

For example, its purposes only cite "civic life" or any other words conveying its meaning only once. Beyond that, the language can be described as a set of platitudes. Yet, as the above argues, the times call for more directed and committed leadership. But before one leaps toward dismissing this effort by the NCSS, the standards themselves – along with any

---

[27] National Council for the Social Studies, *Preparing Students for College, Career, and Civic Life C3.* Here is a list of the Framework's principles:

> Social studies prepares the nation's young people for college, careers, and civic life; Inquiry is at the heart of social studies; Social studies involves interdisciplinary applications and welcomes integration of the arts and humanities; Social studies is composed of deep and enduring understandings, concepts, and skills from the disciplines. The subject, social studies, emphasizes skills and practices as preparation for democratic decision-making; Social studies education should have direct and explicit connections to the Common Core State Standards for English Language Arts.

These are quoted from the NCSS publication.

explanations the publication includes – need to be looked at and considered.

And when one does, one finds a surprise. As one reads the more substantive portions of this NCSS publication, one finds a more "communal/common good" message – one that diverges significantly away from a natural rights bias. For example, here is an introductory statement from the body of the publication:

> Introduction in the College, Career, and Civic Life (C3) Framework for social studies state standards, the call for students to become more prepared for the challenges of college and career is united *with a third critical element: preparation for civic life.* Advocates of citizenship education cross the political spectrum, but they are bound by a common belief that our democratic republic will not sustain unless students are aware of their changing cultural and physical environments; know the past; read, write, and think deeply; and act in ways that promote the common good.[28]

Perhaps this can be the NCSS project's true purpose or principle. This account chooses to believe it is and proceeds to provide instructional ideas based on such a purpose and/or principle.

This targeted aim engenders a central concern, that of content. That is why the emphasis should not be on instructional processes – on how teachers teach, although not totally disregarded – but on the content that civics educators choose to present to students. But the C3 Framework does not, to this point in the document, hold this as its emphasis. Instead, as one reads on, the C3 Framework speaks of the "Inquiry Arc." That

---

[28] Ibid., 5, (emphasis added). This language can basically be an example of good political speech. By couching the effort in terms of college and career concerns, the publication could just be using references the intended audience is likely to see as pertinent. Those concerns are more likely to be in line with natural rights' priorities.

reference aims to have teachers employ inquiry strategies through their instruction.

This brings up a related issue that needs to be addressed. While this writer favors inquiry strategies and tried to implement them in his teaching days, he is also concerned that any policy that mandates such strategies is bound to fail because not all teachers will "play ball." That is a topic for another venue, but this reservation does influence the substance of this book. Here, in this account, the emphasis is on content. That is, this book asks: what does the C3 Framework call for in terms of civics' scope?

Content, the subject's scope, reflects a social philosophy,[29] and nowhere is that truer than in social studies. And that philosophy proffers a view, a set of assumptions, a set of beliefs, and a set of priorities by which it reflects the social world. The challenge here, then, is to see how much the content choices of the C3 Framework in civics reflect the dominant social philosophy of today, the natural rights construct, or how much of it reflects any other political construct.

Of central interest here is: how much do the standards of the C3 Framework reflect or employ the tenets *not* of the natural rights perspective or of the critical theory perspective, but of another perspective: federation theory? Generally, federation theory (what some might call republicanism with a small "r") emphasizes the need for a viable citizenry to be communal, collaborative, and to feel, among themselves, a sense of partnership – that is, to feel *federated*.

The theory also claims that republican governance relies on a diffusion of power as opposed to a centralization of power. It supports a noncentralized political structure.[30] And it also

---

[29] Tyler, *Basic Principles of Curriculum and Instruction.*
[30] Elazar, *Exploring Federalism.*

relies on social/political qualities, social capital and civic humanism.

Social capital, using the thoughts of Robert Putnam, is characterized by having an active, public-spirited citizenry, egalitarian political relations, and a social environment of trust and cooperation.[31] And civic humanism, as Isaac Kramnick describes it, is a political being realizing his/her fulfilment through participation in public life and a concern with public good above selfish ends.[32]

But to this point in the Framework, there does not seem to be such a directed emphasis. Given the already identified biases of the educational establishment – being guided by the natural rights construct – that perspective emphasizes liberty and individualism. Again, the education establishment has favored this perspective, and this can be readily seen in a variety of ways and intuitively, one is disposed to believe that those in charge will not give sway to any challenging view without a fight.

This bias can be found in established institutionalized processes and props. That includes any analysis of the content of civics or American government textbooks that school systems have chosen – more on this later in the book. But that judgement does not address the C3 standards themselves. And here is the surprise: when one reads them – the final and targeted offering of this publication – they *are* written in a more communal language.

---

[31] See Putnam, *Bowling Alone: The Collapse and Revival of American Community*.

[32] Kramnick, "John Locke and Liberal Constitutionalism," in *Major Problems in American Constitutional History, Volume I: The Colonial Era Through Reconstruction*, 97-114, 98. The quote is: "… [it] conceives of man as a political being whose realization of self occurs only through participation in public life, through active citizenship in a republic. The virtuous man is concerned primarily with the public good, *res publica*, or commonweal, not with private or selfish ends."

They assume the acceptance of various communal values and, if followed, instruct teachers and curriculum developers to share with students these values. The developers of the C3 Framework communicate these aims not only by the standards themselves but also by the explanatory remarks the document makes about the standards.

Here is a sampling of the contextual language the C3 Framework provides for the civics standards:

> ... the political system established by the U.S. Constitution is an important subject of study within civics. Civics requires other knowledge too; students should also learn about state and local governments; markets; courts and legal systems; civil society; other nations' systems and practices; international institutions; and the techniques available to citizens for preserving and changing a society. Civics is not limited to the study of politics and society; it also encompasses participation in classrooms and schools, neighborhoods, groups, and organizations. Not all participation is beneficial ... What defines civic virtue, which democratic principles apply in given situations, and when discussions are deliberative are not easy questions, but they are topics for inquiry and reflection.[33]

And,

> Civics teaches the principles—such as adherence to the social contract, consent of the governed, limited government, legitimate authority, federalism, and separation of powers—that are meant to guide official institutions such as

---

[33] National Council for the Social Studies (NCSS), *Preparing Students for College, Career, and Civic Life C3*, 31.

legislatures, courts, and government agencies. It also teaches the virtues—such as honesty, mutual respect, cooperation, and attentiveness to multiple perspectives—that citizens should use when they interact with each other on public matters. Principles such as equality, freedom, liberty, respect for individual rights, and deliberation apply to both official institutions and informal interactions among citizens. Learning these virtues and principles requires obtaining factual knowledge of written provisions found in important texts such as the founding documents of the United States. It also means coming to understand the diverse arguments that have been made about these documents and their meanings. Finally, students understand virtues and principles by applying and reflecting on them through actual civic engagement— their own and that of other people from the past and present.[34]

Sounds good, doesn't it? But, despite the surprise and its turn toward federalist values, a closer, more nuanced look might uncover a lack of direction for teachers.

This non-direction, therefore, is somewhat problematic. The developers of the standards do not provide sufficient theoretical support for what they promote; their legitimacy seems to be taken for granted. It can also be added that they are poorly defined. It is assumed everyone knows what is meant by the language the Framework employs. This area of concern needs to be elucidated as the language of the descriptors and the standards indicate. The twelfth-grade standards are shared below.

Why does the language of the descriptors and standards need to include more of a theoretical basis? Because without

---

[34] Ibid., 33.

such a rationale, resulting language can still be a set of platitudes. They can be easily interpreted from a variety of political biases and subsequently used to mean very different things – at times, opposing messages. If one does not find this problematic, then one is probably in line with natural rights thinking.

And that bias probably finds most attempts by schools to promulgate any values – other than liberty – offensive and even dangerous. But those who hold such a belief are at best unintentionally disingenuous. For if one argues the natural rights argument, one is basically arguing market values. That is not to say that market values are all bad, but they are values. In teaching, and this is no more the case than in teaching social studies, *one cannot escape promoting values of one sort or another*.

So, by watering down a set of socio/political/economic values – which one does when they are ill-defined and lacking in justification – one falls in line with the natural rights credo: "do your own thing." Having stated that, this account does want to commend this communal turn in the C3 document. At least it does pick up on the language of a more communal perspective.

But that turn refers to the language the descriptors and standards have opted to use. While it is safe to assume the developers do not have the term, federation theory, in mind, one can readily see a federalist bent – a turn toward communal and collaborative values – in how the standards are immediately "teed-up."

To further explain what this account sees as wanting with the language of the C3 Framework, the following example is offered. Suppose one is studying the Supreme Court decision, Brown vs. Topeka School Board, in which the previous judicial standard concerning schools and other public accommodations was that it was legal to segregate racially. There was one proviso: the service (such as schooling), if public, was to be "separate, but equal."

That is, school districts could maintain separate school facilities if they *were* "equal." Of course, in segregated systems, they were separate, but not equal – not even close. What if the teacher in this classroom brings up the possibility that at the time of the court case some segregationist or group promoted a program that maintained segregation, but meaningful efforts were made to make schools equal in terms of resources such as decent schoolhouses, textbooks, and qualified teachers.

And further, that person or group, in trying to sell the idea, told African American parents that if this segregated plan were to be put in place, it would avoid their children being subjected to contentious environments among white students and staffs that didn't want them in any mandated desegregated school.

How do the above lists of values – the ones identified in the C3 document – deal with this "accommodation?" This account judges that the language of that document does not challenge this message or the processes a segregationist might use to sell his/her option. Luckily, the Supreme Court, after many deliberations (it heard the case twice) addressed this type of "solution."[35] It saw any segregation unequal *per se*. But the justices were thinking with a more substantive theory of law and federalism that led them to dismiss such a segregationist plan.

Yes, because of their eventual decision, many black students did have to attend contentious settings – contentious for both black and white students. But given the eventual outcomes

---

[35] Armed with sufficient statistically backed studies, the Justices found that segregation of a group of students, in and of itself, communicates the idea that subjects of the separated groups are inferior. Therefore, whether the groups are treated with equal resources or not, segregation communicates the message: "you are not good enough." Of course, that can and usually does have a debilitating effect. Therefore, the practice of segregating students offends the constitutional provision of equal protection under the law.

– significantly more desegregated school systems – their sacrifice can be deemed worthwhile.[36]

Of course, the aim should not be to expect students to be able to render Supreme Court decisions, but the aim should be to lead to good classroom questions – both from teachers and students. It is not that this scenario would necessarily occur in a classroom, but with a clearer and more comprehensive theory, that type of case can assist both teachers and students to devise "federalist" questions that lead students to consider federalist values.

And that is helped by a more substantive theory or narrative of what it means to value equality or liberty, two instrumental federalist values. It also helps to have enough substance by which to judge which one, equality or liberty, is held more important in a given situation. That is, it assists students when they are confronted with situations in which citizens must choose between or among civic or federated values. According to the judgement here, the NCSS offering falls short – at least as they are presented in the C3 Framework publication. But if read with federalist lenses, an acceptable application can be achieved.

To be federated, as just pointed out, the standards need students to consider federalist questions. They include:

- How engaged should citizens be in solving public issues?
- How much are citizens involved in collaborative efforts to solve public issues?
- How much should citizens see public issues as threats to federalist values such as equality, liberty, and most important, societal welfare?
- How much does an issue concern trust levels, over-prioritization of self-interests over communal interests or

---

[36] This is not to minimize what remains in attaining truly desegregated and even integrated American schools. The nation still has a long way to go.

vice versa, power distribution or authority (too concentrated or too diffused), civic morality or immorality among citizens, and/or the viability of groups, associations, or other entities, such as racial groups, within a polity?

In other words, does the content of a civics course, unit of study, or lesson reflect concerns over the health of the commonwealth?[37]

Noting that the C3 Framework's descriptive statements use a central, sought after social/political quality, civic virtue, one should have a clear understanding of what that quality is. Here is how the C3 Framework defines it:

> What defines civic virtue, which democratic principles apply in given situations, and when discussions are deliberative are not easy questions, but they are topics for inquiry and reflection. In civics, students learn to contribute appropriately to public processes and discussions of real issues. Their contributions to public discussions may take many forms, ranging from personal testimony to abstract arguments. They will also learn civic practices such as voting, volunteering, jury service, and joining with others to improve society. Civics enables students not only to study how others participate, but also to practice participating and taking informed action themselves.[38]

This account judges this statement as hopeful. While one can still read into it a more structural concern – it misses the richness of a federated commitment – the use of civic virtue does hint at what direction the standards should take.

---

[37] Social capital and civic humanism, the two constituent values that comprise societal health, are defined earlier in this chapter.

[38] National Council for the Social Studies (NCSS), *Preparing Students for College, Career, and Civic Life C3*, 31.

While it can be questioned as to how targeted the effort is, one can detect a sense of morality. Yet, one can judge the statement as being limited to procedural or behavioral dimensions of good citizenship such as voluntarism. In other words, it lacks any meaningful sense of what one should volunteer to promote or advance. But one can harbor a degree of hope that when these standards are applied, an educator can read into them a federated sense of moral politics.

This book proceeds with the assumption that one can interpret the standards in this more normative and directed fashion. Therefore, this defines a function for this book; it provides a route for using the Common Core standards to advance a federated view of governance and politics. It describes and explains this perspective throughout the upcoming pages, but of special note, this account provides, albeit truncated, a federalist moral code in Chapter 4.

And that accounts for the contextual statements found in the C3 Framework; what about the standards themselves? Do the civics standards offered by the Framework follow this more federated turn? Below, the twelfth-grade standards are highlighted. The reader can logically deduce what the standards are for the lower grades as the listed standards can be considered the logical aims of the lower-level standards.

The Standards

The standards are divided into three conceptual categories: Civic and Political Institutions, Participation and Deliberation: Applying Civic Virtues and Democratic Principles, and Processes, Rules, and Laws. If one reads these standards as reflecting a federalist view as opposed to a natural rights view, one can ask a telling question: how exactly can this be done to determine a civics course's content at the middle or high school levels?

Each of this book's "unit" chapters (3, 4, and 5) and the Conclusion, Chapter 6, attempt to answer this question. But the challenge of this book is to be true to federation theory and at the same time faithfully apply or indicate a way to meet the standards identified by the NCSS publication. All of this is to be done while taking a realistic approach regarding the conditions of American classrooms.

Unfortunately, as present conditions in most civics' classrooms demonstrate, teachers use the assigned textbook to define the curriculum they actually implement. If the reader is familiar with American government textbooks – the most prominent being *Magruder's American Government*[39] – does he/she wonder how much in line these standards are with the content of those textbooks?

In addition, can these textbooks be useful in pursuing a federalist guided content? The answer is yes to both questions, but with some effort, and the entailed challenge should not be underestimated.[40] In a very practical sense, these are extremely important concerns. They reflect, in part, the transformative nature of what reform in civics education means.

As will be demonstrated through this book, the textbook needs to function differently: instead of the fountainhead of civic knowledge, it needs to be but one source of information. Does the language of the standards allow for such a function? Yes, but

---

[39] McClenaghan, *Magruder's American Government*.

[40] In a series of postings in 2015, the blog, *Gravitas: A Voice for Civics* (https://gravitascivics.blogspot.com/), provides an extensive review of this textbook. That review attempts to answer the question: how federated is *Magruder's*? The reader is invited to visit an online site that contains these postings. The URL for this site is accessed through http://gravitascivics.blogspot.com/ , October 23, 2021. The overall judgement is that as used, *Magruder's* serves to define civics curriculum at the high school level and that definition is to convey a mechanical view of government, governance, and politics.

only if the textbook becomes an information source – mostly relating to the structure of government – and not as most teachers use it – as defining the curriculum of the subject matter.

In addition, the various secondary civics and American government textbooks follow the same basic format and just as they do not directly promote a federated view of the subject matter, they do not particularly promote a civic virtue view either. So, not only does an educator need to read into the C3 Framework standards a federalist approach, he/she, to a further extent, also needs to read it into the textbook he/she uses.

Perhaps an establishment publication like the C3 Framework will encourage changes in how these textbooks are designed. Further, if states adopt these standards, the publishers might be more encouraged to do so. Hopefully, the publication of books such as this one can also help. In any event, these outlined changes indicate how difficult the changes presently called for are.

What follows is each of the "12th grade civics standards" and an accompanying commentary that describes how the standard can be interpreted as a "federated" standard. The hope is that the reader can appreciate how creative teachers need to be in their courses to be more in line with federated theory and/or the C3 Framework (as interpreted in this chapter and in the rest of the book).

Category I: Civic and Political Institutions Standards:

Individually and with others, students distinguish the powers and responsibilities of local, state, tribal, national, and international civic and political institutions.

This standard directly addresses what most people think of when they hear the word, federalism. Federal arrangements can be formed among nations or within nations. A federal system that is formed within a nation usually means that the nation has multi-level governments – it is a noncentralized system. This puts into effect a federalist value, dispersion of power.

Of course, the US has such a system with the federal/state governmental arrangement. While there are also local governments – county and city governments – they are creations of the respective states. State governments are not created by the central government, but by the people of the respective states (their inclusion into the US federal system does need the approval of Congress). And to round out this description, the US central government is formed by the peoples of various states and by the states. It is a complex system.

As for this standard, it is "federal" enough as written. This writer might have added a phrase – such as, "to appreciate the concern the founders had for over-concentration of power within the US …" – but to do so would probably have demanded an additional standard that distinguishes the American system from those of other nations or of federated, international systems.

The point is that American federalism – along with what might exist in other nations – allows for local socio-political cultures to express their political biases within the national polity or some level of that polity. Also, as a related issue, nations might have federalist structures, but lack federalist processes. That is, they might lack the processes that are collaborative and communal and have the dispersal of power provisions that characterize federalist arrangements, *a la* Elazar.

To be a truly federated system, the processes – those that encourage or count on a federated populous – are more essential than a federal structure, but that does not diminish the importance of structure.[41] If these ideas of distribution of power are incorporated into this standard, then the standard can be considered a federalist one.

---

[41] Elazar, *Exploring Federalism.*

Individually and with others, students analyze the role of citizens in the U.S. political system, with attention to various theories of democracy, changes in Americans' participation over time, and alternative models from other countries, past and present.

A federalist view sees this standard as an opportunity to make some very important distinctions. The history of the US has been one in which various views concerning various social qualities have risen and gained follow-ship – currently, during the 2020 election, one might see "Trumpism" and the President (who identifies himself as a nationalist) in this light. Ideologies that have had a significant number of followers include socialism, nationalism, populism, progressivism, etc. These constitute, in the language of this standard, various theories.

Also, generally accepted isms, such as the natural right-ism and federalism, have changed in their meanings among the American public. For example, early federalism among colonial settlements was tied strongly to religious beliefs and ideals.[42] Of interest, in these terms, is to distinguish federalist thought vs. natural rights thought vs. critical theory thought and how these vying belief systems are being maneuvered in the national political arena of today.[43]

These last vying perspectives are particularly important among educators, but they are also important in providing context for what a federated American government course or a civics course is attempting to do in terms of this standard. This standard provides justification to studying these "isms" and their relative importance in American political discourse.

---

[42] Guelzo, *The American Mind*. Guelzo points out that the effects of the Civil War dampened this influence by that war's level of carnage and destruction.

[43] For example, there is, currently (2020), the nationalism of President Trump and the socialism of Senator Bernie Sanders. As of this writing, there is also a reported upsurge of socialist – critical theory – influence in the Democratic Party.

Individually and with others, students analyze the impact of constitutions, laws, treaties, and international agreements on the maintenance of national and international order.

All polities come about through one of the following: force, accident, or choice. This standard paves the way for students to look at each of these foundations – their histories and examples – and how the US was not the product of a military/strong "man" development, or the product of a cultural tradition in each territory, but the product of a group of founders getting together and *choosing* to set up the polity through the formulation of various covenants or compacts.

This description can take on more meaning if it is compared to other types of formation. For example, most European nations were formed by a combination of the accidental cultural development they experienced with the strong-arm leadership of the various royal families.[44] This leads logically to the next standard.

Individually and with others, students explain how the U.S. Constitution establishes a system of government that has powers, responsibilities, and limits that have changed over time and that are still contested.

This standard can mark a point of instruction in which a teacher provides the evidence that US constitutions – both at the central and state levels – came about using compacts. As such, they are sacred – in a secular sense – agreements among the citizenry of the respective jurisdictions. This tradition, in the US, originally evolved from a Biblical influence,[45] but through its development eventually took on a secular standing. They should be distinguished from a commercial contract that calls for a *quid pro quo*: something for something in exchange.

---

[44] Ken Follett provides an entertaining account of part of this process in his recent novel, *A Column of Fire*. See Ken Follett, *A Column of Fire*.
[45] Elazar, *Exploring Federalism*.

A compact is something else. That is, a covenant or compact forms a partnership that binds citizens to each other no matter what any citizen does – subject to appropriate sanctions for abuses or other offenses to the agreement. That means that citizens are committed to abide by the provisions of a covenant or compact as equal participants with equal benefits (rights, privileges, and responsibilities). Chapter 6 provides more information on this account by describing the attributes of an association.

Of course, this reflects the history of the nation – stretching all the way back to the *Mayflower Compact* (which was technically a covenant – it called on God to witness the agreement) through the development of the colonies, the development of the national government – the *Articles of Confederation* and the *US Constitution* – and the fifty states.[46] Other portions of this book will review the significance of compacts in federation theory.

Individually and with others, students evaluate citizens' and institutions' effectiveness in addressing social and political problems at the local, state, tribal, national, and/or international level.

This can be a potentially important standard. Of importance, *a la* federalist values, are problems and solutions defined in terms of the common good as opposed to the good of

---

[46] Supporting this claim see Lutz's series of essays. Lutz, "The Mayflower Compact, 1620," 17-23, "The Fundamental Orders of Connecticut, 1639," 24-35, "The Declaration of Independence," 1776, 38-145, "The Virginia Declaration of Rights and Constitution, 1776," 150-165, "The Articles of Confederation, 1781," 227-248, in *Roots of the Republic: American Founding Documents Interpreted.* To be clear, while a covenant calls on God to witness the agreement, a compact does not; the US' constitutions are compacts. For example, the Massachusetts' constitution (written in 1780) recognizes God (expresses gratitude to Him), but it does not call on God to witness the agreement.

individuals, selected groups, corporations, or other organizations that exist within a societal arrangement.

Of course, federalist-based civics instruction would ask those questions that have students consider whether actors are defining their interests in ways that place in priority self-interest over the common interest or the other way around. These types of questions undergird federated instruction. Much of domestic politics can be analyzed through these concerns.

Individually and with others, students critique relationships among governments, civil societies, and economic markets.[47]

This standard does elicit a federalist concern; i.e., it steers instruction to highlight the interaction between and among political actors. Such instruction focuses on the federalist aspect, a concern over the relationship among governments – especially among those governments in a federated structural arrangement. In turn, one can question the motivations those actors bring to their interactions. Therefore, this standard can further center students' attention in the direction of the immediately preceding standard.

Category II: Participation and Deliberation: Applying Civic Virtues and Democratic Principles Standards:

Note: This category has a more targeted offering in relation to federation theory. Using the concept, civic virtue, a directed message is communicated, and it can be logically linked to federated issues and values.

Individually and with others, students apply civic virtues and democratic principles when working with others.

---

[47] National Council for the Social Studies (NCSS), *Preparing Students for College, Career, and Civic Life C3*, 32-33. Each of these Civic and Political Institutions standards is taken from this source.

If one defines civic virtue as a moral quality and that quality places on the individual a responsibility to federate him/herself to others within the polity, then this is very much a federalist standard. The word that most captures this sense is partnership. Here is what Daniel Elazar explains about this quality:

> Federalism involves a commitment to partnership and to active cooperation on the part of individuals and institutions that also take pride in preserving their own respective integrities. *Successful federal systems are characterized not only by their constitutional arrangements in the narrow sense of the word but by their permeation with the spirit of federalism as manifested in sharing through negotiation, mutual forbearance and self-restraint in the pursuit of goals, and a consideration of the system as well as the substantive consequences of one's acts.* Political institutions common to different political systems, when combined within a federal system and animated by federal principles, are effectively endowed by those principles with a distinctive character.[48]

One should think about what a good partnership is; it occurs when the benefit to one partner is to the benefit of all partners and *vice versa*. This might sound a bit too idealistic, especially to those who adhere to the natural rights construct. But there is nothing unreasonable or impossible in having a set of espoused values that one believes are worth pursuing.

A federalist view promotes this spirit; a federalist moral code (in Chapter 4), is offered to guide one's public posture. That one "sins" against it, as with any value commitment, does not mean one should abandon it and its effects to potentially

---

[48] Elazar, *Exploring Federalism*, 154 (Kindle edition). Emphasis added.

encourage "good" behavior. In this sense, it defines what good is and what good citizenship looks like.

For example, this sense of partnership places a reasonable expectation on one exercising his/her judgment as to what is legitimate on moral grounds. There are those policy positions that are unquestionably immoral, but if one is *too* apt to judge disagreeable options in that light, compromise becomes almost impossible. "Tribalism," in which citizens abandon any disposition to compromise, obviously undermines any basis for partnering with others, especially if one uses a judgement of immorality as the basis of such evaluations. Discretion needs to be practiced.

Federal systems count on compromise and if people are disposed to viewing opposing positions as immoral or otherwise distasteful, the citizenry becomes divisive and compromise is beyond reach – nothing gets done.[49] Polities that take on a general, shared sense of extreme individualism – what Elazar calls "radical pluralism" – seem to drift toward such a hostile view regarding compromise. That categorizes how politics in the US has drifted since World War II as Americans have adopted the natural rights construct as the dominant political set of beliefs.[50]

Individually and with others, students evaluate social and political systems in different contexts, times, and places, that promote civic virtues and enact democratic principles.

This standard can lead to lessons that one can consider to be designated a comparative study. By comparing systems

---

[49] In this light, one can direct his/her attention to the role Scottish, common-sense philosophers attributed to benevolence. For them, this proclivity to find benevolence as a naturally-induced good feeling acts as gravity does in the universe – it promotes federated relationships. See Wills, *Inventing America: Jefferson's Declaration of Independence.* It can act to encourage a more compromising disposition that does not abandon principles.

[50] Elazar, *Exploring Federalism.*

generically or a single system over time, one can ask questions that lead to political generalizations – or hypotheses – and that in turn lead to better explanations as to what is effective or moral within the political realm of reality. In doing so, students can look at other systems and develop a better sense of what constitutes their system.

Other systems can have different forms of federalism – consociations, leagues, confederations, etc. – and students should have a good sense of what these options are.[51] In addition, there are republican systems that are centralized, i.e., follow a Jacobin/French model. These latter systems do not, as federalist systems do, emphasize dispersion of power.

And within federal systems, there are various styles or cultural bases by which citizens adopt federalist structural elements conducive to those areas' traditional definitions of what federalism means. Of course, these are too numerous to list here, but they are mentioned to suggest the potential for various lesson topics.[52]

---

[51] Ibid.

[52] Ibid. For example, Elazar identifies three separate subcultural traditions in the US upon which its federal system was formulated. They are the moralistic subculture (originating in the New England colonies), individualistic subculture (originating in the mid-Atlantic colonies), and traditional subculture (originating in the Southern, slave-owning colonies).

In addition, over its history there have been the more nuanced relationship-based views of federalism. One approach looks at pluralism *vis-à-vis* regions of the nation. There have been, for example, neutrality of territory view which is based on market values – prevalent in mid-Atlantic states – and associated pluralism based on membership in service/social associations – such as churches or organizations such as the Lions Club – prevalent in mid-Western states

One approach is radical pluralism based on a disassociation with any groups but relies on individuals seeking their own aims and views of morality – prevalent initially in California, but more recently becoming dominant throughout the nation. This view is not considered by this writer to be federalist at all. Instead, it is an adoption of the natural rights perspective that

Individually and with others, students use appropriate deliberative processes in multiple settings.

A helpful distinction should be made here to better appreciate this standard. Forensic judgements are about what happened in the past. Deliberative judgements are about what happens or should happen in the future. [53] Most meaningful, governing issues have to do with what the government should do in terms of some perceived social/economic condition. Civics, as opposed to history, and despite its potential use of historical information, has a future orientation.

This standard can be linked to the instructional approach, Historical Dialog-to-Action;[54] this account promotes HD-to-A and it is introduced in Chapter 2. Suffice it to mention here, this approach relies on students engaging in dialogue. One form of dialogue is debate. Those who study debate make a distinction between forensic discussions within debates and deliberative discussions within debates. Each has its own processes, and civics, therefore, emphasizes processes that are geared to speculate what it takes to achieve a brighter future. More on this below.

The federalist link depends on how one identifies and defines the problematic nature of the issues that a civics class considers and chooses to highlight. Each of the remaining chapters addresses this aspect of instruction. At its core, educators, using federation theory to guide their content choices, view the contemporary political landscape and find those situations or conditions that offend federalist values. This varies from what curricular developers currently do; i.e., identify what

---

has a historical link to the times in which the *US Constitution* was written and ratified. That tradition has evolved, and the current form is significantly different from its form back in the late 1700s – it is a much more individualistic approach today.

[53] See Atchison, *The Art of Debate – A Transcript Book.*
[54] Reminder: HD-to-A refers to historical dialogue-to-action.

is controversial. Federalist issues might be controversial, but not necessarily.

Further, and this is germane to those who might see instruction guided by a federation theory to be a form of indoctrination, in that a construct helps educators choose the questions a teacher will ask and, by doing so, sets the context in which civics' lessons are conducted. Today, the same is done, but it is the natural rights construct that serves that function. This writer cannot envision an approach that does not do this in some form; it's "baked into the cake."

Individually and with others, students analyze the impact and the appropriate roles of personal interests and perspectives on the application of civic virtues, democratic principles, constitutional rights, and human rights.[55]

Federalist-minded citizens face a recurring, key challenge: how does one conduct his/her affairs within federalist moral standards and, at the same time pursue self-interests? No responsible interpretation of federalist values denies the individual from seeking to advance legitimate self-interests. This can be considered as part and parcel of respecting each citizen's individual integrity, a federalist value. But often, pursuits, even if they are legal, can offend federalist values.

A question is: how do people define their individual interests and how do they act upon them within the realities of a social community or polity? Good citizenship demands that those interests not impinge on what is seen as the interests of the commonwealth. This can be more challenging than what one would intuitively think. Yes, giving up on an opportunity might be difficult when that opportunity has the potential to render significant rewards. But the challenge does not end there.

---

[55] National Council for the Social Studies (NCSS), *Preparing Students for College, Career, and Civic Life C3*, 33. Each of these standards is taken from this source.

Because of other factors, individuals might hurt the common good inadvertently – and sink assets at such times. This is but one sort of development that can make seeking the common good very difficult to attain. But this type of political drama sets up interesting and revealing scenarios for students to ferret out through their instructional experiences.

Category III: Processes, Rules, and Laws

Note: Since the first three standards under this last category are closely related, the commentary will address all three of them simultaneously:

Individually and with others, students evaluate multiple procedures for making governmental decisions at the local, state, national, and international levels in terms of the civic purposes achieved.

Individually and with others, students analyze how people use and challenge local, state, national, and international laws to address a variety of public issues.

Individually and with others, students evaluate public policies in terms of intended and unintended outcomes, and related consequences.

These standards are federal if the related instruction takes a further step. Not only should students make judgements about the performance of governments or government agencies at various levels, but they should also learn how to interact with government personnel and seek policy options those agencies should choose. Yes, this instructional aim is hinted at in previously listed standards, but not addressed directly.

Federalist structures feature a valued attribute that provides for various levels of government to address various types of problems. This attribute also allows citizens to choose which governmental agency – at which level – they address their claims or demands. Further, it allows those choices to match the political resources voters might command.

In relation to this, structural information – information relating to the branches of government, departments, agencies, offices, etc. – can become very important and such sources, such as most civics and government textbooks, can provide important and useful information. Here, one can appreciate a more functional role for textbooks: to render such information in an efficient manner.

On another front, most citizens do not have the resources – political or otherwise – to appeal to the national government, but most can take their demands to local governments. Now this might not be totally satisfying, given that many problems often take on national or even global dimensions. But for the typical governmental concern – e.g., installing a traffic light at a certain intersection – federalism is a highly functional form of governance. One can also claim that even national and international issues or topics have local aspects to them.

And, if citizens get into the habit of interacting with government, such actions can lead to more expanding roles and activities such as: writing to an elected official, volunteering, writing letters to an editor, participating in election campaigns, joining an advocacy group(s), and the like. Not only can this develop, but the student, through appropriate instruction, can also be encouraged to reflect on what constitutes responsible engagement.[56] In addition, there are among interested writers the reporting of current accounts of how essential and effective grass-root politics is.

That is, there have been a series of issues in which "winning" sides have won or are winning because they have

_____

[56] This account points out – see online Appendix – the prevalence of disruptive political engagement in the US as pointed by Charles C. Euchner. See Euchner, *Extraordinary Politics*.

promoted and utilized nationally organized efforts among common folks. One good review of such efforts is provided by Leslie R. Crutchfield in her book, *How Change Happens: Why Some Social Movements Succeed While Others Don't.*[57]

Individually and with others, students analyze historical, contemporary, and emerging means of changing societies, promoting the common good, and protecting rights.[58]

This is the last 12th grade civics standard of the C3 Framework. As such, it serves as a summarizing federalist standard. Admittedly, it could also be the summarizing standard for a civics curriculum of a centralized, republican nation – such as that of France. But the Common Core Standards project is submitted to be applied to the federalist polity of the US. As a matter of fact, by highlighting the common good, this standard recognizes that at least a primary priority of this project is a collective or, better still, a communal one.

Without such a reference, slipping into illegitimate expectations is easy to do. This writer feels that critical theory[59] does this. While he agrees with that construct that most legitimate issues in civics, and in all social studies, have to do with equality, he sees that approach as shortchanging such concerns as incentives; they are mostly overlooked by critical theory advocates. And one can add that often interests – self-interests – are not monetary ones; they can be whatever one's emotions target.

---

[57] Crutchfield, *How Change Happens*.
[58] National Council for the Social Studies (NCSS), *Preparing Students for College, Career, and Civic Life C3*, 34. Each of these standards is taken from this source.
[59] Reminder: critical theory is a construct that claims Western societies, individually and collectively, are ruled by an exploitive class, what is commonly called the 1%.

This aspect of civic behavior often verges on issues related to the maturing process among young people and here, civics instruction has a role. Philip Selznick writes about how individuals deal with maturing issues and how they develop the ability to close the gap individuals create between believed reality and actual reality.

He cites phenomenology and its psychologically oriented study of such conscious issues and how during adolescent years – those years occurring during one's secondary schooling – are marked with such difficulties that are enlarged due to scant use of reason. For example, there is a marked desire for freedom, but a reluctance to accept social restraints or responsibilities.[60]

When it comes time to make socio-political-economic decisions where related values clash, people would be helped by an educational experience that prepares them to make responsible decisions. It is the judgement here that the NCSS's effort is enough of a green light to pursue a civics curriculum that can directly address these challenges, that emanate from the maturing process, and the related forces one feels during those years.

They are forces that undermine the societal health of this nation. The natural rights perspective is wanting in this concern due to its over individualistic approach to governance and politics. Equally wanting is the critical theory view that shortchanges very human frailties that interfere with productive, responsible choices. Federation theory promises a more responsible view, one that addresses the concerns of the other two views without radicalizing those concerns as those constructs tend to do.

This chapter and the next is an overview of the instructional approach this book promotes and uses to design subsequent unit strategies (in Chapters 3, 4, and 5). By doing so,

---

[60] Selznick, *The Moral Commonwealth.*

the chapter encourages the reader to appreciate how these standards can be used in a federalist fashion.

CHAPTER 2: APPLYING FEDERATION THEORY

A Guiding Light

Can any institution reverse a cultural tide such as a prevailing high level of un-civic behavior? Here is a thought: those who oversee a basic institution such as education have a moral obligation to look at the realities affecting their institution and, in as honest a way as possible, react to any dysfunctional realities. They should do that by steering that institution in as useful a direction – defined by the needs of sustaining and advancing societal health – as the existing realities allow.

Usually that means that relevant efforts appropriately meet that institution's needs, purposes, and processes and, where wanting, work toward remedial changes. If drastic change is called for, be it procedural or transformative, those who oversee the process should attempt to incorporate as much of that institution's or the nation's historical tradition as is possible.

Unfortunately, what is called for in terms of civics education today is transformative change. Change is daunting enough, and any possibility of sustaining a semblance of a common past will soften the sacrifices that are entailed by such a challenge. At the same time, the change must promote institutional elements that will cure or ameliorate those conditions and beliefs responsible for the dysfunctionalities plaguing that institution.

The previous chapter describes the National Council for the Social Studies' C3 Framework. That chapter encourages the reader to see that framework's standards as an opportunity to steer civics curricula toward advancing the nation's civic virtue (using the Framework's language).

The standards are not so much dictating or even suggesting specific lesson plans; that's the role of lesson objectives. Standards – to a degree of specificity – guide lesson planning in terms of content or subject matter. While that content can be about skills – such as political skills – the emphasis is on the scope – the content – of the subject.

Further, that chapter broods over the vague term, civic virtue, and suggests how it can be given a more tangible meaning by referring to two socio-political qualities: social capital[61] and civic humanism.[62] In turn, those qualities are used in this presentation as the elements of what, along with societal survival, constitutes societal welfare or health.

The NCSS, as an establishment organization, undertook this effort as part of the US Department of Education's program, the Common Core Standards. But it is also believed here that it has been undertaken because, as already pointed out in the Introduction and in the online Appendix, the state of civics is in trouble. In short, civics education needs drastic change.

If that change includes a shift in how educators view civics' substance, then the process of change itself becomes a point of concern. If teachers', administrators', or parents' view

[61] This book, to remind the reader, uses the writings of Robert Putnam, who defines social capital to mean a societal quality characterized by having an active, public-spirited citizenry, egalitarian political relations, and a social environment of trust and cooperation. See Putnam, *Bowling Alone.*

[62] Civic humanism is defined as a communal bias which holds that citizens are, through the polity, in a partnership. As such, the individual is disposed to sacrifice personal interest for the common good or, if not, at least arrange for personal interests not to be antagonistic to the common good. Above, the idea of civic humanism can be sourced to Kramnick, "John Locke and Liberal Constitutionalism," in *Major Problems in American Constitutional History, Volume I: The Colonial Era Through Reconstruction*, 97-114, but here is another source: McDonald, "The Power of Ideas in the Convention." in *Major Problems in American Constitutional History, Volume I*, 160-169. McDonald gives the reader a sense of how essential the sentiment corresponding to civic humanism was in the thinking and feelings of the founding fathers.

of governance and politics is part of the problem, then these perceptions become part of what needs changing and, therefore, the proposed change becomes transformative and very challenging.

In other venues, this writer has made the argument as to what view is presently prominent in American thinking, how that view has shifted from political ideals prior to World War II, and how the previous political ideation sprang from the nation's colonial past.[63] The remaining pages of this chapter give the reader a partial account of this development.

This chapter's concern is how a historically established political, mental construct can be implemented; that is, what those involved with the teaching of civics – teachers, parents, administrators, and others – can do to implement another perspective. Specifically, the call is for those actors to adopt federation theory as their dominant view of governance and politics and, in turn, to develop congruent instructional plans in civics while advancing the C3 Framework.[64]

---

[63] Gutierrez, "The Prevailing Construct in Civic Education and Its Problems," *Action in Teacher Education*, 24-41 AND "The Predisposition of High School Students to Engage in Collective Strategies of Problem-Solving," *Theory and Research in Social Education*, 404-428 AND "Moral Code for the Current Secular State of Affairs, *Education*, 353-372 AND "Our Federalist Roots: A Neglected Past?, *Theory and Research in Social Education*, 218-242 AND "What Can Happen to Auspicious Beginnings: Historical Barriers to Ideal Citizenship," *The Social Studies*, 202-208 AND "Rekindling Concerns over Moral Politics in the Classroom," *The Social Studies*, 113-119.

[64] This writer wants to point out an important belief he harbors. Federation theory does not demand the implementation of any one methodological approach to instruction. Federation theory can work with didactic methods (lecture and other presentations) or inquiry methods. This account will emphasize inquiry to be in line with the C3 Framework. Inquiry also matches what the theory calls for in terms of an ideal citizenry, i.e., a collaborative and actively participating populace. This chapter gives the reader a "feel" for this bias.

From his teaching experience, the writer also believes that insistence on an inquiry method is a non-starter for any reform effort. Why? Because

A Concern for Instruction

An educator, in accomplishing this change, has various chores to perform. One is to address how teachers look at the function of their assigned textbooks. This was pointed out in the last chapter. Most teachers consider their textbooks as not only providing a source of information but also as defining the curriculum they are to follow. Yet, the C3 Framework's approach depends on either another function for textbooks or the unlikely abandonment of the current textbooks being used.

To be realistic, teachers need to be convinced of the former option. Hopefully, this book can be helpful in that pursuit. Toward that goal, a good understanding of the implications surrounding the adoption of the C3 Framework would be useful. If one reviews the Framework, one can see that its developers placed significant emphasis on the content – hopefully, the reader agrees with that judgment after reviewing the twelfth-grade standards in Chapter 1. But they also highlighted the inquiry approach to instruction.

The publication that presents the standards promotes an "inquiry arc," and when one looks at the standards themselves, one can detect what that means. The reader is invited to read the verbs used in the standards: distinguish, analyze, explain, evaluate, critique, apply, and use. These verbs indicate that the Framework is calling on students to discover facts, formulate concepts, and arrive at generalizations that, with the content the standards indicate, eventually lead to civic virtue. To understand this direction, the reader should review a bit of history.

Without getting bogged down in that history, social studies became part of the post-Sputnik reaction. It, with federal government support, attempted to have teachers apply the "scientific method" to social studies' various subjects including

many, if not most, teachers simply will not consider adopting the reform if this element is included, much less insisted upon. The reason for this is a topic for another venue, but it has to do with what these teachers feel comfortable doing in the classroom.

history and civics. [65]   Known as the New Social Studies, this inquiry approach has taken several turns since the sixties – today the term is critical thinking – but the overall concern was/is for students to *discover* knowledge – usually through some problem-solving process – instead of being told what it is.

Since its inception, there have been other instructional methods introduced in the inquiry mode.   Donald Oliver and James Shaver introduced one method not so dependent on a "scientific" methodology and called it the jurisprudential approach.[66]   This other offshoot re-introduced normative questions into an inquiring methodology that relied on argumentation.

This account relies on Oliver and Shaver, but their material relied on the too open-ended concept of "constitutional values."   It relied heavily on two sources for its content: a concept, called American dilemma, offered by Gunnar Myrdal,[67] and on court decisions.[68]

While their prescriptions reflect a value system, this book, while inspired by Oliver and Shaver, presents what its writer considers a more comprehensive political perspective, i.e., federation theory.   By doing so, this book initially offers a well-

---

[65] See, for example, Fenton, Fow, and Bartlett, *A New History of the United States*. Fenton's contributions began in 1955. See Carnegie Mellon University Libraries, "Edwin Fenton Papers," Carnegie Mellon University.
[66] Oliver and Shaver, *Teaching Public Issues in the High School* AND Newmann, and Oliver, *Clarifying Public Controversy*.
[67] Myrdal, *An American Dilemma*.
[68] The reader can review the work of Oliver, Shaver, and another collaborator, Fred Newmann, and judge whether, from a substantive perspective, those theorists provide sufficient guidance to teachers. These theorists presented their efforts shortly after the Warren Court's liberal interpretations of both individual rights and group rights – such as in the decisions affecting racially segregated facilities. They saw this judicial swing as a rich body of content for what they were attempting to do. While this writer is a fan of their work, in trying to apply their theory, this writer – as a teacher – had to fill in a lot of substantive content.

directed sense of what constitutes constitutional values by offering a firm explanation of where these values come from – a long-standing perspective that traces its roots to the colonial days of the nation. Various portions of this book address these roots, albeit in a somewhat cursory fashion.

An approach derived from federation theory attempts to have students do the appropriate analyzing, explaining, evaluating, etc. And so, while claiming a substantive model – federation theory – it can rely on any style of teaching (from didactic methods to inquiry/discovery methods), though the inquiry approach is more conducive to the theory's content and congruent with the C3 standards. This writer will only add, *if instruction, regardless of approach, does not call on students to reflect on the instructional material being taught, students will not learn it.*

The Look and Feel of Being Federated

So, this account aims at advancing federalist values. Can one describe what that means? Here, in an extended citation, is what the French political writer, Alexis de Tocqueville, offers. It is a view of a federated disposition among Americans of an earlier time – the 1830s:

> It is not impossible to form an imaginary picture of the surpassing liberty which the Americans enjoy; some idea may likewise be formed of the extreme equality which subsists amongst them. But the political activity which pervades the United States must be *seen* in order to be understood. No sooner do you set foot upon the American soil than you are stunned by a kind of tumult; a confused clamour is heard on every side; and a thousand simultaneous voices demand the immediate satisfaction of their social wants. Everything is in motion around you; here, the people of one quarter of a town are met to decide

upon the building of a church; there, the election of a representative is going on; a little further, the delegates of a district are traveling in a hurry to the town in order to consult upon some local improvements; or in another place the labourers of a village quit their ploughs to deliberate upon the project of a road or a public school. Meetings are called for the sole purpose of declaring their disapprobation of the line of conduct pursued by the Government, whilst in other assemblies the citizens salute the authorities of the day as the fathers of their country. Societies are formed which regard drunkenness as the principal cause of the evils under which the State labours, and which solemnly bind themselves to give a constant example of temperance.

The great political agitation of the American legislative bodies, which is the only kind of excitement that attracts the attention of foreign countries, is a mere episode or a sort of continuation of that universal movement which originates in the lowest classes of the people and extends successively to all ranks of society. It is impossible to spend more efforts in the pursuit of enjoyment.

The cares of political life engross a most prominent place in the occupation of a citizen in the United States, and almost the only pleasure of which an American has any idea is to take part in the Government, and to discuss the part he has taken. This feeling pervades the most trifling habits of life; even the women frequently attend public meetings, and listen to political harangues as a recreation after their household labours. Debating clubs are to a certain extent a substitute for theatrical entertainments. An American cannot converse, but he can discuss; and when he attempts to talk he falls into a dissertation. He speaks to you as if he was addressing a meeting; and if he should chance to warm in the course of the discussion, he will infallibly say "Gentlemen," to the person with whom he is conversing.[69]

To this writer, this cited passage gives the best description he has ever read of a people politically engaged in the affairs of their community, i.e., of being federated among themselves.

It portrays an imagery of citizenship that civics teachers should value and strive to instill in their students. How accurate is this account? Mark Twain's description of Americans of that time, in *Huckleberry Finn*, gives a very different image.[70] Yet Tocqueville was a respected professional political writer of his time and he wrote these cited words in real time, not years later, and from personal observation. Accurate or not, the description above can serve as an ideal – maybe one this nation will never (again) achieve, but one for which it can strive.

A Dialogue Progression

The following pages introduce a methodological commitment by which to present civics that builds on this type of citizenry. This writer calls it "historical dialogue-to-action" (HD-to-A). It will be an instructional approach that does not count on the scientific method; citizens don't conduct either experiments or survey research when they "talk" politics.

Instead, they engage in discussions, arguments, and/or debates about what they perceive to have happened, what should have happened, or what should happen at some future time. HD-to-A calls on students, with some rigor and a future orientation, to perform these types of dialogue to increasing levels of

---

[69] de Tocqueville, "Political Activities in America," in *Alexis de Tocqueville: On Democracy, Revolution, and Society*, 78-101, 78-79.

[70] Twain, *The Adventures of Huckleberry Finn*.

sophistication. When performed in communal settings, these activities assist students in meeting those standards that promote social capital and civic humanism, what the C3 Framework calls civic virtue.

The overall course described in this account identifies various progressions: through taking a student from the familiar to the foreign – local-national-global political landscapes and issues; through those skills students develop in terms of their dialogue – discussion-argumentation-debate; and through their action within their political environment – designing-implementing-evaluating an action strategy. In each case, the course aims to take a student from the more basic and familiar to the more complex and foreign.

Consider, as an example, the progression in dialogue. The following pages describe it for an American government course at the high school level. It progresses from, at the beginning, engaging in discussions; then, during the middle units, to students participating in arguments or the development of arguments; and finally, in the last units, to competing in formal debate. In the following three chapters (3, 4, and 5), each, in turn, provides an example of each phase.[71]

This development has students, during the first stage or phase – the discussion stage – choose between offered opinions, usually between two polar-opposite opinions that address a chosen topic. The goal in this phase would be to have students identify and provide supportive data – factual information – for their chosen opinion.

This discussion stage simply has students express their opinions concerning the issues that the content highlights. So, for

---

[71] Students are called upon to discuss the opioid crisis in Chapter 3, argue a legal position in Chapter 4, and participate in a debate over foreign trade in Chapter 5. Each of these phases will further the ability of students to formulate and express logical arguments – more on this below. And each chapter will further describe the dialogue skills that chapter addresses.

example, an early topic, one close to the student, can be a look at the civic nature of families and a related issue might be divorce. If the teacher using this issue brings up a suggested policy change in the divorce laws – making it more difficult to secure a divorce – students would be called upon to react to the suggestion.

Perhaps the former state of New York's standard can be discussed, in which divorce was granted only if one of the parties engaged in an extra-marital affair. New York began allowing "no-fault" divorces in 2010. Given that the national divorce rate is presently at 40 to 50 percent, and all the disruptions that causes, should the divorce laws change and become more stringent, possibly reinstating the New York standard of old?

This could make for a spirited discussion. But the aim would be to make students comfortable with expressing an opinion allowing for little to no criticism. The relevant lesson might take on a modified brainstorming format or an "opinion session," in which students express what they think without having to defend their positions.

A historical study of New York's law could accompany this discussion and be beneficial as it would expose how law can affect family relations. Also, the discussion should limit consideration to one optional policy change: for example, should the old New York law be reestablished? Yes or no? That unit aims to have students begin developing a comfort level in expressing their beliefs, opinions, or related knowledge within the constraint of limited options.

To further illustrate this progression, Chapter 3 reports on the development of a unit concerning how local communities politically deal with the opioid crisis. That treatment assumes the "opioid" unit appears early in a course and addresses a local community issue. It therefore aims at advancing discussion skills.

The course then moves to the next stage, argumentation. Instruction can encourage the student, who is now hopefully comfortable with expressing opinions, to engage in an argument.

Students, under an argumentation format, entertain two or more options. These can be policy positions, legislative bills (or a part of a bill), or suggested actions. The class conducts arguments, with the teacher being highly conscious of detecting illogical arguments.

Students should be, during this stage, instructed on the basic components of a sound and meaningful argument. Relying on Stephen Toulmin's model (more fully described below), the components consist of the following: a conclusion, supportive facts (datum statements), warrant statement(s), backing of a warrant statement(s), qualification(s), and reservation statement(s).[72]

Meaningfulness concerns how the argument relates to federalist values and how many people are affected by its provisions. For example, if a proposed policy affects the equality or health status of millions of people, that is meaningful. Students don't naturally appreciate conditions that affect others. Generally, HD-to-A aims to have students become more sensitive to the fate of others.

In this second phase, students argue a position that should be more specific than what was called for in phase one. This is of course, to a great degree, determined by the questions asked by the teacher and the information students are provided or are called upon to find through their research. Teachers' questions ask students to be more concrete in their arguments as they consider more options.

That is, should the government do X or Y or even one of more options? To illustrate using tort law as an issue (the topic of Chapter 4) the following is offered. Should the US call on its 50 state legislatures or its national legislature to reform tort law by enacting statutory provisions governing tort issues or to basically, as it is now, mostly rely on common law? Or, still more complex, consider an extensive combination of the two,

[72] Toulmin, *The Uses of Argument.* Model is more fully explained below.

taking into account various nuances within tort suits? Here, students can supply either supportive or contradictory information for a given option.

If the teacher believes that his/her students have sufficiently mastered argumentation skills outlined above, the students can advance to the debate stage. Chapter 5 relates to a unit, the last one of the proposed course of study in American government, in which students are ready to engage in formal debate. HD-to-A designates formal debate as the final dialogue phase.

In that phase, students take on the responsibility of conceptualizing the chosen issue area into subtopics and policy considerations. This is at a more complex level, and a teacher again should exercise judgement as to what his/her students are prepared to do. In all of this, the process is organized by what constitutes a logical argument and asks students to get a good handle on how logical arguments are composed or constructed as they apply to debates.

This final stage also calls on students to perform these skills by assuming roles in a formal debate. A debate is a competition and students are to take one of various roles. Here, students apply all the skills they have acquired during the two prior stages. As Chapter 5 (in which students debate a policy-question relating to foreign trade) describes, there are various roles such as an advocate, judge, or interrogator, which a student can play in a debate.

When students reach the level of sophistication in which they can take part, effectively, in a debate, instruction should have already introduced them to certain elements of debating – nuanced questions and arguments, the use of information, and the attributes of logical argumentation.

In terms of debating, the teacher needs to introduce additional concerns. Many have to do with maintaining debates within manageable terms. Debates can become unruly as perhaps experiences with argumentation might have already been demonstrated to readers. The discipline of order, as Selznick warns, can be challenging.[73] One way to harness order is to appropriately focus a debate. That is, preparation for a debate needs to find that aspect of the issue that is truly under contention.

Often, when a teacher presents a debate issue, it turns out that the debaters probably agree on a lot of its aspects. Therefore, initially debate preparation needs to separate the aspects debaters don't agree upon from those they do. In terms of foreign trade, for example, all or at least most students agree that foreign trade should advance American interests. But perhaps students disagree as to whether the US should manipulate its currency or set higher tariffs on more products.

Of course, such narrowing is part and parcel of devising potential policy positions. And useful discussions, arguments, or debates are those that limit student attention to specific aspects of disagreement; this is called the point of stasis and students should be taught what that is and how to establish it.[74]

Another source of "disruption" can be traced to the federalist bias this book promotes. Regardless of how close or foreign an issue is, federalist analysis calls for identifying how an issue affects a local area. So, for example, the approach here looks at more removed issues and has students looking into how those issues affect local social/economic/political conditions. This approach can make the "far away" have a local stake potentially making it more emotional. Therefore, it might keep certain perspectives potentially virulent in the eyes of students and, perhaps, their parents.

---

[73] Selznick, *The Moral Commonwealth*. Below, this account describes Selznick's "the Five Pillars of Reason." Order is the first pillar.

[74] Atchison, *The Art of Debate – A Transcript Book*.

That is, local stakes introduce varying biases or prejudices. Teachers need to be conscious of those. For example, if the issue is again foreign trade, that trade can possibly have local negative effects; it might have eliminated employment opportunities for local workers. In those cases, an educator needs to be honest, sensitive, and at times brave in handling unpopular aspects of that situation. Aspects of formal debate suggest techniques that can defuse such controversy, such as identifying the point of stasis. But there are other aspects in debating that can help.

For one thing, instruction should look at not only negative consequences, but also the positive ones. In the case of foreign trade, one should not forget that products produced by cheaper labor lead to cheaper consumer prices; it allows one to find a winter jacket at Costco or Walmart for twenty dollars. The point is, without whitewashing the problems, all aspects need to be addressed – the positive as well as the negative.

Finally, debaters, as opposed to discussants and arguers, engage in a competition. And in determining which side of the competition wins, there is the addition of a third-party judge. Determining who wins a debate is a matter of subjective opinion and, therefore, calls on the role of a judge or judges to provide that opinion. He/she/they also provide accompanying reasons for that determination.

The addition of judges has various consequences. Debaters address their comments to judges and, consequently, emotions will be less likely to escalate as might be the case if remarks are aimed at the adversary. Therefore, more reasoned, logical arguments tend to be expressed (below see Selznick's "pillars of reason").

And then there is nuance again. Nuance can't be stressed enough, as it helps the speaker be more accurate. By adding qualifications and reservations, speakers can better say what they mean to say. Nuance also helps prevent derailing debates from what they were intended to be. Often, unruliness stems from someone or a group stating arguments not really meant.

For example, instead of saying, "I believe that everyone should be allowed to say what he or she wants to say," the person's claim could be more nuanced and say, "I believe that adults should be allowed to say what they want to say as long as their speech does not endanger someone else's safety." Perhaps, to make this point, a teacher can think of several unnuanced statements, ones that might be misinterpreted and taken as disruptive and have students rephrase them in a more diplomatic and more accurate way by adding nuance.

Also, with these elements in mind, a teacher, in previous units, can better direct students' discussions and arguments, preparing them to be more effective debaters. Teachers should see the progression from discussion to debate as a continuous and reinforcing process, and furthermore as one in which skills – pertaining to discovery and logic – can be perfected. [75] Along these lines, effectiveness – in discussion, argument, or debate – is enhanced if the person conducting the dialogue uses reason, appropriate passion, and disciplined self-control.

And with that, the progression of dialoguing, in terms of its phases, comes to an end. Here are its highlights: the number of options considered by students should become more numerous and more nuanced; students should demonstrate higher levels of sophistication in their arguing skills and in implementing various logical elements in their arguments. In short, students develop the knowledge and skills to become effective participants – as dialoguers – within the nation's citizenry and its polity.

---

[75] To further his/her development in the elements of effective debating, the teacher might find it useful to acquire related instruction in formal debating. For example, one such instruction is offered by the Great Courses program. One can purchase the transcript for the course, *The Art of Debate*, featuring Professor Jarrod Atchison. Atchison, *The Art of Debate – A Transcript Book*.

In terms of logic, toward the end of this chapter, this account describes what constitutes logical argumentation. Perhaps readers who have a good foundation in logical argument need not review this information. But for those readers who are not that familiar with this discipline or have not considered it for some time, a review of the elements of logical argumentation is provided toward the end of this chapter starting with the subsection, "The Discipline of Reflected Argument."

The Action Part of the Deal

To this point, this account features the HD-to-A approach as seeking to make a connection between historical information to dialogue with a promise that all that talking leads to action. But talking does not *necessarily* lead to action and, if it does, it does not necessarily lead to the action one would judge beneficial or logically derived from such talk.

One can say dialogue is a precondition, but other factors play a role in persuading people to act in ways that advance what a group – federated or not – wants to accomplish. And action, irrespective of its aim, functions to institute new or maintain an old condition, be it a social, political, and/or economic one.

In terms of student action, either one or the other option is possible. Students might choose to act to help maintain a status quo even if that state is an anti-federalist reality. Change theory serves up relevant insights whether one sets out to change or maintain some reality.

Those who study this area of behavior readily confirm that relating to change or social action, the issues can be very complex.[76] In terms of change, those who are dedicated to

---

[76] For example, see Benne, "The Current State of Planned Changing in Persons, Groups, Communities, and Societies" in *The Planning of Change*, 68-82. This is but one article in this classic collection of articles regarding change theory. AND a recent work provides case data on successful national efforts – e.g., anti-smoking movement. See Crutchfield, *How Change Happens*.

facilitating change – the emphasis below – need to be conscious of that complexity and understand that there is no sure recipe for success.

A dialogue, whether competitive or not, allows a person to voice concerns over obstacles standing in the way of implementing a plan. Students, within the context of a dialogue, can review their own feelings, those of their fellow students, and those of the community or other significant people who would be involved in such an effort. These are essential elements of a responsible change strategy.

With that context, this next portion of the chapter shares some ideas of what kinds of actions students can initiate and work to accomplish. Based on the work of various researchers, the argument for students being actively involved in developing and implementing political-action plans has been made by respected change experts.[77]

Educational researchers offer empirical evidence to suggest that experiential education (learning from actual, real life experiences) succeeds in many of the aims that federation theory highlights.[78] That is, by students dealing with the people affected by social and governmental policy and practice, they more readily engage emotionally and develop a sense of self in relation to the concerns they are investigating and upon which they are acting.

Experiential education should not replace classroom instruction, but it can have a viable place in a civics course. And in doing so, a teacher needs to be observant of what students are learning in the field and that they are in safe environments. Pamela J. Conover and Donald D. Searing offer an insightful description of this concern: "while most students identify

---

[77] "Civic Education," *Stanford Encyclopedia of Philosophy*.
[78] For example, Eyler, "The Power of Experiential Education," Association of American Colleges and Universities.

themselves as citizens, their grasp of what it means to act as citizens is rudimentary and dominated by a focus on rights, thus creating a privately oriented, passive understanding."[79] This is another indicator of the prevalence of the natural rights view.

To usher students away from this self-serving and unengaged social view, nothing is more effective than political participation. But it needs to be focused on relevant, local concerns and accompanied by legitimate questioning that centers student attention on the relevant facts. Teachers should strive to have students think about governmental and political realities by looking at what immediately affects them and those who live nearby, not from a self-centered point of view but one guided by federalist values.

More specifically, some activities, such as voting and donating to political campaigns or to favored advocacy groups, do not do enough; students need to engage in political action aimed at enhancing social capital and civic humanism. And that, in turn, calls for direct communication and other interactions with those who are affected by the issue in question.

William Damon, the Stanford educator, points out that, in terms of moral education, experiential encounters are beneficial; they "engage students directly in action, with subsequent opportunities for reflection." This he considers to be a positive form of instruction. [80] And, in a relatively open society, students have a multitude of opportunities to exploit such learning experiences.

---

[79] Conover and Searing, "A Political Socialization Perspective," in *Rediscovering the Democratic Purposes of Education*, 91-124, 108.
[80] "Civic Education," *Stanford Encyclopedia of Philosophy*. This source offers a useful summary of various action options that educators can employ in a civics course. Interested readers can find this source at https://plato.stanford.edu/entries/civic-education/ .

These actions can include showing up for and taking part in political gatherings, scheduling and holding political meetings which can be occasions to express political opinions or demands, organizing and carrying out fund drives; canvassing an area to gather signatures in support or against legislative bills or other initiatives, seeking to serve on political boards, joining or starting a political club, and/or performing political theatrics.

Any one of these activities needs to be set up by collecting from affected groups relevant information regarding some problematic situation.[81] Too much? Perhaps, life is full of responsibilities leaving little time for such activities, but a civics course can promote a more engaged ideal. A course of study that adopts the HD-to-A model needs to allow enough time for students, individually or in groups, to carry out such an activity. The course can assign an experiential project as a course-long assignment – perhaps its final product taking the place of a final exam.[82]

---

[81] Ibid., Here is a quotation from Stanford site that offers its list of action options, some potentially applicable by teachers, others as part of a person's array of possible behaviors:

> We can think of civic action as participation that involves far more than serving, voting, working or writing a letter to the editor. It can take many other forms: attending and participating in political meetings; organizing and running meetings, rallies, protests, fund drives; gathering signatures for bills, ballots, initiatives, recalls; serving on local elected and appointed boards; starting or participating in political clubs; deliberating with fellow citizens about social and political issues central to their lives; and pursuing careers that have public value.

By the way, teaching is such a career. Note that being exposed to illegal dealings is not included.

[82] This option of substituting a report or other work product is suggested also at the unit level of the course by calling on some work product being used to substitute for a unit test.

Lessons can also include activities more associated with students' school experiences: participating in debates or other deliberations over a social and/or political issue relevant to student lives and possibly starting an educational plan that leads to an occupation or a life-long activity that has public value. This writer is aware of two organizations that are dedicated to advance students in the pursuit of these types of activities. They are The National Action Civics Collaborative (NACC) and SOS Outreach.[83]

But before leaving this concern, there is one area of special interest. As Theodore Sizer points out, the school site can do more to teach democratic values than any other source.[84] With an aim to impart a commitment to social capital and civic humanism, this can include everyday concerns such as student discipline, bullying, or instances of sexism or racism. Professional oversight should be included. In choosing actual policies in which students could have a say, a teacher or perhaps an administrator needs to give that choice some reflection.[85]

Progressing through a Course of Study

As indicated, the next several chapters provide descriptions of several units of study that could be part of a middle school civics course or a high school American government course. The unit chapters, as they appear in this book, are developed for twelfth graders. A lower grade application needs to accommodate those

[83] The writer is not recommending membership in these organizations. His knowledge of them is limited to his awareness that they exist and is mentioned here to be of assistance.

[84] Sizer, *Horace's Compromise*.

[85] Further, when one talks about a school-wide effort, the supportive philosophy needs to be widely shared among that school's faculty and staff. If a teacher who wants to engage in experiential learning strategies stands alone in terms of these ideas in a faculty, he/she needs to be conscious of that fact and plan accordingly. But, if he/she is committed to applying this experiential learning approach with a bit of creativity, this writer believes the opportunities are there in most schools.

units – as described on these pages – so that resulting instruction is age appropriate.

Here is a potential list, in the form of a course outline, of appropriate unit topics:

Unit 1: The individual – short term interests vs. long term interests, deciding on educational options or entrepreneurial ambitions – e.g., under a federalist mindset, how does one determine the limits of ambition? – balancing personal interests with the common good

Unit 2: The family – the effects of divorce, the marital compact or covenant – the level of seriousness the law should consider nuptial promises – should constraints on divorce be implemented? – considering potential, communal intrusion into personal life decisions

Unit 3: The neighborhood – meeting neighbors' needs – how do debilitating drugs affect one's ability to meet communal responsibilities? – local efforts to handle a drug crisis such as the opioid epidemic

Unit 4: A small business – business regulation *vis-à-vis* the size of businesses; the level of regulation – do regulations and their intended aims add or detract from the common good, given the potential disincentives they pose to business activities? – local entrepreneurship

Unit 5: A citizen association (such as a labor union) –treatment of employees, the legal standing of labor unions – should state law change its labor laws and how they relate to "right-to-work" provisions? – equality issues regarding labor

Unit 6: A large corporation – product safety, the ravages of hazardous products – how should governmental policy relate to the health emergency presented by the availability, distribution, and consumption of hazardous products (such as firearms) – corporate, "individual" rights

Unit 7: A local government (either city or county) – zoning or racial/ethnic divisions or failures of oversight functions such as water policy in Flint, Michigan – what are the rights of citizens in any legal claims against local jurisdictions? – approachable governance

Unit 8: A state and/or federal government agency – issues surrounding water management or laws concerning the use of deadly force (e.g., "stand-your-ground" laws) – what does the Second Amendment prohibit states from legislating? – communal dispositions of bureaucrats, do they exist and, if so, to what extent?

Unit 9: Congress/Legislatures – the extent that money (donations) is influential over such issues as health care or environmental policy – should the federal government provide a national health care program such as Canadian or European programs? – the right to health care, does it exist?

Unit 10: The White House/Chief Executives of Governmental Entities – leadership that exploits divisive politics such as the "Southern Strategy" – should the chief executive promote inclusion into forming a winning coalition in an election? – federating the electorate

Unit 11: The courts – the role of interpreting constitutional principles or how courts handle tort claims – does the reliance on common law in tort cases lead to non-federalist results? – justice among legal adversaries

Unit 12: Society – during emergencies such as wars – what are the parameters surrounding special demands on citizenship? – the decision to shelve the draft; the possibility of instituting a mandated service obligation

Unit 13: International associations – levels of interdependence between nations, US foreign trade policy – should or how should federal policies promote job availability *vis-à-vis* countries with cheap labor? – liberal or constrained trade policies

As the reader can see, each unit is listed by stating its main area(s) of concern (e.g., Congress) and a related issue that, if studied, would address a societal health topic. Each unit addresses some incidence of federalist values being challenged. The above content choices are recommended for those localities where the mentioned issues have targeted import. They are, as described above, concerns students can choose to act upon through an action assignment.

But before moving on, a bit of warning needs to be extended. And to make the point, the opioid crisis (Unit 3) example is used. This crisis is an ongoing societal problem that abuses federalist values. HD-to-A has students engage in a political or otherwise voluntary activity meant to help end or ameliorate the local manifestation of such situations.

If the issue, as exemplified by the opioid crisis, involves illegal activities, if chosen, teachers need to *guarantee* that students do not come into physical contact with any of its illegal aspects such as selling or buying the drug. For example, students cannot be exposed to any handling or being in the proximity of any illicit drugs or with those who engage in its trade.[86] If the readers reaction is, "well, duh", that is a good sign, and this writer is thankful for it.

In Review: the HD-to-A Model

The historical dialogue-to-action (HD-to-A) approach has students review the historical record relating to an issue. The conditions of that issue reflect some social reality in which a federalist value is being to some degree defiled. Those involved

---

[86] This can become touchy if a student's relative(s) or friend(s) engages, in any way with the drug's trade. Perhaps those students should limit their interaction with people who are – from a community effort to a law-enforcing attempt – working, from afar, to address either the market conditions under which this drug is distributed or the consequences of its sales and consumption. Students should avoid witnessing the actual sale or consumption of the drug.

use history to decide what should be done to solve or ameliorate related problems that people face. That has a future orientation.

In any of its forms, dialogue, when using historical information, can be utilized for one of two purposes: forensic uses or deliberative uses.[87] That is, to ask about the past to devise the reasons for what happened – forensic questioning – or to ask about the past to decide what should happen – deliberative questioning. Civics is about the future and, therefore, dialogue should be a deliberative exercise.

By way of review, here is an overall instructional model that incorporates the HD-to-A progressions outlined above:

Phase One: Reflect on one's interests and concerns (based on personal, communal, national affiliations) relating to some political reality that offends federalist values and has a local presence. That could be any one of the topics this book highlights in its "unit" chapters (opioid crisis, tort law, or foreign trade and job availability) or other concerns.

Phase Two: Investigate how that issue/topic/problem area is experienced locally.

Phase Three: Identify local agents (government officials, media personnel, victims or perceived victims of the concern with the exception of those who would expose students to illegal activities).

---

[87] Forensic questioning asks: what happened, why did it happen, and what should have happened? This form of questions is suitable in historical studies and, as these questions indicate, the study or dialogue emphasizes the past. Deliberative questioning, on the other hand, asks: based on past events or developments, what is likely to happen, why will it happen, and what should happen? A civics course deals with policy questions and therefore, has a future, deliberative orientation. See Atchison, *The Art of Debate – A Transcript Book.*

Phase Four: Set up appropriate information gathering protocols such as interview sessions of affected people or identify relevant recorded information sources (e.g., recorded testimony)

Phase Five: Gather information.

Phase Six: Review various action options (identified above) as a final work product, e.g., organizing and running meetings of interested parties and citizens.

Phase Seven: Perform action.

Phase Eight: Coalesce resulting information in a report that can include written materials, tapings (such as interviews), etc., and a set of recommendations for further action.

Phase Nine: Submit the report and be able to describe, explain, and defend its findings in terms of how comprehensive it is and the anticipated effectiveness of what it advocates.

The Discipline of Reflected Argument

With this curricular approach, this account turns to the elements of a logical argument. As stated above, the approach promoted here holds as central the function that logical argumentation plays in determining and implementing citizen action. The HD-to-A approach has students, in evolving levels of sophistication, engage in dialogue about political issues.

The progression in this approach includes instruction in those skills that are associated with discussions, arguments, and finally, debates. The works of Philip Selznick and Stephen Toulmin offer useful ideas in the planning of relevant lessons. For readers who have not had formal training in logic or if it's been a while since they have had such instruction, what follows serves to introduce or refresh the reader in logical/reasoned dialogue.

This account succinctly reviews the discipline one needs to apply in the use of reason, a central tool in legitimate argumentation. What Selznick[88] provides is a useful list of qualities upon which reasoned arguments are based. He calls them the five pillars of reason. The qualities are order, principle, experience, prudence, and dialogue. Their consideration leads to legitimate ends and one can improve upon them by practicing them and attempting to meet their demands.

As indicated, each "pillar" can be referred to as a discipline. The definitions of these disciplines are:

- Order: It calls on a person to be able to functionally objectify the information relevant to an argument by keeping in check any emotions that hamper an objective-based analysis. While a person sees things ultimately through biased eyes, he/she can work on being more objective.

- Principle: It calls on a person to keep in focus ultimate goals of the argument-formation-delivery process. "Reason is end-centered: the fate of comprehensive or long-term objectives is always to be kept in mind, always open to intelligent assessment."[89] Some call this ability the ability to reconceptualize (or, in the current parlance, to reconstruct).

- Experience: It calls for a willingness to subject a formed hypothesis to experience – aka, empirical information – from various sources. Arguments can most *explicitly* derive that information from experimentation, but more practically from historical information. The aim is to seek information from reputable historians, journalists, and other researchers. At times, if applicable, interviews with eyewitnesses or other affected subjects are useful.

---

[88] Selznick, *The Moral Commonwealth*.

[89] Ibid., 59.

- Prudence: It calls on a person to demand a critical review of any derived theories or models against ongoing experience, what Selznick calls "practical wisdom."

- Dialogue: It calls on a person to honor diversity of ends in terms of others' goals and understandings by engaging with them in mutual efforts – as they act as honest agents – toward seeking truth and/or prudent policy. At times, this discipline relies on negotiation and compromise, but in any event, it helps in checking biases of oneself and others.

In the study of government and civic affairs, a person is likely to be involved with making and evaluating arguments. Federated citizens seek this eventuality and are disposed to demonstrate the related skills in their verbal interactions. Participants try in political interactions to determine what is good policy; should the government do this or that?

Not far below the surface of social niceties is the reality that sought-after assets are scarce to the point all compete to attain them. To be federated is to be in agreement that the participating parties agree on a grand protocol where all have their integrity and basic needs met within reason. That relates to the essential reasons to establish a polity among the people.[90]

A "good" civics education program wants students to be able to determine the soundness and reasonableness of arguments. As Selznick points out, this does not mean that arguments should follow the tenets of rationalism in which only reason is used to construct and accept an argument.[91] A reasoned argument has room for emotions, but one needs to be disciplined in the use of reason *and* emotions. However, they should avoid

---

[90] A good accounting for the natural basis of this competitive nature of social life is provided by Steven Pinker. See Pinker, *How the Mind Works*.
[91] Selznick, *The Moral Commonwealth*.

86

sentimentalism – arguments based only on emotions such as tenderness, sadness, or nostalgia.

Yet all behaviors begin with an emotion that motivates the person to act or think in a given way.[92] Not only that, but in everyday experiences, a person is led by emotional or intuitive thinking and reasoning only plays a role to justify – to others – already determined conclusions.[93] One, to be effective, needs to achieve a balance between reason and emotions and this is difficult but possible.

In this, one can find undeserved legitimization in certain types of arguments. Some arguments or positions held by even reputable sources are, upon reflection, radicalizations of some theory, ideology, religious belief, or philosophic position. A possible or even likely outcome here is a person promoting a belief or claim of knowledge as being true and that, in turn, should trump all other relevant considerations. Such an approach assumes perfect knowledge, something at which humans have been proven to be quite deficient. "Ain't nobody perfect."

In general, then, students should be on the "look-out" for such arguments. To do so, Selznick's disciplines help; they – when melded with skills *a la* Toulmin – lead to logical argumentation.

Toulmin's Elements of a Logical Argument

To be effective in this approach, a teacher needs to be informed as to what constitutes a sound argument and, in turn, he/she needs to develop certain skills. Toulmin's model[94] is useful because it provides a set of elements for logically sound argumentation, but it also lends itself to instructional elements by targeting specific, useful skills. Examining arguments can assist one in this development. Here is one that can be useful; while not a

---

[92] Pinker, *How the Mind Works.*
[93] This is simply how people think and act. Haidt, *The Righteous Mind.*
[94] Toulmin, *The Uses of Argument.*

particularly good argument, it will demonstrate the elements of a sound one.

It goes as follows: Since Paolo was born in Italy, he is therefore a Roman Catholic because eighty percent of Italians are Catholic according to the latest census reported on Wikipedia (81.2%), unless Paolo happens to be in the roughly twenty percent of the population that is non-Catholic and assuming Paolo is a human being and not, say, a cat or a dog.

Now, here's a not so sound argument: Since Jane smokes marijuana, she will therefore eventually be addicted to serious drugs such as heroin because most addicted people at one time smoked marijuana as numerous surveys of addicted people reveal, unless Jane does not live to "graduate" to harder drugs and supposing that she is not subject to arrest or an addiction prevention program before an addiction is formed.

The first argument is sound but does not convey anything meaningful. The second is not sound but does attempt to convey a meaningful, albeit illogical message. The soundness of each relates to how reasonably it includes the factors that make up a logical argument. Training in syllogistic reasoning assists one in seeing this inclusion.[95] So, by stating that 80% of the population of Italy is Catholic and qualifying the argument that Paolo could be part of the 20% that is non-Catholic, therefore, the entire population of Italy is included.

But in the second argument, when one states that just about all hard drug-takers began their use of illicit drugs by consuming marijuana, one is not totally inclusive – not in terms of establishing a causal relationship or even a useful correlation. For example, how many marijuana smokers have never tried hard drugs? Probably many more than have tried them.

---

[95] For a delightful, short overview of syllogistic reasoning, see Bow, "Logic," *Mathematics*, 18.

Yet, most people have heard this second argument – linking marijuana smoking and hard drug use – and without much reflection, many have accepted the conclusion that marijuana smoking will result in acquiring a hard-drug addiction or be highly instrumental in doing so. While there *is* a correlation among those who are suffering from a hard drug addiction and earlier use of marijuana, a more telling statistic – a more meaningful one – would be how many marijuana users eventually "graduate" to hard drugs.

In that, the numbers are small and, therefore, it is difficult to conclude that marijuana leads to hard drug use.[96] So, one can make a more useful argument. For example, the more meaningful factor *could be* attitudinal: how disposed is a person to break the law or irresponsibly seek experiences that defy social norms.[97] These "rebels" are apt to look for ways to counter any behavioral standards that society considers moral or responsible. Such people are readily known by most other people as individuals who "live on the wild side."

To construct a good, sound argument entails performing certain skills. And if one not only wants to convince others of a point of view, but also to assure oneself and others that the point of view is true or responsible, one needs to develop those skills. A dissection of a sound argument, such as the one about Paolo, reveals what those skills are.

Toulmin[98] provides a model for argument structure that is helpful in this endeavor. The first argument begins with a factual statement: Paolo was born in Italy. Toulmin's model classifies this as a datum statement. These statements are the who, what, when, where, and how statements. The skill involved in this first stage is to make sure that the datum statement is true. For example, journalists who are professionally involved in searching

[96] "Is Marijuana a Gateway Drug?," National Institute on Drug Abuse .
[97] Of course, of late, several states have decriminalized certain uses of marijuana. What is conveyed here assumes this has not taken place.
[98] Toulmin, *The Uses of Argument*.

truthful claims have a protocol to heighten the likelihood of reporting truthful statements.

Before accepting a factual claim, journalists need to hear it from two separate, independent sources unless the substance of the claim is personally viewed or otherwise perceived by the journalist. Whether that is sufficient is a matter of judgment, but as a requirement, it demonstrates a concern over the truthfulness of any claims.[99]

With the use of reason, facts can lead to some conclusions. For example, Paolo is a Roman Catholic is derived from the fact that Paolo was born in Italy. Using syllogistic reasoning, the fact – Italian born – would be a minor premise (such as in the standard example: Socrates is a man). In Toulmin's model, the fact leads to a conclusion: Paolo is Catholic.

But that's a big jump; one needs some connector statement to make such a conclusion reasonable. Toulmin calls that sort of connecting statement a warrant statement (in a syllogism it would be a major premise). In this simple argument, that would be 80% of Italians are Catholic (in the standard example: All men are mortal).

The reasoning of inclusion from the syllogistic model goes as follows: All men are mortal (major premise), Socrates is a man (minor premise); therefore, Socrates is mortal (conclusion).[100] But Toulmin's model arranges the argument in a different order and adds a few more elements.

---

[99] A good, dramatic depiction of this process can be appreciated by viewing the feature film, *All the President's Men*. In that movie, one can view how even this process can result in untruthful claims. Pakula (director), *All the President's Men*.

[100] This basic structure of a logical argument is attributed to Aristotle. See, for example, Bow, "Logic," *Mathematics*, 19.

To begin with, the warrant statement (or major premise) is supported with backing statements (according to the latest census and reported on Wikipedia). It should be added that in either using syllogistic reasoning or using Toulmin's model, major premises or warrant statements are called for, whereas in everyday arguing they are mostly assumed and unstated. Such assumptions lead to faulty dialogue in that many conclusions are stated without linking facts to what the conclusion is claiming.

In terms of backing statements, what becomes an issue is: is there sufficient evidence, reasonable claims, or other reputable basis for making the claimed connection? In Paolo's case there is census information. In general, one can use scientific findings, reasoned generalizations, or insights emanating from reputable experts or reputable organizations (for example, government agencies) or gathered data to back a warrant statement.

In addition, the conclusion, in Toulmin's model, is qualified using an "unless" statement (Paolo is part of the 20% that is non-Catholic) and a reservation (assuming Paolo is human and not a dog, for example). These elements add richness to the argument or nuance and, therefore, the conclusion is more apt to be truthful or accurate. By the way, truthfulness is never guaranteed, but its probability is increased by using logic.

But the addition of these elements results from someone employing skills. They are finding truthful, factual statements, deriving from the facts a logical conclusion, tying the facts to the conclusion with a powerful enough warrant that justifies the connection, identifying the backing information that validates the warrant statement, and including the necessary qualifiers and reservations that prevent an overstatement – unjustified inclusion or overgeneralization.

If one applies such skills to the issue addressed in the second argument above, the one about marijuana, perhaps one can more meaningfully derive the conclusions that would help resolve the drug problems of this nation. Such argumentation is not easy, especially when one is not merely attempting persuasion, but is attempting to derive the truth or effective policy (the elements of a legitimate argument).

Keeping an Argument on the Straight and Narrow

How do arguments go astray, i.e., end up being illogical? This will be addressed with a distinction being made; that is, pointing out the difference between sound argumentation that can be aimed at both truth sharing and being persuasive and those cases in which arguments are meant only to be persuasive. People who use arguments – truthful or otherwise – for the sake of persuasion engage in rhetoric.

Rhetoric is usually noted for clever uses of language. Those arguments that happen to be illogical and used for rhetorical purposes are common in everyday news coverage. Effective listeners can detect them. One should remember what the aim of political speeches is to convince others of a political position or to act in a given way – such as voting for a candidate. In every case, politicians engage in rhetoric and, therefore, what they say is not *primarily* meant to share truth.

As such, rhetorical arguments might be based on out and out lies. Some arguers are very good at lying. But another approach of dishonest rhetoric is not to tell untruths, *per se*, but according to Richard A. Lanham, to engage in illogical argumentation that *sounds* logical and truthful.[101] In civics classes, teachers should make rhetorical analysis a recurring activity.[102]

Lanham identifies two sorts of supports: real and synthetic. Real support refers to evidence such as eyewitness accounts, documents, scientific reports or analysis, and laws.

---

[101] Lanham, *A Handlist of Rhetorical Terms*.

[102] For example, a teacher, after sharing an example of political rhetoric, can ask students to determine what support the speaker uses to convince someone. This encourages students to be critical listeners.

They are factually based claims about reality; what Toulmin calls datum statements. Usually, a single datum statement does not prove the conclusion, but when added to other testimony, it can support the conclusion, perhaps even prove it. For any conclusion of any complexity, the usual argument lists several facts and each one can begin with the words "since" or "whereas."

On the other hand, there is synthetic support. "Synthetic" does not necessarily mean untrue or unreal. It is a statement of reality that is not necessarily a logical supportive statement or does not sufficiently, despite its claim for truthfulness, prove the conclusion. Despite that, it is used to support a conclusion and takes on one of various types.

In the Paolo example, if one says that he is Catholic because Mr. X says so and Mr. X has a good reputation or good character, then this argument is based on a synthetic support. It is supportive but does not logically prove the case. The ancient Greeks noted the use of reputation – argument using the good name of its advocate – and called it "ethos." Of course, ethos can help in formulating a successful argument. Good reputation naturally lends force to an argument – people tend to be lured by it – but it does not make the case.

Also aiding an arguer can be a pleasant mood or generation of a positive feeling, what the Greeks called "pathos." One is encouraged to believe Paolo is Catholic because one is Catholic, and one likes Paolo and one would like to believe his afterlife is more secure if he is Catholic, according to that speaker's biases. A use of good feeling can be expressed in the argument and increase the likelihood of its acceptance. But again, it is not enough to prove a conclusion and, as such, it is synthetic.

Then there is the argument that sounds logical whether it is or isn't and that is known as the use of "logos" according to the Greeks. For example, an argument might state that one knows

Paolo is Catholic because one saw him attend a Catholic mass. While illogical, it attempts to sound logical. That is, while the proof here is based on a real event – Paolo attended a mass – it is not enough to logically conclude he is Catholic. One does not need to be Catholic to attend a Catholic mass. Here, the support is synthetic because the argument is illogical.

Again, a rhetorical device does not make the conclusion false, but if the device is synthetic, it is illogical, artificial, *or* incomplete argumentation (as is the case of Paolo attending a mass). Yet while illogical or insufficient, the illegitimate uses of ethos, pathos, or logos are all used to convince the listener of a conclusion and not to *necessarily* share a truthful and/or logical argument.

But good arguers should keep these three qualities in mind and be disposed to use them in legitimate ways. That is, an arguer is assisted by holding a good reputation, promoting good feelings, and of course, being logical. [103] Also, to be an effective arguer or debater, one needs to develop "an ear" for these devices to evaluate what others are saying and how those arguments stack up in terms of logical requirements.

Another concern is that certain mental operations need to occur if a person is to follow a "proof." Here, one is on more familiar ground. There are two mental operations: inductive reasoning and deductive reasoning. Inductive reasoning focuses on factual claims and deductive reasoning focuses on warrant statements.

By relying on datum statements, one's main concern in inductive reasoning is to ask: are there enough datum statements to account for all the incidents relevant to the conclusion or is it

---

[103] Bishop, "Legal and Legal Practice," *Law School for Everyone*. Ms. Bishop applies the concepts of ethos, pathos, and logos to the art of good argumentation in the courtroom. Their use, therefore, is not, in and of itself, illegitimate, but can be part of a responsible and effective argument.

based on a partial – insufficient – number of incidents? As this question indicates, induction relates to logos, as described above.

For example: Maria is Italian and Catholic; Carlo is Italian and Catholic; are those enough cases to logically prove Paolo is Catholic since he was born in Italy? Obviously not, but that is the concern when thinking inductively.   There must be enough cases to prove the argument or what statisticians would demand: the "n" number must be large enough. Short of that, one is talking about levels of probability in making a conclusion. In the illustration above, there is an 80% probability that Paolo is Catholic assuming he is a person. Even significant correlations end up being probable conclusions, but if the "n" is big enough, one is prudent to accept its validity.

This leads to another concern.   Reasonable dialoguers also note whether their conclusions identify relationships between or among factors that are correlations or causal connections. Do many cases associated with a conclusion reflect a situation in which the cases cause the conclusion or are they all caused by some other, at times unidentified, factor? [104] Perhaps the reader can think of an example.

Growing up, the writer was told that colds are caused by cold weather, after all, winter is when people were much more likely to catch them. Now, he is led to believe that cold weather is not the direct cause; instead, cold weather causes people to stay indoors near others. This makes being in closed-in areas the

---

[104] Gaarder, *Sophie's World*. This is a delightful review of western philosophers. As to the point being made: this claim is more in line with David Hume's contribution. The important lesson is that there is a distinction between things as they are and things as they are to the person perceiving them. Empiricists – that is, scientists – today readily succumb to this reservation over what is causal. They, in their research, do not contend that they discover cause and effect relationships; they merely report correlation. That is, they issue "X happens, Y happens" sort of statements – it is their theorizing that makes cause and effect contentions and even then, they are hypothesized.

cause since in those areas the contagiousness of viruses is more apt to occur. Therefore, it's not cold weather, but the avoidance of cold weather – staying inside – that is to blame. As this example illustrates, induction can be tricky.

On the other hand, in terms of deduction, an arguer concerns him/herself with whether the warrant statement – the claim that establishes the logical relevance or connection between the datum statements and the conclusion – conclusively or probably connects the two. Careful: the reference here is to the viability of the warrant statement, not the datum statements, and not a conclusion statement.

The claim, for example, that all Italians are Catholic is a generalization – and it links the fact that Paolo is Italian with the conclusion that he is Catholic. As stated, the assertion – the warrant statement – is conclusive (but not true). Offering an alternative warrant claim, the overwhelming number of Italians are Catholic, is a qualified generalization which makes the conclusion probable – Paolo is probably Catholic – and true in its probable form. These are the determinations one looks for when analyzing deductive reasoning.

For each of these various elements, at least one analyzing question can be derived (e.g., how many people observed a reality claim?) and teachers can devise them so that students can analyze arguments such as in politicians' speeches. A possible assignment: students can "diagram," according to Toulmin's model, a famous argument, such as the one expressed in the *Declaration of Independence* (limiting the number of datum statements to two or three).

Fallacy Types

As alluded to above, political argumentation makes up much of what is reported on the news. To further assist teachers in having their students analyze arguments, this chapter provides a partial listing of illogical arguments – fallacy types – that seem to reoccur in common speech, the media, and in political rhetoric. There are recurring forms or types of fallacies. They are so common that logicians have been able to classify them.

One can readily find a list of fallacy types, including the following list (it is drawn from a list of fourteen types), including their definitions, and an illustration of each:

- Appeal to authority – Also known as "argumentum verecundia" (argument from modesty); if someone is respected for his/her knowledge and believes/believed in some conclusion, it must be true. Since the genius, Albert Einstein, rejected the unpredictability attached to quantum mechanics, it must not be true.

- Appeal to public opinion – Since something generates a public emotional bias, statements that apply that bias must be true. Example: Since football (American style) is so popular, it should not be regulated in terms of its alleged effect on brain injuries.

- Association fallacy – Also known as "guilt by affiliation;" something is wrong, untrue, or immoral because an unsavory person believes or ascribes to it. Example: Since my political opponent is backed by the leader of the opposition, voters should reject him/her.

- Attacking the person – Also known as "ad hominem;" it attacks a position by insulting the person or group espousing it. Example: Why would anyone listen to a proposition offered by that jerk?

- False causation fallacy – Also known as "cum hoc ergo propter hoc;" stating something is the cause of something else only because it preceded the second event; often considered a superstition. Example: They moved to Baltimore and six months later, they are getting a divorce. Baltimore ruined their marriage.

- Slippery slope – Simply because one allows an event to happen, it will lead to more serious and detrimental events to happen. Example: If a few illegal immigrants commit serious crimes, then being lenient on illegal immigration will lead to uncontrollable crime rates.[105]

Often, civics teachers confront one or another type of fallacy as students might repeat it from what is said at home, in their neighborhood, or from some politician on TV. These concerns are so central to the instructional approach this book suggests that a teacher would be well-served to begin several lessons with an example of an illogical argument and hold a quick contest as to which type of fallacy it is. If done regularly, students would experience a significant amount of practice in detecting illogical arguments.

Some Instructional Concerns

This presentation needs to review some instructional issues before it begins the first of three-unit chapters. These concerns pertain to each of the units presented in Chapters 3, 4, and 5. Overall, a general assumption is that just about any problem or issue, if instruction opts to treat it as a local concern, is more likely to be seen as relevant by the student.

This is commonsensical but difficult to find research to support it. Research is overwhelmed by national issues and problems – e.g., immigration, the national economy, drug problems, etc. But in the education literature, one can find the following type of argument being made:

> Sara Bernard [of Edutopia writes] … "If a student acquires new information that's unrelated to anything already stored in his[/her] brain, it's hard for the new information to get into those

---

[105] For a complete listing of the fourteen types see Gutierrez, "Fallacy Types," *Gravitas*.

networks because it has no scaffolding to cling to. Effective teaching helps students recognize patterns and put new information in context with old – a crucial part of passing new working memories into the brain's long-term storage areas."

Students need a personal connection to the material, whether that's through engaging them emotionally or connecting the new information with previously acquired knowledge. Without that, students may not only disengage and quickly forget, but they may also lose the motivation to try.[106]

And this is further enforced by the fact that what is local is more familiar and more apt to have an educational effect on young people. Therefore, one can make the following claim: local landscapes – be they of a physical sort or a mental sort – have a strong educational quality and exploiting that advantage makes sense.

In addition, as suggested above, if a course initially considers an issue such as the opioid crisis as experienced in those communities, it can further motivate the student to not only engage with this early material but also set a tone of relevancy for the course in general. Each of the problems identified in this book does have a potential local element and a teacher would be wise to at least point that out, if not emphasize it.

Also, this treatment of a suggested course of study suggests the teacher assign a *course*-wide assignment in which students, in groups of three to five, can plan and implement a *local* community action plan. Generally, this project can relate to the opioid crisis (Chapter 3), tort law (Chapter 4) or foreign trade

---

[106] Briggs, "How to Make Learning Relevant to Your Students (and Why It's Crucial to Their Success)," Inform Ed.

(Chapter 5) or any of the topics identified in the above suggested course of study. Of course, there are many other issues that can fulfill this function.

A teacher who is aware of which topic a group of students is planning while the course implements the relevant unit, can check with that group and ask for a "progress report;" how well are they doing? Instruction can have students investigate what local efforts are afoot during the related unit and assist those groups regarding their action component.[107]

And perhaps the final work product – the plan and its resulting materials and evaluation – could substitute for a final examination and be handed in during the last week of classes or during the designated exam period. Instead of students taking an exam, they can present their findings to the class and be subjected to appropriate questioning.

While conducting any targeted, local research, students, beyond usual information sources, can engage in interviewing local people – victims, professional responders, or media agents covering the issue – who are involved with the topic. Presentations can be augmented with videos or audio tapes of these interviews or having appropriate local responders invited to speak.

This is a good point at which to remind the reader, teachers, parents, administrators, especially if the topic relates to illegal behavior, that students are not to be exposed to illegal activities. Proactive steps should be taken to assure this exposure does not occur.

Also, the course early on (before Unit 3 begins) should dedicate time to reviewing the steps a student should follow in

---

[107] A proactive step a teacher can take is to research his/her community and identify community workers in each of the topic areas that is highlighted during the course.

devising and implementing a plan (in accordance with the HD-to-A action model presented above). Students should not wait until the topic is "covered" in class before they proceed to initiate their investigations and it should be remembered that the assignment – as suggested here – is not only to investigate, but also to devise and implement an action plan.

The action should emanate from their investigation. In turn, their end-of-course presentation should include a review of what their action was, what their reactions to the action are, and what lessons they draw from the entire experience. Students should incorporate the information gathered in their instruction and how it informed their action choices and enhanced – or diminished – their experiences. Of course, this reporting should be honestly and responsibly critical of the overall instruction during this course of study.

Local incidence of a problem – e.g., the opioid epidemic – presumably provides the real-life opportunities to seek out those who are dealing with the problem. The above (in the text and in a footnote or endnote) identifies a list of actions upon which students can embark. Here is a sampling of those options: organizing and carrying out a fund drive and canvassing an area to gather signatures in support of or against a bill or another initiative.

The overall goal of any of the following described units of study is to expose the students to what it means to be federated with their fellow citizens. To be federated means to care, to be interactive and collaborative with others, and to be aware of how social/economic/political realities affect the welfare of themselves and of others. Perhaps a mental image of that sort of citizen is provided by Tocqueville in his description of 1830s Americans. That can serve as a targeted exemplary image.

One More Contextual Point

Among the populace there is little awareness of how divided the fields of civics education and social studies, in general, are. This account, while its goal is not to give an extended report of this division, maintains that that division affects what this book is about since the disagreements are over what civics and social studies should teach. That is, the field does not agree on what the subject should be; each party has its own view or construct (general explanation) of what *is or should be* civics' content.

So, those who abide by each of the different constructs are competing for the allegiance of the field's professional groupings and of the general public, especially parents. To summarize these varying views, the chart below is offered. It summarizes key elements of the three constructs to which this account refers. They are federation theory, the natural rights perspective, and critical theory.

Figure 1: Chart of Vying Perspectives in Civics/Social Education

Construct	Ultimate or Trump Value	View of Equality	View of Liberty	Application to Civics/Social Education
Federation Theory's Liberated Version	Societal Welfare: Societal Survival & Health	Regulated Condition or Regulated Equality: Gov't regulates to assure human dignity, integrity, and the ability to participate while relying mostly on markets to distribute values – a sense of partnership prevails	Federal Liberty: Freedom to do what one should do	Historically, Parochial/Trad. was the dominant view of gov't/politics from colonial times up to the years following World War II – Newer version, Liberated Fed'ism, sheds parochial biases to be inclusive of all legal entities w/in a partnership
Natural Rights Construct	Natural Liberty	Equal Condition: Equality before the Law especially in regarding market relationships	Natural Liberty: Freedom to do what one wants to do (respecting others to have the same) – a sense of transaction prevails	The dominant view of gov't/politics since World War II; basic view of educational establishment
Critical Theory	Equality	Equal Results: To share equally in society's wealth; comradeship under a sense of solidarity prevails	Freedom from the exploitation by dominant class – Truly free to determine one's humanity	The dominant view of American academics particularly in socially related fields of study

The placement of this chart here can be questioned – a lot of its elements have not been addressed up to this point, but given the general aim of this chapter, its placement seems reasonable given the options the writer has. The information contained in this chart will be explained through the various sections of this book – particularly those theoretical sections accompanying the lesson chapters and in the Conclusion chapter.

General Aims in Applying Federation Theory

Hopefully, the reader can benefit from reviewing the chart because it provides foreshadowing of important claims this account makes. Picking up on the recommended approach that this chapter describes, federation theory, there are four main elements upon which a civics course should be built. In summary form, they are:

- One, the course should highlight political problems that offend federalist values and progress from local to national and then to international issues and arenas.
- Two, the course aims for students to progressively develop dialogue skills, from discussion to formal debate, by using ever more sophisticated modes of discourse.
- Three, the course should introduce students to action, i.e., to participate in more proactive political engagements through developing an action strategy that denotes development, implementation, and evaluation; i.e., the implementation of the HD-to-A Model.
- Four, the course through these activities sets out to implement the C3 Framework standards and have students evaluate political maneuvers through civic virtue concerns.

And with that short summary, it's time to look at specific units of study guided by federation theory and that implement the C3 Framework standards.

CHAPTER 3: A LOCAL POLITICAL CHALLENGE, THE OPIOID CRISIS

A General Aim

This book suggests that civics teachers focus on local civic problems or highlight the local aspects of national or international issues. By doing so, a civics course of study can illustrate how governmental institutions operate locally and provide opportunities for students to engage within those institutions in realistic and viable ways – what one can call political action. In this chapter, that civic problem or issue is the opioid crisis.

Such subject matter matches what the C3 Framework highlights, the civic areas in which a student can express civic virtue.[108] This chapter, the first of three, attempts to implement this general aim by calling for the utilization of federation theory to guide that implementation of the C3 Framework.

In terms of the unit presented in this chapter and quoting from the C3 Framework, the following standards seem relevant to this topic: "Individually and with other students evaluate citizens' and institutions' effectiveness in addressing social and political problems at the local, state, tribal, national, and/or international level ... apply civic virtues and democratic principles when working with others [and] ... analyze how people use and challenge local, state, national, and international laws to address a variety of public issues."[109]

---

[108] See National Council for the Social Studies, *Preparing Students for College, Career, and Civic Life, C3.*

[109] Ibid., various pages distributed through several portions of the publication. It is these standards that *most directly* guide the content that this chapter's unit of study will address. Other standards in the C3 Framework can also support this general aim.

This and the following two chapters follow a format: a general introduction to the problem area, an overview of how federation theory pertains to the problem area, a short history of the problem area, and lesson ideas a teacher might consider in teaching such a unit; these are suggested instructional ideas and materials. Here, then, are some introductory remarks.

A Definite Local Crisis

Unfortunately, for those victimized, the opioid epidemic has ravaged many communities across the US and, therefore, provides a serious offense to federalist values. It could be treated either as a national problem or a local one; there is even an international angle to this challenge. This chapter will treat it as a local concern. As such, if the resulting unit were to be situated within a course of study, it is recommended that it be placed toward the beginning of the course.[110]

As a third unit, it falls roughly in the third to fourth week of a high school course or the fourth to sixth week in a middle school course, assuming it is a year-long course. Of course, the high school version should be more sophisticated than the middle school version. As always, a teacher's judgement should be used to determine how much of what follows should be included at either the middle school level or the high school level – what follows "overshoots" in its identification of relevant information.

To many Americans, the opioid crisis of addiction seems to have suddenly mushroomed, a problem that befell the nation all at once. But this problem has a history and knowing and understanding it seems essential to finding solutions to meet its challenges. The detrimental use of prescription and non-

---

[110] In Chapter 2, it is suggested that the opioid crisis could be the focused issue when studying the neighborhood – Unit 3 of either an American government course (senior high level) or a civics course (at the middle school level). This progression – from local to international – runs counter to how adopted textbooks deal with government. Those books begin with a national orientation and only deal with local concerns as an afterthought.

prescription opioid drugs, in notable numbers, began in the late 1990s. Since then, as the statistics below demonstrate, their use has escalated.

What are opioids? They are a collection of painkillers that doctors have often prescribed to relieve both short-term pain – for example in post-surgery treatment – and chronic pain. They include, but are not limited to the following: oxycodone, hydrocodone (Vicodin), and the synthesized drugs such as tramadol, methadone, fentanyl, and carfentanil.

In terms of killing pain, they work well – although some question their effectiveness – and despite the concerns, patients in pain seek them and opioids readily come to doctors' considerations when choosing medications for those patients. Also, of note here – and further explained below – is the aggressive marketing strategies certain pharmaceutical companies have employed to bolster their popularity among prescribers.

As euphoric inducing drugs, they are also popular for recreational purposes. They have addictive qualities and resulting overdoses have potentially fatal effects. Below, as this chapter looks at how these drugs affect the individual, human biology plays a role in their addictive qualities. So, the epidemic portrays itself as both a medical problem and an abuse problem.

American use and in many cases misuse of opioids have generated a slew of statistics that reflect a very serious situation. With those figures, one can readily understand why the terms "epidemic" or "crisis" are being used. It turns out that the epidemic causes heightened misery in certain localities. It is those communities that might find it useful for students to take a close look at what is happening and ask what *should* happen regarding this malady.[111]

---

[111] The reader is reminded of the warning Chapter 2 states: illicit drug trade, by definition, is illegal, and students should not be exposed to that trade.

A legitimate place to "look" or led to look can be their civics classes – not because it is a "popular" or "controversial" issue, but because it offends federalist values. It does so by rendering the victims as ineffective partners within the grand partnership under the auspices of the *US Constitution* and of the various state constitutions. The abuse of opioids offends relevant federalist ideas and ideals.[112] And as with any federalist treatment of the problem, a local emphasis is quite appropriate and should be emphasized.

Beginnings and the Centrality of Federalism

By defining this problem as one that offends federalist values, one gleans how central to the constitutional character of the nation such a concern is and how understanding that character helps one identify the governmental/political aspects of its effects. While on the surface it might seem a bit off base, a good place to start this development goes back to the nation's colonial past.

Why? Because much of the opioid crisis could have been avoided or ameliorated if there had been in place a strong federalist sense among the people of local communities, the type exhibited by early Americans. The reportage of Sam Quinones, for example, does more than hint at this; it provides ample evidence in current America. [113]

Therefore, federalist ideas and ideals (as experienced in an earlier America) are not foreign to the American political culture – they were behind the issuance of the *Mayflower Compact* – but they do not have the prevalence they once had. While not all scholars agree, many believe that they held strong influences over American thinking about governance and politics up to the mid-twentieth century.

---

[112] Chapter 4 will present a formal presentation of what constitutes a federalist moral code. In doing so, it presents a list of federalist values.

[113] Quinones, *Dreamland*. See Chapter 6, toward the end of this book (the one being read); it provides a powerful example of how in one exception to the general trend, meaningful community action can turn lives around.

The claim here is that federation theory, in its parochial/traditional form, held dominance from the colonial period to the years following 1945.[114] Since then, the nation has shifted to a highly individualistic view of the natural rights construct.[115]

Chapter 2 offers some evidence of the earlier bias by sharing Tocqueville's observation of 1830s American political thinking and behavior. That quote describes Americans as not only disposed to local political discussion and action but also relishing in it. The resulting interaction is described by Tocqueville as a "clamour." Can a teacher recreate, within reason, this form of "clamor" in the classroom?

As one reads the information below relating to the opioid epidemic, one might remember Tocqueville's description of what resembled such a problem in the 1830s, that of drunkenness and the proactive community action to combat it. One can readily sense the difference in social/political attitudes between what exists today and what existed then. No, this is not an argument for temperance (as Tocqueville's account describes an early American aim), but an argument for caring.

---

[114] The intellectual history of the nation cannot be whittled down to one train of thought. As with any nation, the history of the US can be noted for a diversity of ideas and aspirations. A good review of this history can be found in Guelzo, *The American Mind* AND Elazar, *American Federalism* – to be clear, Elazar felt, to the point of his passing in 1999, that federalism continued to be the dominant political perspective among Americans – AND Gutierrez, "Our Federalist Roots: A Neglected Past?, *Theory and Research in Social Education*, 218-242 AND Gutierrez, "What Can Happen to Auspicious Beginnings: Historical Barriers to Ideal Citizenship," *The Social Studies*, 202-208.

[115] Elazar, *Exploring Federalism*. Elazar uses other terminology; he describes this level of individualism as the prominence of radical pluralism, a subcategory of federalist thinking. In terms of its earliest influences, the claim here is not that federalism stood alone or that it was a singular view. For example, within its time of dominance, there were opposing sub-theories. And before the theory was highly developed, there was a high degree of overlap with other views, even the early view of natural rights. The introduction of natural rights (*ala* John Locke) was not as individualistic as it is today.

The reader might question how extensively these values were held; after all, wasn't there slavery, the prejudicial acts against the most recent immigrant group, and the treatment of the indigenous peoples? There are ample examples of such un-federated behavior reflecting un-federated sentiments among the American people then and today. Unfortunately, there were, in the earlier years, various aspects of the nation's politics that fell short of federalist ideals.

The general trend of this earlier version or form of federalism treated these victimized groups as not part of the people who instituted the nation's constitutional agreement.[116] Therefore, they – those not included – were not subject to certain provisions, particularly regarding the federation's benefits (generally, they were not excused from its obligations).

Consequently, this account refers to this earlier version as *parochial*/traditional federalism. And the contributions of parochial/traditional federalism were/are important. It introduced federalist principles to the American continent; it functioned to define the constitutional tenets incorporated into the American constitutions (that of the nation and of the various states), and it was the source of basic governing and political values that guided the nation's activities and, one can argue, *set the stage* for what eventually led to more inclusion.

Unfortunately – at least in the eyes of this writer – these federalist values have either been degraded or disregarded entirely in the years since the mid-point of the twentieth century. One can argue that the nation's slowness to address the opioid crisis reflects this development.

What led to this shift toward a more individualistic perspective? Naturally, the answer to that question lies within the nation's history. Parts of that history challenged federalist values and changed the relative power of the constituent governments making up the federalist system. An appreciation of

---

[116] For example, read that Chief Justice Roger Taney's opinion in the Dred Scott decision was based, in part, on this idea. See Ellis, "Roger B. Taney and the Leviathan of Slavery, *The Atlantic*.

that history helps empower a person trying to address the opioid problem or any problem in which federalist values are challenged. It points out the depth of the challenge.

A partial rundown of these challenges is as follows: the introduction, in the mid to late eighteenth century of John Locke's ideas concerning individual rights (though not as individualistic as portrayed today);[117] the introduction of transcendentalism from Europe that popularized individualism and a bias toward self-reliance;[118] the Civil War[119] and Civil War Amendments (*Thirteenth, Fourteenth*, and *Fifteenth*) that, while ending slavery, downgraded the relevant strength of localism – an effect quickly softened.

On the economic front: the rise of industrialization by national corporations that treated workers as just another natural resource (leading to exploitation and undermining a sense of partnership); in response to industrialization, the Progressive Movement and the New Deal arising in which individuals were lost in mazes of large bureaucracies (the government opted for corporatist structures)[120] but, as a result, an anonymity formed,

---

[117] Guelzo, *The American Mind*. This account gives a good overview of how the federalist view (using other terminology) competed among different governing models (for example between the congregational view of the Puritans and the hierarchal view associated with the Church of England and within its own set of ideas as illustrated by those who ascribed to classical republicanism and those who ascribed to liberal republicanism).

[118] Santayana, "The Genteel Tradition in American Philosophy."

[119] This is not to include the emotional effects that the Civil War (and later, World War I) rendered among Americans – the level of slaughter was more than sobering. Yet, at no time was an optional mode of governance considered – the federalist model never came under debate or was threatened. See Guelzo, *The American Mind*.

[120] The history of the Progressive Era is a bit complicated. There developed two views: the New Nationalism of Theodore Roosevelt that can be described as approaching a corporatist view of government. But there was also an opposing view led by such national figures as Supreme Court Justice Louis Brandeis, who opted for a more federalist view. Neither side prevailed and shortly after Woodrow Wilson's term as president, a *laissez faire* view of governance and economics took hold. See Urofsky, *Louis D. Brandeis*.

availing people a new means by which to express their individualism.

And the political consequences to industrialization included the rise of a predominant central government, again at the expense of local government which led to a more national and then global political landscape; and finally, the furtherance of de-localizing politics and social consciousness with the advent of modern technologies – especially TV and computers. TV, for example, promotes a simplistic sense of reality[121] and encourages a less social life, in that homebound entertainment became the norm.

In terms of the New Deal, John Dewey, the philosopher usually associated with education, in 1936 made comments on the difference between a natural rights view and a more social view of rights. These comments were offered in response to critiques of the New Deal reforms of the FDR administration. Natural rights advocates – those who saw rights as natural ascriptions to human nature – considered the New Deal as an affront to natural rights – particularly those rights of businesspersons. Dewey defended the arguments of Supreme Court Justices Holmes and Brandeis by writing, "... their defense of civil liberties [is notable] but even more [notable] for the fact that they based their defense on the indispensable value of free inquiry and free discussion to the normal development of public welfare, *not upon anything inherent in the individual* as such." He goes on to write,

> The only hope for liberalism is to surrender, in theory and practice, the doctrine that liberty is a full-fledged ready-made possession of individuals independent of social institutions and arrangements, and to realize that social control, especially of economic forces, is necessary in order to render secure the liberties of the individual, including civil liberties.

This gives one a flavor of the battle between sets of assumptions of those who held a more social view, one can read "federalist" view, and natural rights view. See Dewey, "John Dewey on Liberalism and Civil Liberties, 1936," in *Major Problems in American Constitutional History, Volume II: From 1870 to the Present*, 245 (emphasis added) and 246.

[121] Postman, *Amusing Ourselves to Death*. In general, for an account of this whole movement toward noncommunal social landscape, see Putnam's *Bowling Alone*.

In total: the world becomes "smaller" and as such, problems initiating in far off locations call on national and international, as opposed to local, responses. The reader should not read into this listing of developments a negative judgement; they are merely presented here for their explanatory qualities. Each of these, one could say, was inevitable but did pose a threat to the nation's commitment to federalism.

For example, court decisions in the late 1800s and into the twentieth century legally defining laissez faire economic policy did much to undermine a federalist view of the economy.[122] Yet, it should be remembered that that construct survived as the dominant view of those developments that took place before 1945. Those court cases, for example, provide evidence to this claim; they mostly overturned laws passed by popularly elected legislatures.

But the federalist construct did succumb in the later years of the twentieth century. In its place, the dominant construct has been – to this day – the natural rights construct – as it is currently defined. This presentation does not dedicate much space to explain this other construct. Interested readers are guided to the writer's treatment of this view.[123] Suffice it to write, the newer dominant view, the natural rights perspective, enshrines an individualistic view of politics or what is known as classical liberal thought.

Unfortunately, when it comes to social pathologies such as the opioid epidemic, a natural rights view encourages indifference in the general population. If the problem does not offer an immediate tragedy or other problems to a person or his/her close family and friends, it can and often is ignored by those not so affected.

---

[122] See Hall, "Laissez-Faire Constitutionalism and Liberty in the Late Nineteenth Century" (introductory remarks to Chapter 2), in *Major Problems in American Constitutional History, Volume II: The Colonial Era Through Reconstruction*, 23-25.
[123] Gutierrez, "The Prevailing Construct in Civic[s] Education and Its Problems," *Action in Teacher Education*, 24-41.

Centrally, liberal thought believes, as an ultimate or trump value,[124] that individuals should be free to form their own values and goals in life along with the freedom to act toward fulfilling those values and goals. As alluded to above, Elazar[125] calls this radical pluralism: every person pursues exclusively his/her aims. This writer takes a further step and states that this is not federalism at all.

The value, liberty, following John Locke's standard, is the right to pursue one's value choices, limited only by the rights of others to do likewise. As an ultimate or trump value, the sanctity of a person to be such a free agent has been identified by the term, *individual sovereignty*.[126] Or as John Locke stated this key idea, "every man has a Property in his own Person."[127]

Here, *a la* John Winthrop, is one way to see the difference between how federation theory and the natural rights construct view liberty:

> ... Winthrop's "On Liberty" sought to disaggregate two notions of liberty, namely, natural liberty [aka natural rights] and civil or federal liberty. Winthrop identifies "natural liberty" as the liberty "common to man with beasts and other creatures." It is, in other words, the "liberty to do what he lists; it is a liberty to evil as well as to good." *Importantly, this type of liberty*

---

[124] As explained below, federation theory, as presented in this account, relies on a consequential model of moral thinking (as opposed to categorical moral thinking). Something is immoral because it leads to something, more inclusively immoral. This leads one up a chain of moral values until one gets to an ultimate or trump value. This type of thinking follows the pragmatic philosophic view of morality.

[125] Elazar, *Exploring Federalism*.

[126] Reiman, "Liberalism and Its Critics," in *The Liberalism-Communitarianism Debate*, 19-37. Adding to this view was Locke's notion that the social contract was formed by unencumbered individuals. Anthropological evidence and common sense undermine this view.

[127] Dan-Cohen, *Harmful Thoughts*, 296.

resists all authority and ultimately, is the source of moral evil.

On the other hand is civil or federal liberty, which Winthrop also calls moral liberty. This *"federal liberty"* is liberty governed by covenant. Winthrop gives examples of the "covenant between God and man" as well as "politic covenants and constitutions amongst men themselves." ...

This distinction between two types of liberty—liberty of the individual free from society and the liberty of the individual upon entering society—is not entirely unique to Winthrop. In fact, one finds a similar basic framework in social contract thinkers, including Hobbes and Locke. The similarity is not a coincidence. As John Witte has argued, social contract theory owes a debt to the Calvinist theology that also forms the foundation of Winthrop's Puritan theology.[128]

Yes, Locke, as he originally proposed his thoughts, was not so Lockean as he is understood today.[129] But to the point being made here, it is this notion of federal liberty that first initiated, on these shores, a love for liberty and a more communal sense by which to define it.

According to Elazar, federalism is/was the glue that bound constitutionalism, democracy, and republicanism together.[130]

---

[128] This theme will be central to distinguishing the natural rights construct and federation theory. This quote is found in "The First 'On Liberty,'" Intercollegiate Studies Institute: Educating for Liberty. Emphasis added.

[129] Locke's concerns are interesting to look at – a revulsion against the parasites of the surviving noble class on the British Isles. See Kramnick, "John Locke and Liberal Constitutionalism," in *Major Problems in American Constitutional History, Volume I*, 97-114.

[130] Elazar, "How Federal Is the Constitution? Thoroughly" *Readings for*

How? It contributes to enhancing basic social knowledge, promoting basic social/political skills, and casting in a positive light the role citizens play – or should play – by federating themselves one to another. It is in this spirit that an attack on the opioid crisis – and the other problem areas identified in the next two chapters – is sought.

Understanding the lack of such concerns for fellow citizens allows one to better understand how an opioid crisis can get started and spread. On the other hand, a federal liberty imposes civic roles and if such roles are exercised in the spirit of social capital, a different social landscape is formed.[131] Inescapable in such a landscape is federalism's inherent communal bias that opposes such a view of civic indifference. It is truly a "we are all in this together" sentiment originating with the Calvinist theological-political origins of the New England colonists.[132]

A Short History of the Opioid Crisis

With the above account of federalism and its emphasis on localism, one can review a short history of the opioid epidemic that follows.[133] This is a bit of a jump from one emphasis to another, but one should keep in mind that the aim is to link federalist values to the crisis and perhaps to a better response among Americans. First, though, two "housekeeping" issues

---

Classes Taught by Professor Elazar. There is a bit of disagreement about whether federalism still functions in this manner.

[131] *A la* Robert Putnam, social capital, a social quality, is characterized by having an active, public-spirited citizenry, egalitarian political relations, and a social environment of trust and cooperation. See Putnam, *Bowling Alone.* This quality plays a central role in the construct presented here; i.e., federation theory.

[132] Elazar, *American Federalism.*

[133] Thanks to Wikipedia for providing the general outline this history follows and the identification of many of the cited sources this history uses.

need to be addressed: a useful definitional distinction and the role and quantity of facts.

This account uses the word, factoid, to indicate a "parcel" of related facts. As the following history demonstrates, America's affair with opioids has created a winding narrative, one with various turns. In each turn, many facts make up the substance of that narrative. Here, in this history, is only a sample of those facts. To supplement this history, there is an online site[134] with a listing of factoids *and* insights for students to consider. Students can access the site to bolster their research, analysis, and evaluation, *a la* the C3 Framework.

As for the definitional distinction, the following is offered: Historically, people used the term opiates to indicate all drugs derived from opium. Later, the term, opioids, was used to distinguish between opiates from synthetic opiates. Today, the term, opioids, is generally used to include both categories.

With those points made, here is a short history. A more extended version stretches back to the 1800s when opiates were introduced to the US. During the Civil War, morphine, an opiate, was an effective pain reliever. Afterwards, the famous company Bayer (as in Bayer Aspirin) sold heroin (1898 to 1910) as a cough-suppressant, claiming it was non-addictive. [135] Apparently, experience proved otherwise and, in due time, concern among doctors was expressed by their increased reluctance to prescribe opiates.

This led to Congress enacting the Harrison Narcotics Act in 1914 which imposed a tax on opiates and still later, the Anti-Heroin Act of 1924, making the importation or manufacturing of heroin, also an opiate, illegal. Despite this legislation, one can

---

[134] See "Factoids and Insights Describing the Opioid Epidemic," submitted by Robert Gutierrez. To gain access use http://gravitascivics.blogspot.com/ , October 23, 2021.
[135] Moghe, "Opioid History: From 'Wonder Drug' to Abuse Epidemic," *CNN*.

describe the general awareness among Americans at that time to be quite limited.

One can also detect during the 1950s a belief that an addiction problem existed among Americans, but the problem was limited to jazz musicians. The mere presence of heroin in the country was considered a frightening condition but not an extensive one.[136] This writer remembers this general aversion to illegal drugs at that time.

Then, during the years of the Vietnam protests, a shift occurred in public opinion. In the 1960s and 1970s, a popularization of drugs among certain segments of the population – such as college students – took place. Chief among the favored drugs were marijuana and hallucinatory drugs, aka psychedelics. Their consumption became somewhat common and they were often depicted in popular media. There was even a much-highlighted event, the Woodstock music festival, where young people were readily shown consuming drugs.[137]

The war in Vietnam became a contributing factor in spreading a drug problem to the US since soldiers, coming back from the war zone, often came with addictions, such as to heroin. In Vietnam, these drugs were easily acquired. A Congressional report stated that 10 to 15 percent of returning vets were addicted to heroin.

In addition, there were highly publicized events; e.g., the overdose death of the singer, Janis Joplin, that furthered the general awareness of the problem.[138] This drew the attention of President Nixon; he declared drug abuse the nation's number one enemy.[139] In 1973, the estimate was that 1.5 deaths per 100,000

---

[136] Caldwell, "American Carnage: The Landscape of Opioid Addiction," *First Things*.
[137] Ibid.
[138] See Clear, "How Vietnam War Veterans Broke Their Heroin Addictions," *Behavioral Psychology (Habits)*.
[139] "Interview: Dr. Robert DuPont," *Frontline*.

people were due to overdoses and that was considered unacceptable.[140] Yet, this level of deaths due to drugs was only an introduction.

In the later years of the twentieth century, Americans expressed an increasing demand for what are now called opioids. In the 1970s, two drugs started to become common – Vicodin and Percocet (brand names for two potent opioids). Despite initial apprehension, doctors began to regularly prescribe these drugs in the 1980s, even though there were warnings.[141]

Unfortunately, in 1980, a short letter appearing in the *New England Journal of Medicine*, by a group of Canadian researchers, seemed to indicate that these drugs were not as dangerous as initially thought. Their findings determined that only a handful of people who took opioids became addicted – at least that is how many people interpreted the letter.[142] Years later, an author of that letter claimed that his intent was not to give a green light to prescribing these drugs and that the initial letter was based on use among hospitalized patients, not people in general.[143]

As the 1980s progressed, another non-opioid drug, crystalized cocaine, took center stage. Its popularity began during the 1970s, but has a history stretching back 3500 years in South America. There, the coca plant, from which cocaine is derived, has been used for a variety of purposes such as fatigue, depression, and intimacy dysfunction.[144]

---

[140] Caldwell, "American Carnage: The Landscape of Opioid Addiction."

[141] Waismann, "The Devastating Effect of Opioids on Our Society," *The Hill*.

[142] "Opioid Crisis: The Letter That Started It All," *BBC*. AND Porter and Jick, "Addiction Rare in Patients Treated with Narcotics," *The New England Journal of Medicine*.

[143] Leung, MacDonald, Stanbrook, Dhalla, and Juurlink, "A 1980 Letter on the Risk of Opioid Addiction," *New England Journal of Medicine*, 2194-2195 AND "Opioid Crisis: The Letter That Started It All," *BBC*.

[144] MacLaren, "Cocaine History and Statistics," *DrugAbuse.com*. To add a bit

By reacting to cocaine's upsurge in popularity in the US, the government established policies to counter a crack cocaine epidemic and, later, to initially meet the opioid epidemic. In the 1980s, government officials called those policies the War on Drugs.[145] Under this general governmental posture, the opioid crisis grew, starting in the late 1990s and into the new century. It became more identified in the nation's consciousness as it resulted in vast devastation to a growing number of American communities.

Some noted members of the drug industry developed a well-thought-out marketing strategy (during the years 1996-2001) for the opioid, OxyContin. The strategy aimed to alleviate concerns over the addictive qualities of that drug.[146] Prominently, a private pharmaceutical company, Purdue Pharma, organized more than forty promotional meetings in three locations in both the southeast and southwest regions of the US.

Using the term, "Partners Against Pain," this was a marketing strategy that offered a bonus system to incentivize sales of OxyContin, derived from Oxycodone. In part, the instigators of this strategy aimed to relieve fears about the addictive danger of the drug. They claimed that addiction affected less than 1 percent of users. Along with incentives, this claim encouraged doctors to liberally prescribe the drug.[147] Resulting sales indicate the strategy worked.

When it comes to recreational use of opioids among Americans, these two forms, Oxycodone and OxyContin,

---

of history: the German chemist, Friedrich Gaedcke, in 1855 isolated and purified the drug and Albert Niemann, in 1859, further "improved" the drug and gave the drug the name cocaine. Also, the coca plant is used to make cocaine and cocoa plant is used to make chocolate.

[145] Scott and Marshall, *Cocaine Politics*.

[146] Van Zee, "The Promotion and Marketing of OxyContin: Commercial Triumph, Public Health Tragedy," *American Journal of Public Health*, 221-227.

[147] Ibid.

constitute the most used, non-heroin opioids. According to the US Department of Health and Human Services report, circa 11 million Americans consume an oxycodone drug for recreational or non-medical reasons. As such, Oxycodone accounts for a large portion of this epidemic.[148]

Oxycodone has its own history in the US. It began in 1939 when it was first made available on these shores. But it took until the 1970s before US authorities in the Food and Drug Administration deemed this drug to have a high probability of being abused and potentially causing addiction. This government agency did this by classifying it as a schedule II drug.[149]

To get around the addictive quality of the drug, Purdue Pharma in 1996 introduced OxyContin. This "controlled" formulation of the drug was meant to make the resulting product less apt to be addictive, so the FDA approved it. Unfortunately, it wasn't long before consumers learned how to derive a purer oxycodone drug by simply crushing the controlled release tablets. They then could consume the derived drug by various ways: swallowing, inhaling, or injecting it. Any of these modes renders a very powerful opioid.[150]

---

[148] "Opioid Crisis Fast Facts," *CNN Library*.

[149] A schedule II (some sources capitalize the "s" in schedule) are defined by the US Drug Enforcement Administration as follows:

> Schedule II drugs, substances, or chemicals are defined as drugs with a high potential for abuse, with use potentially leading to severe psychological or physical dependence. These drugs are also considered dangerous. Some examples of Schedule II drugs are: Combination products with less than 15 milligrams of hydrocodone per dosage unit (Vicodin), cocaine, methamphetamine, methadone, hydromorphone (Dilaudid), meperidine (Demerol), oxycodone (OxyContin), fentanyl, Dexedrine, Adderall, and Ritalin[.]

See "Drug Scheduling," DEA.

The derived drug, when consumed, results in an upgraded "high" that is described as being "morphine-like." Purdue Pharma's eventual testing in 1995 demonstrated how users, by crushing their product, could extract a 68% oxycodone.[151] All of these developments cost Purdue Pharma; in 2007, the company paid a $600 million fine for making false claims about their product, specifically regarding its risks.[152] Today, this company still faces legal challenges.[153]

Then, in 2010, the company issued a newer version, a reformulated OxyContin. By using a polymer, they made their pills very difficult to crush or dissolve. In turn, this made the product significantly less apt to be abused. Predictably, as a result, documented use of the drug declined slightly, which in turn hints that a portion of its consumption was due to non-medical reasons.[154]

Despite this development, in 2012, Canada's government decided to strip OxyContin from its approved drug list. In 2017, the FDA requested the producers of oxymorphone, an injectable

---

[150] Van Zee, "The Promotion and Marketing of OxyContin: Commercial Triumph, Public Health Tragedy."
[151] Ibid.

[152] Meier, "In Guilty Plea, OxyContin Maker to Pay $600 Million," *The New York Times* AND "Purdue Pharma Lawsuit: Sackler Family Sued over Toll of Opioid," *CBS News*. Purdue Pharma's estimated worth, according to this *CBS News* report, is $13 billion. The woes through the years have continued. As of this writing, the company is considering bankruptcy to sidestep a high number of lawsuits. See Heisig, "How OxyContin Maker Purdue Pharma's Potential Bankruptcy Filing Would Stall Thousands of Lawsuits before Federal Judge in Cleveland," *Cleveland.com*.
[153] Purdue Pharma has filed for bankruptcy. See Hampton, "What Americans Don't Know about the Purdue Pharma Bankruptcy Hurts All of Us, *Time*.

[154] Hwang, Chang, and Alexander, "Impact of Abuse-Deterrent OxyContin on Prescription Opioid Utilization," *Pharmacoepidemiology and Drug Safety*, 197–204.

form of the opioid, to remove it from the domestic market. The agency determined that the risk of the drug is greater than its benefits. This marked a turning point for the FDA since it was the first time it issued such an order due to fears of abuse.

Nationally, the uptake in prescriptions and subsequent consumption led to a national death rate of 10.3 per 100,000 population. At the state levels, in New Hampshire, a death rate of 30 per 100,000 was reported and in West Virginia, a rate of 40 per 100,000 was reported.[155] In a 2016 national survey, conducted by Substance Abuse and Mental Health Services Administration, stated that more than 11 million people in the US misused prescribed opioids. In addition, one million used heroin and 2.1 million formed an addiction to prescribed opioids including heroin.[156]

From 2010 to 2017, overdoses of illicit opiates tripled. One can find signs, as the dangers of this type of drugs has become more readily known, that that upsurge has leveled off.[157] This writer began to see (in 2018) public service announcements informing viewers of the dangers involved.[158]

There have been state and local government reactions. Given the local nature of this unit of study, these local efforts should be emphasized.[159] The main reaction has been legislation

---

[155] Caldwell, "American Carnage: The Landscape of Opioid Addiction."

[156] Doherty, Gottlieb, McCane-Katz, Schuchat, and Volkow, "Federal Efforts to Combat the Opioid Crisis: A Status Update on CARA and Other Initiatives," National Institute on Drug Abuse.

[157] Dowell, Noonan, and Houry, "Underlying Factors in Drug Overdose Deaths," *JAMA*, 2295-2296.

[158] In a story on an opioid overdose reversal drug, naloxone, *CBS News* broadcast a heart-wrenching account of how an opioid addiction can present tragic consequences to a seemingly middle-class family. See "Saving Your Child from an Opioid Overdose," *60 Minutes*.

[159] Somewhere in this account should be stated the detrimental effects of being over-local or over-parochial in one's approach. Teachers should remember that the *US Constitution* is a national compact and students should be reminded that all of the US is "in this together." Perhaps a national

to block those prescribing protocols that have led to "high-risk" prescribing practices. For example, there are now laws against doctors and clinics prescribing the drug on long-term bases.

There have been four categories of laws: laws mandating a sign-up database of all patients who have been prescribed "controlled substances" – known as the Prescription Drug Monitoring Program (PDMP); laws mandating that any time a doctor or clinic worker is about to prescribe an opioid, he/she is to check the PDMP; laws limiting the amount and duration over which these drugs can be prescribed; and laws that establish the necessity to monitor clinics – some known as "pill mills" – to drastically decrease the opioid prescriptions they issue.[160]

Of late and of special concern, fentanyl has caused a heightened deleterious effect on the health of tens of thousands of Americans. The National Institute on Drug Abuse offers the following definition of that drug:

> Fentanyl is a powerful synthetic opioid analgesic that is similar to morphine but is 50 to 100 times more potent. It is a schedule II prescription drug, and it is typically used to treat patients with severe pain or to manage pain after surgery. It is also sometimes used to treat patients with chronic pain who are physically tolerant to other opioids. In its prescription form, fentanyl is known by such names as Actiq, Duragesic, and Sublimaze. Street names for fentanyl or for fentanyl-laced heroin include Apache, China Girl, China White, Dance

---

perspective of this issue can more readily do this, but since its pain is felt locally, this account sticks to its decision to treat it as a local issue.
[160] McGinty, Stuart, Alexander, Barry, Bicket, and Rutkow, "Protocol: Mixed-Methods Study to Evaluate Implementation, Enforcement, and Outcomes of U. S. State Laws Intended to Curb High-Risk Opioid Prescribing," *Implementation Science.*

Fever, Friend, Goodfella, Jackpot, Murder 8, TNT, and Tango and Cash.[161]

This deleterious effect can be measured in terms of deaths, as cited above, and economic costs. Generally, the economic cost of misused prescription opioids is estimated to be $78.5 billion a year. That includes healthcare, lower productivity, treatment, and costs related to criminal activities.[162]

The drug problem has been in the US for a long time. If one considers alcohol a drug, it has been part of the American story almost from the beginning. But with the opioid chapter – and especially regarding fentanyl – that story seems to have taken a significant turn. Christopher Caldwell of *The Weekly Standard* states: "… the scale of the present wave of heroin and opioid abuse is unprecedented. In Maryland, the first six months of 2015 saw 121 fentanyl deaths. In the first six months of 2016, the figure rose to 446."[163]

Within that context, one can consider a couple of insights when studying the fentanyl effect:

- At sites where accidents have occurred, incidences of first responders inadvertently suffering overdoses – from merely touching the fentanyl – has changed protocols. This is because fentanyl is very difficult to detect and because it is very potent. Now, applying DEA recommendations, they send collected material to laboratories for analysis.[164]
- The dangers of fentanyl have to do with its undistinguishable characteristics in granulated form (a white substance that is odorless and tasteless), surprising victims when they find out that they are in the hospital

---

[161] NIH: National Institute on Drug Abuse.
[162] "Opioid Overdose Crisis," *National Institute on Drug Abuse*.
[163] Caldwell, "American Carnage: The Landscape of Opioid Addiction."
[164] "Briefing Guide for First Responders," U. S. Department of Justice/Drug Enforcement Administration.

because their intended heroin fix was laced with fentanyl.[165]

As of the writing of this history (the beginning of 2019), there is one more development to that story. Last year, the US Senate passed the Opioid Crisis Response Act of 2018 and the House previously passed similar legislation. Both need to be reconciled and Congress is expected to do so.[166] In the words of the bill, its goal is "to address the crisis, including the ripple effects of the crisis on children, families, and communities, help states implement updates to their plans of safe care, and improve data sharing between states."[167]

The opioid crisis includes a regional character; its manifestation has been concentrated. For example, in 2016, West Virginia, the most affected state, had an overdose death rate of 52 per 100,000 population. West Virginia was followed by New Hampshire and Ohio with each reporting 39 deaths per 100,000.[168] Chapter 6 has, toward its end, a special tale to tell relating to this problem in Ohio.

But one cannot avoid noticing that this development seems to be experienced with little to no community reaction. There have not been, by local concerned citizens, significant protests of pill mills, for example. Public revulsion should be targeted and aimed at these sites. Yet, from what is reported either from this short history or the factoids and insights found listed on a related online site, [169] the common citizenry, except for some noted exceptions, has not been engaged.

---

[165] Cutway, "Orlando Man Pleads Guilty to Selling Heroin Mixed with Fentanyl," Orlando.com AND Howard, "Why Opioid Overdose Deaths Seem to Happen in Spurts," *CNN* AND "Opioid Data Analysis," Centers for Disease Control and Prevention.

[166] "Senate Passes the Opioid Crisis Response Act of 2018," *Revenue Cycle Advisor.*

[167] "The Opioid Crisis Response Act of 2018," U. S. Senate. A follow look in February 2020 indicates the bill has not become law.

[168] Caldwell, "American Carnage: The Landscape of Opioid Addiction."

[169] Reminder, the accessing URL is http://gravitascivics.blogspot.com/ ,

Yes, at the state and federal level, representative bodies have reacted and that might reflect citizen reaction, but it took too long to materialize, and one is not sure what is motivating these political/governmental actions. Surely the reaction – or lack of it – does not resemble the Tocqueville America described earlier in the last chapter.

This account provides this history as only part of the story. In addition, it refers to the just cited online site for more parcels of information and a set of insights (generalizations or explanations) that add to the story. For example, it looks at the controversy over whether countermeasures should include the use of opioid drugs or not.[170] Students can access that information as a starting point for any research they might undertake. Note: the site is augmented with citations of other online sources.

Related Lesson Ideas

With an overall short history, development of a unit of study can begin and is assisted by individual lessons that target the various elements of this epidemic. The lessons below address parts of the history shared above. They include: the issue as a challenge to federalist values, the challenge of opioid addiction at the individual level, counter therapies, production and distribution of opioids, demographic aspects of the crisis, and governmental reactions.

A teacher can choose from this list, do them all, or opt to include other elements of the narrative – other aspects are identified below. Instruction that informs students of the above historical account – which could be distributed, totally or in part, as a lead-in reading – prepares them to investigate these aspects. As such, each aspect can potentially serve as an organizing

---

October 23, 2021 AND in terms of lack of public reaction to this crisis, see Macy, *Dopesick* AND Quinones, *Dreamland.*
[170] Goodnough, "," *The New York Times* AND Macy, *Dopesick.*

concept for a single lesson or several of them can be lumped together in a single lesson.

Summarily, those concerns would reflect promoting the general societal qualities of social capital and civic humanism.[171] These, then, are some of the issues that instruction needs to address. Instruction does this by calling on the teacher to ask certain questions and provide certain materials. It is not by insisting that students accept a list of values, but consider these values in their research, their dialogue, and their action.

Appropriate "federalist" questions could include, but not be limited to, the following:

- How does the opioid crisis affect the individual integrity of people?
- How does an addiction to opioid drugs affect the ability of the individual to meet his/her communal responsibilities? What are those responsibilities?
- To what extent – magnitude – does the over-use of opioids manifest itself in *this* – the student's – community? What kinds of assets or resources promise to be effective in meeting the problem locally?
- What are the local responses to this epidemic? Are there private-non-profit organization efforts, local government – city and/or county – responses, state and/or federal government resources addressing the epidemic? If so, what are they?
- How is this crisis affecting people locally in relation to income distribution, racial divisions, cultural divisions, and/or other prominent divisions among the local population?

---

[171] Reminder: Putnam, "Bowling Alone: America's Declining Social Capital," *Journal of Democracy*, 65-78 AND McDonald, "The Power of Ideas in the Convention," in *Major Problems in American Constitutional History, Volume I* 160-169, 162-163.

This unit assumes that both teachers and students are willing to discuss these and other concerns associated with the opioid crisis, and relate them to federalist values. The fact that the emphasis is on the local manifestation of the crisis should help in this regard.

This account will now provide a short description of a one-week unit made up of five instructional, 50 to 60-minute lessons, with the last lesson dedicated to a unit evaluation. This overview offers an outline (organized by lessons with the number of days for each) and is followed by added information provided to enrich the reader's understanding of the various instructional elements. The outline of this unit is as follows:

Lesson 1 (one day) has students define the opioid crisis or epidemic in terms of federalist values and, through those values, surmise how the problem area challenges the ability of citizens to pursue civic virtue. Of note, Chapter 4 provides a list of federalist values.

Lesson 2 (one day) has students investigate how the opioid crisis affects people on an individual basis.

Lesson 3 (one day) has students, through their readings and talking to local people, discover existing counter therapies available for addicted people. Therapies can consist of counter drugs, targeted therapies, and/or participation in support groups.

Lesson 4 (one and a half days), through groups, has students research and report on one of the following topics: production and distribution of opioids, demographic aspects of the epidemic (where consumption of opioids is more prevalent), and various government reactions to the crisis. Note: this lesson calls for a work product to be verbally reported and submitted on the last day of the unit – its test day.

In terms of defining the issue *a la* federalist values, the above history or some version of it would be helpful. That reading can be distributed a few days before the unit begins. It is further augmented by many of the factoids and insights the teacher (and students) can find on the supplemental, online site.[172]

As for the history, the aim should not be to have students memorize this history, but rather to have a "conversational" familiarity with that history. Students who can recite a general knowledge of how long the problem has plagued the nation and its major deleterious effects would probably be knowledgeable enough to engage in a meaningful study of the other aspects of the problem.

If this unit appears early in the course, it should be remembered, according to the HD-to-A approach, that the dialogue skills to be expected have to do with discussion. In an early unit, therefore, this aim is limited. Here, students are merely asked to express opinions in classroom interchanges. This unit has students express their opinions over the various elements of this issue. It *introduces* students, in a conversational way, to logical requisites of reasonable dialogue and, in turn, useful self-evaluation of their discussion points.

In doing so, teachers might ask for reasons why a student holds an opinion; suggest, in a conversational tone, the reasons it is or is not logical; and briefly express why that is the case. If the teacher finds an above average sophistication level among the students, he/she can, in an informal way, introduce what warrant statements (insights that connect factual information to conclusions) are and how they are supported by backing statements.

Perhaps some instruction, through the implementation of the unit, can highlight the functions that warrant statements and

---

[172] That site is repeatedly referred to below. The teacher can cut and paste those portions of the site he/she cares to use or simply inform students what the site's URL is so they can read it themselves. As a reminder, here is that site's address that instruct the reader to gain appropriate access, http://gravitascivics.blogspot.com/ , October 23, 2021.

datum (factual) statements play. Reminder: datum statements serve as the "whereas" or "since" claims in an argument and warrant statements serve as the "because" claims.[173] In general, "whereas" or "since" statements are factual claims and "because" claims tend to be generalizations or insights.

To give the reader a sense of what types of information the factoids (bits of factual information) and insights contain on the online site, here is a sampling. The teacher can share whatever portion of that list with his/her students in an initial lesson of this unit.

Factoids:

Concerning heroin –

- The last decade or so has seen significant increases in heroin use. Those numbers include an increase from an estimated 374,000 Americans using heroin in 2002-2005 to 607,000 in 2009-2011.[174]
- By 2014, as a reflection of a leveling-off progression, the number was estimated to still be over half a million.[175]

Concerning fentanyl –

- Fentanyl has been named the deadliest drug in all of history. It is attributed to causing the deaths of 18,000 Americans in 2016.[176]

---

[173] To further remind the reader: *Since* Aristotle is a human (datum statement), he is therefore mortal (conclusion) *because* all humans are mortal (warrant statement in the form of a generalization). This argument uses the Toulmin format. The reader is given a presentation of logical argumentation in Chapter 2.

[174] Anderson, "Heroin," *Drugs.com.*

[175] "What Science Tells Us about Opioid Abuse and Addiction," *Abuse, National Institute on Drug.* This site is no longer posted. Instead see "Opioid Epidemic," *Wikipedia.*

[176] *NBC Nightly News with Lester Holt*, broadcast December 12, 2018. Apparently, there is an even more toxic opioid making its presence felt. That is carfentanil.

- Between 2013-2016, the death rate linked to fentanyl consumption rose 113% per year.[177]

Insights (or generalizations):

Concerning opioids in general –

- The epidemic is more acutely felt in rural areas due to over-users in those more remote areas not having medical and therapeutic services that are readily available elsewhere.[178]
- Opioid use results in an addiction rate of 56% as of 2018.[179]

Other entries in the insight list identify the role that the debacle of coal mining and the loss of jobs to foreign cheap labor countries have played in rural communities, seriously disposing them to drug addiction.

Concerning heroin –

- Opioid users who shift to heroin tend do so because heroin is cheaper than prescribed opioids and can be readily obtained through black market outlets – *without* a prescription.[180]
- The profit margin of heroin is 600 percent which readily motivates an ongoing sells force.[181]

---

[177] Ibid.

[178] Oliver, "Opioids," Last Week Tonight available on YouTube. A further word on this site. Oliver presents a very good review of the problem in terms of its present (mid-2018) manifestation. An educator, though, should be aware that despite its usefulness, it is riddled with satire and profanity including sexual references. Teachers should review the site before considering assigning its viewing.

[179] Macy, *Dopesick*.

[180] Kolodny, et al., "The Prescription Opioid and Heroin Crisis: A Public Health Approach to an Epidemic of Addiction," *Annual Review of Public Health*.

[181] Macy, *Dopesick*.

Of course, as with any of these lesson ideas, the teacher is encouraged to be "choosy" in what he/she includes. In no way is this account insisting the teacher use any of the material; the aim is to be helpful. But in terms of what follows, the different lists offered here are aligned with the way the unit is visualized by this writer.

This review has noted that a list of federalist values is listed in the next chapter. But here, a word or two adds context. Those values summarily advance the societal qualities of social capital and civic humanism (or, in terms of the C3 Framework, civic virtue). In this unit, the student should be able to communicate how the crisis undermines the central federalist concerns or values in that the US is a grand partnership among its citizens.

In any endeavor, partners seeking to achieve shared aims and goals who find themselves compromised – be it for any reason – will probably not be able to fulfill their responsibilities as partners and in turn, will, to whatever degree, hinder the partnership in fulfilling its aims. As the crisis grows, this can be significant, especially in local areas.

This point does not mean to belittle the very human concern for those victimized. Federalism counts on the eventual, if not initial, sense of caring that either coordinates or encourages communal efforts. Somewhere, this writer has heard the saying: "Benevolence is the gravity of humanity." But the problem transcends the personal costs it has on individuals, and a mature consciousness insists on melding the personal with communal needs.[182]

In lesson 1, students discuss the history of the crisis and ask: how and why did the nation find itself at the level of crisis

---

[182] Selznick, *The Moral Commonwealth*

that the history describes? And questioning by the teacher should have students consider the opioid crisis as one that challenges federalist values both from the perspective of individuals and of the community.

In lesson 2, the emphasis is on how difficult an opioid addiction can make a person's life. The addiction to those affected becomes central in that person's consciousness. For example, Beth Macy gives a lurid description of how debilitating "dope sickness" can be.[183] In turn, getting the next fix becomes central. This leaves little room for other concerns such as being a family member, an employee, or a community member. And those consequences do not mention the possible medical problems, even death, that over-use can very likely cause.[184]

For example, medical consequences have social costs, but one should remember, they also have economic costs. Among the economic costs as mentioned above are lost productivity, but also emergency costs and related medical expenses that are often met by public funding since many affected addicts are not insured.

The basic question this second lesson addresses – and expects students to address – is: what are the symptoms of an opioid addiction? Supportive questions include: how do individuals acquire opioids? And how has the medical establishment interacted with affected individuals? One added concern that probably causes more of an emotional response is: how do opioids physically interact with a person's body?

In pursuing these questions, the lesson can have students creatively write, in class, a "day-in-the-life" of an opioid addict. The format can be in the form of a journal entry. This can be collected at the end of the class period or start of the next class period. Here, the teacher can evaluate the resulting narratives by

---

[183] Macy, *Dopesick.*
[184] See "Opioid Overdose Crisis," National Institute on Drug Abuse.

seeing how well students include the relevant factoids and the insights upon which the accompanying material reports, especially from the provided history and the referred-to online information the teacher chooses to include.

The aim would be to engender in students an empathetic sense of what it means to be so victimized. And with that focus, here is how the body is affected: opioid's sedative qualities are caused by the effect on that part of the brain – the respiratory center in the medulla oblongata – that controls breathing. The drug, if the dose is sufficiently large, produces a euphoric sensation that can be very strong. High enough doses can depress respiratory processes, potentially resulting in respiratory failure and even death.[185]

If students know first-hand about such cases, they can include, in their narratives, the related information they know to be true, but they should be instructed to respect the confidentiality of these peoples' identities and other personal information. Also, assisting students in this assignment can be cited sources – identified in this chapter's footnotes/endnotes and in the cited online site – to round out their narratives with relevant information.

Lesson 3 deals with counter therapies. The teacher can give students a list of such counter therapies for the various opioid drugs that drug responders have developed. Overall, counter therapies take the form of prevention strategies, prescriptions of counter drugs such as methadone (which has been controversial), behavioral therapies such as 12-step programs, and individual and group therapies.[186]

---

[185] "Information Sheet on Opioid Overdose," World Health Organization (UN).
[186] See "Opiate Withdrawal Timelines, Symptoms and Treatment," American Addiction Centers AND Veilleux, Colvin, Anderson, York, and Heinz, "A Review of Opioid Dependence Treatment: Pharmacological and Psychosocial Intervention to Treat Opioid Addiction," *Clinical Psychology Review*. Of

If a list of factoids and insights is distributed before students arrive in class once the period begins the teacher can potentially launch a discussion about the possible political forces at play when opioid policy is considered. For example, representatives of the opioid industry worked to make that industry's interest known in the halls of Congress and state capitols and worked to secure "friendly" policy positions.[187]

For those students who have chosen the opioid crisis for their course-wide assignment, an emphasis on local, counter therapies is one aspect upon which they might focus. They can investigate which local counter resources, be they therapies or other approaches, are found in their communities. In addition, if there is time, the teacher can request that these students voice their opinions and back them up with stated factual or insightful information they have been given or found in their research – again, in an informal way.

As the next class period approaches, the teacher might note that there are only two more class periods left in this unit. The development of this unit of study has already determined that it should last five periods (assuming each period consists of fifty to sixty minutes). Therefore, Lesson 4 presents a tactical problem: the challenge is to provide instruction for three more aspects of the problem area – production and distribution, demographics, and governmental reactions – in the remaining time.

To cover the last three aspects, it is suggested that the students be divided into three equally (or as close to equally)

---

note, an accompanying countermeasure is the use of buprenorphine. For its benefits see Schwartz, "My View: New Approach Needed for Opioid Epidemic," *Portland Tribune* AND Macy, *Dopesick*.

[187] If the teacher has an interest in this aspect of the crisis, he/she might find the role Purdue Pharma played in the initial phases of this drug's popularity. See "U. S. City Sues OxyContin Maker for Contribution to Opioid Crisis," *NPR*.

numbered groups. Each group is assigned one of the remaining aspects. The teacher can guide students' attention to that portion of the online site with the list of factoids and insights that pertains to their assigned aspect (either by having students view the information online or a teacher prepared handout with the information).

This fourth-class period can be dedicated to having students work on their assigned aspect by researching "its literature" in their assigned groups. The question guiding this research is: given your assigned aspect, how has it contributed to or affected the opioid crisis? Each group during the class period conducts its research. This is preparation for the next class period when the students will be given an opportunity to express any findings or opinions they wish to express within a limited time frame.

That is, each group during the fifth-class period, within a fifteen to twenty-minute period, reports and includes any opinions and findings it wishes to express. If a teacher follows this suggested instructional plan, he/she would substitute the reports for a traditional test – the reports can be given a comparable test grade. Of course, if the teacher wants to administer a test, the fifth-class period would need to be conducted in a different way.

Another option during the "test" period is for students, after their short group presentations (perhaps being limited to ten minutes), write a report. They will have roughly twenty minutes to write a one-page report – no more, no less – with the assistance of any notes to answer a general question regarding the crisis.

One such question can be: how well is the local community meeting the incidence of opioid abuse by local community members? If this option is used, students can, from their investigation of local efforts, answer the question: how well does the community address this challenge? The teacher might inform the students what this question is beforehand.

If students are aware of this option, they can arrive prepared to fulfill this requirement. Again, the suggestion here is for the reports to be considered comparable to a unit test. This type of test can be meaningful if students are encouraged to include what information they found and considered important regarding this epidemic.

And that completes this chapter's suggestions about how to conduct a unit of study dedicated to having students reach informed positions about the opioid crisis. If successful, the student will be well-positioned to take an active role in his/her community to address its battle with this epidemic.

And now, the next chapter turns to a national concern.

CHAPTER 4: A NATIONAL POLITICAL CHALLENGE,

TORT LAW

And Now There Is Tort Law

This chapter reports on the development of another unit of study. Tapping tort law as its issue, this chapter presents it through an analysis of three legal tensions – strict liability vs. negligence, misfeasance vs. nonfeasance, and factual causation vs. legal causation – that characterize that portion of the law. But initially, this chapter shares a few thoughts about how this legal area classifies as a political challenge.

One might more specifically identify tort law as being that hidden political challenge. That is, what follows demonstrates how a political decision can affect the non-political processes of the courts. And by doing so, students can acquire an appreciation of how powerful expertise with a dash of legitimacy can be. The judiciary system of the US depends on these bases of power. [188]

Notice that by not choosing for this chapter a politically contentious field of interest – the processes of tort law are by and large not controversial – the writer avoids identifying a specific issue or problem. But through this analysis, the student can question the boundaries of federalist biases – its values – and by doing so, he/she can get a finer understanding of what being federal in one's politics means.

---

[188] French and Raven, "The Bases of Power," in *Current Perspectives in Social Psychology.* French and Raven's five bases of power are coercion, reward, legitimacy, expert, and referent powers. Without armies or police forces – that are usually lodged under executive offices of government – courts exert enormous power.

The course outline offered in Chapter 2 identifies a Unit 11, "The Courts."[189]   Of the unit headings listed in the outline, "The Courts" seems like the obvious place to situate this legal/political topic.   Since what is anticipated in terms of content affects the courts equally throughout the nation, a national focus seems most appropriate.

As with the other two units described in this book, this development includes an explanation regarding the relevancy of federation theory, a short history, and lesson ideas – all offered below.   The only difference is that the information used is not in the form of factoids and insights, but in cited cases that illustrate precedents and how they are used.

While a review of tort law can stretch back to England's history before English colonization in America or even all the way back to Ancient Greece, this presentation limits its review to that of case law in the US (with a case or two emanating from British courts).   In doing so, this account starts by making a distinction between two approaches to tort law: common law (based on precedent) and statutory or civil law.

So, what is tort law?   Tort has to do with one party damaging another party.   When one person drives his/her car into another person's car, that situation provides a simple example. The damaged party, to seek relief from the resulting harm, files

---

[189] Reminder: The course of study identifies the following units: Unit 1: The individual, Unit 2: The family, Unit 3: The neighborhood, Unit 4: A small business, Unit 5: A labor association (such as a union), Unit 6: A large corporation, Unit 7: A local government, Unit 8: A law enforcement agency, Unit 9: Congress, Unit 10: The White House, Unit 11: The courts, Unit 12: Society, and Unit 13: International associations.

[190] Tort law can also include the issuances of injunctions that are issued to order a party to do or refrain from doing some action.
[191] This eventuality questions the claim that judges should not make law. In the common law tradition, judges, from time to time, do make law.

suit against the alleged party who stands accused of being responsible for the harm.[190] Usually, courts dispense relief in the form of a monetary award to the damaged party by the party found to be responsible. But within the Western world, there are two approaches to this process.

The reasons for this variance are basically historical. England opted for a common law tradition and mostly stuck to it. Common law uses case law; that is, what is considered binding depends on previous decisions – what previous courts, either judges or juries, have determined to be correct in each area of dispute between litigants.[191]

Therefore, prior cases produce the sum of all judicial decisions, known as case law. Courts divide case law between criminal law and tort law, and tort law in the US is mostly based on common law. On the other hand, people who are charged with breaking a law – i.e., a statutory law – face the provisions of criminal law.

Law in terms of criminality depends on enacted statutes – e.g., laws against fraud – not common law. Within this category, when statutory laws do deal with private affairs (tort cases), that is known as civil law. Most Western nations, such as France, use this approach in dealing with tort cases; they do not depend on common law. There are examples of civil law in the US regarding tort issues, but this nation limits them to certain areas of concern (e.g., aspects of employment).

The US has inherited this reliance on precedent (even in Louisiana with its French traditions) from the British. Can legislatures and executives of the state and federal governments in the US bring areas of tort law under the provisions of statutes? Yes, they can, but usually have not done so. Americans, by and large, feel comfortable with common law tradition when it comes to tort issues.

Admittedly, if one draws a Venn diagram that illustrates the boundaries among these various "laws" (case law, common law, civil law, statutory law, criminal law) it would be quite complex. What is important for the purposes of this chapter is that the US is a common law nation when it comes to most tort cases and that tradition calls on courts to settle tort cases according to prior decisions.

This account sets out some initial observations that have led to the development of tort law and how it changes over time. When court decisions define tort law, as opposed to statutes, that law is relegated to slow change, but change does happen. How? Some courts, from time to time, cannot completely abide with what has previously been decided and its relevant precedents – they might not, in some respects, fit the facts of the cases before them. And those courts, usually appeals courts, change the law which reflects a slow change process.

It is slow for a reason. Laws function to provide predictability. Change counteracts that benefit. Judges avoid, whenever possible, disregarding an old precedent and making a new one. Common law tradition in the US abides by this element of common law – applying precedent – and the legal institution gives this bias a name: the doctrine of *stare decisis*.

When judges take it upon themselves to make a change, this can and does suggest a concern. Should one judge or a panel of judges – such as in an appeals court – have such powers? Or should such change be the product of the law-making process emanating from a legislative body such as a state legislature or the US Congress?

When it does happen, courts see the change as essential. One can ask, which specific issue(s) cause change? At times, new technological changes make a precedent non-applicable to a tort claim or the precedent would obviously lead to an unjust finding. Culturally based opinions, such as on race, can have an effect. And related to this last factor, changes in statutory laws can have both direct and spill-over effects on how issues are defined and interpreted.

In evaluating this nation's adjudication of torts, citizens can and perhaps should question this basic alignment that supports common law. And in turn, one should understand that to keep a common law system, as opposed to shifting over to civil law, one is dealing with a political decision. It should be mentioned that there have been efforts to rely more on civil law.[192]

But common law is the "name of the game" in tort law today. Therefore, to know what a common law provision is, one needs to look up the appropriate precedents. By focusing on these "weird" cases, the ones that have issued new binding precedents, a telling-history can be told. This is the approach the short history below takes. By looking at those cases, one can get a good sense of how the judiciary has pursued justice when it comes to tort cases.

There are exceptions to this general approach – a full rundown of all relevant cases would extend this chapter beyond reasonableness. Therefore, this upcoming history will describe the development of these tensions (strict liability vs. negligence, misfeasance vs. nonfeasance, and factual causation vs. legal causation) in a truncated fashion; for an extended version, the reader is guided to an online site, see http://gravitascivics.blogspot.com/ , October 23, 2021, to gain access.[193]

---

[192] But what are the concerns over common law that motivate such "reform" discussion? Reformers cite several concerns, many regarding the quality of juries. This topic that transcends how citizens view tort concerns highlights the overall system's reliance on common law and, therefore, zeroes in on the system itself. The history reviewed in this chapter addresses this question.

[193] This site beyond a historical account of tort history also has a list of significant tort cases.

But relying on case law to tell the story of tort law has an inherent difference from most historical accounts: it is not a sequential narrative. It is episodic. The rendition of this history develops logically from the conceptual arrangement that the above tensions provide. The history below follows that progression: strict liability vs. negligence, misfeasance vs. nonfeasance, and factual causation vs. legal causation, in that order.

Regarding another contextual point, since tort law involves court action dedicated to settling claims emanating from harm, one might see this pursuit as being straightforward. While that basic descriptor sounds simple, in real life, torts can easily become complex. The cases mentioned in the history demonstrate that potential.[194] While this unit cannot address all of these complexities, there is a set of basic concepts that can help interested laypersons have a working understanding of the related issues and thereby be better able to protect their interests.

To encourage students to view citizenry as a partnership, instruction can point out and/or evaluate how court procedures aim to advance justice. Instruction can ask: for a given tort issue, do courts' reliance on common law optimally support a just

---

[194] Relatively simple cases demonstrate how complex tort law can be. Here is such a case. A driver pulls into a golf course's parking lot and does not see a beer can that was left in the parking space the driver chooses and he runs over it. The can slices the bottom of the tire. The driver does not see any damage. Low and behold, a few hours later – after finishing his round of golf – the driver finds the tire flat. The compensation to make the driver whole – acquiring a tire that is comparable to what he had before the flat – results in a bill of $200.

Who should pay that bill? The driver, the unidentified person who left the can, or the owners/managers of the golf course? And what if the golf course is a municipal course? Municipalities are sued all the time and the resulting queue for pending litigation is long and possibly frustrating for the next adversary. This "simple" event has complicated the life of this driver, assuming he insists on being made whole.

judiciary? Who has a duty when harm occurs? How does one define related legal principles in a given, harm-inducing situation? How do the evolving realities – such as technology – affect responsibilities that parties might have in tort situations? And is the best way to handle tort law one that utilizes common law?

And these questions lead one to consider how a study of tort law can advance students toward developing a sense of civic virtue. This turns on the relative C3 Framework standards. Reminder: the C3 standards function as guidelines with a "touch" of specificity. This writer counts eight of the C3 standards as being relevant to the issue of this chapter. Here are three of them – the ones most relevant: Those standards are: Individually and with others ...

- students analyze the impact of constitutions, laws, treaties, and international agreements on the maintenance of national and international order;
- analyze the impact and the appropriate roles of personal interests and perspectives on the application of civic virtues, democratic principles, constitutional rights, and human rights; [and]
- analyze how people use and challenge local, state,

---

[195] National Council for the Social Studies, *Preparing Students for College, Career, and Civic Life C3*, excerpts from various pages. Other relevant standards include: Individually and with others, students distinguish the powers and responsibilities of local, state, tribal, national, and international civic and political institutions; ... analyze the role of citizens in the U.S. political system with attention to various theories of democracy, changes in Americans' participation over time, and alternative models from other countries, past and present; ... evaluate citizens' and institutions' effectiveness in addressing social and political problems at the local, state, tribal, national, and/or international level; ... use appropriate deliberative processes in multiple settings; ... and evaluate multiple procedures for making governmental decisions [such as court decisions] at the local, state, national, and international levels in terms of the civic purposes achieved.

national, and international laws to address a variety of public issues as well as other standards. [195]

In this context, one can further ask: at the systemic level, do the ways in which tort cases are settled advance or detract from the common good? This last question can be asked substantively of court decisions and of the process that courts follow to arrive at those decisions. Those concerns include the legal principles applied or established in identified cases.

One last introductory point: The aim of this unit is not to encourage students to consider a legal profession. This "national" unit chose tort law because it points to an area of social interaction in which federalist values are tested. In a court of law, one is concerned primarily with one's interests – not the general welfare – and one is wise to assume all the parties involved – perhaps apart from the judge – are looking at the experience in the same way.

What can one say? Are federalist concerns simply not applicable? When one's self-interest is highly in jeopardy, can one maintain a federalist commitment to advance the common welfare or, if not, arrange one's self-interests so they are not contrary to the common welfare? In the thick of a tort "battle," this might be hard to do, but if one strongly holds a commitment toward justice, the task, while not easy, becomes easier. And this observation leads to the next topic, a federalist moral code.

A Federalist Moral View

With these introductory notes, the chapter is sufficiently set to shift gears and present an organized moral view that could serve as a foundation for a federalist guided civics curriculum. By doing so in *this* unit, tort law can be judged: does the way the nation's courts handle tort claims protect the integrity of individual citizens and the moral guidance of federation theory?

Ultimately, these concerns transcend politics and governance; they even transcend law. They reach a moral sphere.

How and why this is true can be addressed only through a theoretical approach. The following pages attempt to do this, albeit in a cursory fashion using common language. While theoretical, what follows aims to be practical in that the ideas and ideals expressed are applied to the substance of the unit this chapter presents.

This context is derived from the tradition established by Aristotle, who centered his relevant concerns over behaviors as those that advance the interests of the polity, the common interest or the public good.[196] Aristotle states:

> In all arts and sciences[,] the end in view is some good. In the most sovereign of all the arts and sciences – and this is the art and science of politics – the end in view is the greatest good and the good which is most pursued. The good in the sphere of politics is justice and justice consists in what tends to promote the common interest. [197]

---

[196] For interested readers, this presentation is based on the relevant contribution of writers from the Western philosophic tradition. That includes the following:
Aristotelian ethics promote a morality anchored with the concerns of the polity – a communal sensitivity; Utilitarianism, while it supports a self-centered sense of human happiness, does establish a consequential moral system; David Hume points out that while what is believed to factually exist (the *is*), cannot indicate or determine what – for normative reasons – is correct (the *ought*); yet, one is reminded that certain factual conditions do correlate to certain desired outcomes and that values can be warranted only by sentiments; Immanuel Kant argues that any resulting view must not sacrifice the integrity of each person and that there are categorical imperatives that ultimately determine what is good or evil – a non-consequential moral system; Pragmatism highlights a future orientation through pragmatic thinking, an inexorable connection between means and ends, and the tie between what is moral and the interests of associations; and John Rawls argues two claims: one, through the utilization of a mental exercise, any person would seek true equal opportunity if he/she does not know *a priori* his/her position in a formulated polity or society. And two, advantages are arbitrarily distributed through natural causes (genetic factors and natural environments) or communal conditions (social factors). In either case, the individual has limited control over the level of advantage he/she enjoys.

In this spirit, one is directed toward identifying an ultimate or trump value. For one who wishes to abide by a federalist moral code, he/she holds prominent, as a trump value, the common interest or, stated in other words, societal welfare – defined in terms of societal survival and societal health. So, this account takes a first step; it identifies an ultimate value but needs to state a rationale for that choice; first, some definitions.

An ultimate or trump value refers to the need to identify a final or "highest" value in a moral code that relies on a consequential moral approach. That is, something is moral or immoral – using a Pragmatic view – because that something, usually an act, leads to a higher good or an eviler consequence. In turn, that good or evil leads one to an even more righteous or maligned outcome, etc. This leads logically to an ultimate or trump value. As this line of reasoning illustrates, a federalist moral code utilizes a Pragmatic approach to moral thinking.[198]

The other term, survival, is just what it implies – extending the life of a society that might be threatened by either internal or external dangers or a combination of such forces. This code assumes that societal survival is advanced by a value commitment to certain societal qualities. These qualities are social capital and civic humanism, what basically constitutes societal health.

---

[197] Aristotle, "Aristotle: The Politics," in *The Great Political Theories*, 64-101, 87.

[198] A consequential moral approach can be distinguished from a categorical-imperative approach introduced by Immanuel Kant. This categorical approach is one that is composed of two steps: first a person asks when confronted with the question if one should do something, he/she further asks what would happen if everyone behaved that way. If the answer is judged to be a detrimental result – if everyone lied, no one could be trusted, and all social cooperation would become suspect, if not impossible – one should not do that thing; it's immoral. It is always immoral and, therefore, should never be done. The reason for avoiding such an approach will be made clear in this chapter. See "The Categorical Imperative: An Ethics of Duty," City University of New York. For a more sophisticated analysis of Kant's ethics, see Timmons, *Significance and System*.

Why is this value designated as the trump value? Simply stated, without a societal existence, all other social – and for that matter, all personal – potentials are impossible to attain. Human beings are social animals; their existence on this planet cannot proceed to attain any personal or collective goals or aims without a healthy enough social landscape.

Therefore, all aspects of a civic, governmental, political, economic, or any other social/personal endeavors are dependent on a societal existence and a healthy societal reality to some minimal level; this is existentially vital. But really, doesn't any moral system hold this as the ultimate value; isn't it just understood?

Not necessarily. Without an extended review, there have been leaders who were disposed to sacrifice the existence of a society before succumbing to an enemy. Some might argue that Japanese leadership maintained that nation in World War II beyond its complete destruction and then capitulated only to save the Emperorship. After the US dropped two atomic bombs with the promise of more, Japan did surrender, and one can argue that the Japan that emerged is fundamentally different from the society it was before its invasion of Manchuria in 1931.[199]

Admittedly, in a complex example, stories are told about how President John F. Kennedy was not going to give in to the Soviets over the Cuban missile crisis, threatening a nuclear war. This is debatable but as a case study, an interesting example of a leadership balancing factors that one can argue, considered nuclear inhalation as a very possible outcome in this nation's conflict with the Soviets.

The threat was from an actor who was trying to achieve world communism. This possible eventuality was defined as intolerable and one that can be equated with losing one's society,

---

[199] Kingston, "Why Did Japan Surrender in World War II?" *The Japan Times*. Yes, Japan is still a "rice-growing society" but its entire view has taken a more Western turn.

the difference being that one possibility was to lose the society with a "bang" or lose it with a "whimper."[200]

The reader might wonder if this is going astray. Perhaps to a degree it is, but interested parties need to understand the level of commitment a trump value needs to be held to or cherished to be considered a true trump value. If it is not, it is not by definition a trump value. Federation theory, *in terms of governance and politics*, as defined here, holds societal welfare to that degree, at least to the degree a nation can have a trump value to begin with.

With a trump value identified, this account can present more substantive elements of a proposed construct. In terms of values, it promotes a hierarchal system of values which can be divided into three layers: an ultimate trump value, instrumental values, and operational values; each layer is logically derived from the layer above it.

In terms of their application, one is dealing with definite values, but he/she should not, except for the trump value, apply these values in absolute terms as one finds in Immanuel Kant's categorical-imperative approach.[201] Federation theory promotes that this code be applied to American society, but it has a universal quality. Here is a partial listing of those values:

- Trump Value: Societal welfare (as experienced through societal survival and societal health)
- Key Instrumental Values: constitutional integrity (as federal liberty), equality (as regulated equality), communal democracy, democratic pluralism and diversity, compact-al arrangements, earned trust, loyalty, patriotism, justice
- Operational Values (partial listing): political engagement,

---

[200] For an account of this reasoning and how it affected White House discussion, see Thomas, *Robert Kennedy*. This banter is described on pages 136-137.

[201] See footnote/endnote #187.

due process, legitimate authority, critical and transparent deliberation (or collaboration), inclusive problem-solving, countervailing powers, privacy, universality of human rights, tolerance, non-violence, responsible ambition, teamwork, consideration of others, economic sufficiency, security, localism, expertise[202]

And here are abbreviated definitions of those values most relevant to tort law concerns:

- justice – commitment to giving everyone his/her due based on a realistic view of dispersed or accumulated advantages
- constitutional integrity – a basic value that promotes individual rights as defined by the US *Bill of Rights* or the *Universal Declaration of Human Rights*; aka liberty, but more in the vein of federal liberty (as opposed to natural liberty)
- equality – defined as equal opportunity in a realistic fashion with a commitment for minimal welfare standards as promoted by John Rawls[203] (described as regulated equality – more on this in Chapter 5)[204]
- covenantal/compact-al arrangement – a value that supports social conglomerations based on mutually agreed upon values, structures, processes, and is formalized in a perpetual agreement – a covenant or compact (more on this element in Chapters 5 and 6)
- earned trust – reasonable expectations of veracity and reliability in others

[202] While many of these entries, as stated, sound like structural/procedural elements, they are not meant that way. Instead, they are presented as values. For example, due process, while it is a process, its inclusion is meant to identify a valuing of policy derived by open and even-handed processes.

[203] Kukathas and Pettit, *Rawls*.

[204] Here is a more generalizable definition: Equality is a social quality based on the belief that despite inequality in talent, wealth, health or other assets, it calls for equal consideration of all persons' well-being, that all have an equal right to maintain their dignity and integrity as individual persons.

- countervailing powers – the sense that any social arrangement should disperse power to avoid a concentration of it, actuated through a non-centered power arrangement (e.g., the three branches of government)

The overall thrust to these values promotes social capital and civic humanism.

This account offers a hierarchy of values for two reasons: one, a hierarchy assists conceptualizing possible scenarios in which value commitments are in conflict as in dilemmas (an eventuality highly probable in tort litigation); two, it lends to a consequential approach – as is encouraged by Pragmatism – when considering moral questions.

This latter reason refers to avoiding categorical determination of value choices or in seeing uncontextualized moral shortcomings as described earlier. Federalist ideals call for a more means-ends view of morality as is promoted by Pragmatist philosophy. Again, something is good because it leads to a more central good or it is bad because it distances one from a more central good. In terms of goodness, that refers to the choices that lead to an ultimate trump value.

These values guide the study of civics toward certain subject matter and that should be the content of civics. That is, it guides civics educators to choose content that facilitates the accomplishment of the following goals:

- Teach a view of government as a supra federated institution of society in which, in terms of an ideal purpose(s), it protects and advances the communal interests of the commonwealth.
- Teach, through a variety of venues (prominently civics instruction), that the role of government is to be the guardian of this grand partnership within the citizenry. Those who pursue this aim can do so by addressing both the individual and associational levels of society.
- Establish and justify a political morality that accounts for the realities of the current political world but does not lose sight of the responsibility citizens have in advancing the

common interest – nowhere is this more challenged than in the nation's courts.

- Emphasize the integrity of the individual both in terms of liberty (constitutional integrity or federal liberty) and equity in which each citizen is a member within a compact arrangement and whose role is legally, politically, and socially congruent with the partnership the nation's constitution establishes.

- Point out political strategies that respect the function of expertise at the national level but at the same time, express a reasonable preference for local, unsophisticated participation in policy decision-making and implementation – grassroot politics. The former informs the latter, the latter serves as a reality basis for the former. The history of reform points out the essential role that grassroots politics plays in such efforts.[205]

In summary, citizens confronted by a tort action, either as plaintiffs or defendants, have one perspective in mind: self-interest. Surely, tort law holds a place on the boundaries between federated theory and the natural rights construct. So, to meet this challenge, this chapter presents the above, federalist moral code. Why? One reason is to further assist students (and their teachers) in their analyses of tort cases; they can analyze court decisions while considering their morality. Instruction can ask: Does what a judge or jury say and write enhance or detract from this code?

Short History of Tort Law

---

[205] Crutchfield, *How Change Happens*. This book outlines qualitative research over what constitutes successful change efforts, e.g., reducing smoking practices among Americans. In reviewing her descriptive accounts of successful strategies, Crutchfield uses systems language – considered here unfortunate – but if one looks at the elements of her derived model, the overlap with federation theory is striking. Chief among its prescribed elements is localism or relying on grassroots politics.

Again, this account addresses tort law with the above moral code because that law challenges that code most directly by its very nature. Hopefully, the teacher, in his/her instruction, does not lose sight of this overarching concern. The following history, at least in the writer's intent, helps a teacher have his/her students analyze and consider tort law as a challenge. How well do the above values operate in the real world of judicial courts?

Early on, this chapter mentioned three tensions: strict liability vs. negligence, misfeasance vs. nonfeasance, and factual causation vs. legal causation. Tensions are reflections of realities that, by their nature, oppose each other. The nation's judicial system has been dealing with these tensions since the mid-1800s. Some argue that the main force sustaining these tensions has been technological change. Others argue that economic/political forces have been at work. These arguments provide the backdrop for a historical tale.

The presentation here provides a truncated history of these tensions – as such, not all the relevant cases are cited. Space dictates this form of presentation. But to supplement this history, as mentioned above, there is online an extended list of relevant tort cases. For each case, reference to another site with additional information concerning the listed case is provided along with a more extended version of this history.[206]

Strict Liability vs. Negligence

To begin this history, a common situation is helpful. Inevitably, from time to time, one does something that causes harm. For example, while a visitor to a neighbor's house is carrying an urn of hot soup, the pet of the house runs across his/her path and the visitor trips. This results in the hot soup spilling all over an expensive sofa, staining it. The accident

---

[206] Reminder: the URL for this cite is http://gravitascivics.blogspot.com/ , October 23, 2021.

causes a meaningful cost to the owner of the sofa. Is there a legal aspect to this event?

To generalize, a resulting legal question could take the following form: should a person be held liable for a resultant harm if the person caused the harm, but, as in this example, was not at fault? This question, perhaps difficult to answer in some cases, was not difficult before the mid-nineteenth century.

Then, if a person caused a harm, he/she was held responsible and liable. But the law does change and that includes case law. This shift from automatically holding the person who caused a harm liable – called strict liability – to the more commonly held standard today, holding the person who is at fault liable – called negligence – was a profound change.

And before getting into that change, a distinction is further helpful, i.e., intentional acts that result in harm as distinct from those that are unintentional. The latter, as just pointed out, is called negligence. The former, when one purposely causes harm and there is a corresponding law prohibiting such an act, is called criminal. Tort law basically addresses negligence.

What is negligence? The case, *Blyth v. Birmingham Waterworks Co.*,[207] helps one answer that question. In that case, a harmed citizen sued the local waterworks company and ironically based the suit on a local statute. The statute incorporated Birmingham Waterworks to supply that city with water. Further, the statute provides language as to how the resulting piping should be maintained.

The defendant or respondent, Birmingham Waterworks Co., had laid piping near the plaintiff's property. Due to cold weather, that main leaked and caused damage to the plaintiff's house. This led to the lawsuit in which the plaintiff accused the defendant of negligence. The court, after hearing the evidence,

---

[207] *"Blyth v. Birmingham Waterworks Co.," Case Briefs.*

decided in favor of the plaintiff. In doing so, the court provided what has become the primary definition for negligence. Paraphrased, that definition is:

> Negligence is the failure to do something a person of ordinary prudence would do or the taking of an action that a person of ordinary prudence would not take. A mere accident that is *not* [in the first instance] occasioned by the failure to take such an action or the taking of such an action [in the second instance] does not qualify as negligence.[208]

In other words, *trying* to circumvent the double negative, when a person of normal intelligence does something a person of normal intelligence (broadly defined) would not do or does not do something a person of normal intelligence would do – and harm results – he/she is negligent. This definition illustrates certain concepts of duty and reasonableness. The examples below will make this clearer.

From a historical perspective, one question becomes central: why did the courts shift in this way, from strict liability – in which whoever causes a harm is held responsible – to the negligence standard in the mid-1800s? Apparently, chief among the theories explaining the change has to do with the effects of industrialization. Intuitively, this makes sense.

Industrialization transformed the size and distribution of the American population. Prior to industrialization, the nation, while large, was agricultural. Consequently, the population was thinly spread throughout the nation's landscape. Further, such a sparse population found it rare that people got into what are called joint accidents (when two or more parties are involved in an accident).

---

[208] Ibid. Emphasis added. Below, this history reviews the "but for" standard to establish causation, but that factor refers to another tension: factual causation vs. legal causation.

Strict liability, when rare accidents took place, satisfied any contention that arose due to any harm. "You did something [e.g., laying pipe]; you're responsible" could have summarized how people saw such events. But industrialization changed all that. It caused the population to be drawn into denser factory towns. Also, financial centers such as New York City or Chicago became both industrial centers and supportive service centers.

Their populations exploded. For example, the New York urbanized area in 1850, with a population of 590,000, grew to 16,207,000 by 1970.[209] With those numbers, one can readily visualize the incidence of joint accidents becoming ever more frequent and with that, one can also visualize the vast array of factors and conditions leading to those accidents.

Yet strict liability, in terms of assigning legal blame, doesn't much care about such factors. With strict liability, in a typical car accident, driver A pays for driver B's harm and vice versa. One doesn't ask who was at fault. With industrialization and the advent of automobiles, for example, strict liability made less sense. If driver A was at fault – perhaps ran a stop sign – then he/she should pay for all the damages assuming driver B demonstrated no negligence.[210]

And so, such events naturally, with their incidences of negligence, incorporated fault in deciding court decisions. But there is another view that a legal expert, among others, develops:

> [Morton] Horwitz ... maintains that the fault theory of negligence was not established in tort law until ... judges ... sought "to create immunities from legal liability and thereby to provide substantial subsides for those who

---

[209] "New York Urbanized Area: Population & Density from 1800 (Provisional)," *Demographia*. While the population numbers are estimates, they are based, in part, on Census data.

[210] Or if the accident is no one's fault, still each driver pays for the other's damage or harm. With strict liability, fault plays no role in assigning liability.

undertook schemes of economic development." The modern notion of negligence, then, was incorporated into tort law by economically motivated judges for the benefit of businesses and business enterprises.[211]

This more economic and political explanation, by shifting to a negligence standard, affected judges as they took a pro-business posture and, in effect, began to provide businesses, especially big businesses, substantial subsidies by allowing them to escape sizable judgements against them.

The strict liability standard particularly hurt one industry, the railroads. They, given the technology of that time, caused or provided many opportunities for harm to be inflicted. When one considers these spark-producing machines roaming the landscape, causing fires in open fields, having their boilers explode, or hitting people and other vehicles, one can understand how a strict liability was highly detrimental to that industry's bottom line.[212] And such calculations put political pressure on the system to change and so it did.

But before one casts strict liability to the dustbin of history, one can observe that it has made a limited, but important comeback. Dating to the 1960s, the courts have reestablished the strict liability standard in product liability cases. If one buys a product and it causes a harm, a harmed victim does not need to prove negligence.

For example, one buys an electronic appliance, and it is wired incorrectly. At home, that person uses the product, causes a spark that hits an accelerant, and the house burns down. Is there negligence? Probably, but by whom? Some worker on the assembly-line? Again, probably, but which one? And if the

---

[211] Kaczorowski, "The Common-Law Background of Nineteenth-Century Tort Law," Fordham Law School.
[212] Cheng, "Torts," *Law School for Everyone*, 230-445, 246.

worker is identified, can he/she afford to make the homeowner whole? Probably not. In those cases, the standard has again become strict liability and that liability falls on the business that produced the product.

Yes, the company can question whether the buyer of the product used the appliance incorrectly and that contributed to the fire. If so, there can be relief for the company, but in the main, courts today utilize strict liability when it comes to assigning responsibility in tort claims against companies that produce and sell consumer or industrial products.

Today, there is a complex landscape of tort law in which there is a mixture of standards. That field is composed of a few intentional tort cases (when someone intentionally causes harm) – potentially treated as criminal matters – many negligence cases, and a much smaller number of strict liability cases. See the extended version of this history online for more cases.

Misfeasance vs. Nonfeasance

One can now look at a second type of tension, misfeasance vs. nonfeasance. This tension centers on a moral-legal distinction in analyzing tort cases. One might claim that nowhere is there a greater gap between the value orientation one can ascribe to a federalist perspective – or most moral systems – than exists between legal duty and moral duty as defined by the courts' findings regarding feasance liability. For a supporter of federalist values, a person might be motivated to work politically to change this aspect of tort law.

And nowhere is this tension more exemplified than the boilerplate example – hopefully fictitious – of the flailing baby. That is: a flailing baby finds him/herself in a puddle of water and is about to drown. The baby only needs for a nearby person to grab or move him or her, but that person does nothing. The baby drowns. Is that "nearby" person liable to any legal jeopardy, be it a tort suit or criminal liability?

To answer, a look at a more common, everyday example might be more telling. Say a person is driving down a deserted street. To make the point more poignant, the person is a good-sized man in his thirties. The driver then faces a moral demand; he looks left and sees an elderly man climbing the steps of a church when the old man clutches his chest and falls.

The driver, who could easily pull over to where the old man lies and provide him some help, doesn't. He merely keeps driving. As it turns out, the old man suffered a heart attack and died a short time later. He could have been saved if someone – the driver, for example – were there to assist him by applying CPR or using a cell phone and calling 911. No other person was there to do that. So, the older man died.

Later, church officials look at what a security camera videoed; it shows the above event and it also spots the driver who ignored the emergency. The old man's daughter, seeing the video, is incensed. Can she sue or file a criminal complaint against this driver? Can she, in other words, claim the driver had a duty toward her father?

No,[213] the governing legal standard that common law provides in such cases can be summarized as follows: "no duty to a stranger." And that lack of duty applies to a person who ignores a flailing baby in a puddle. In either case, the generally accepted moral duty does not translate to mean a legal duty. Among other conditions, a plaintiff in a tort action needs to establish the defendant's legal duty toward the plaintiff. And as these examples demonstrate, just being able to help someone is not enough.

What *is* enough – or needed – for a tort claim to have a chance in court? While one does not owe a legal duty to a stranger, there are situations or relationships that do. One owes a

---

[213] Unless the local jurisdiction has a statutory law that establishes a duty, which most do not.

duty to reasonably not be the *cause* and to behave without negligence in relation to someone else's harm. That is, a plaintiff needs to meet three elements in a claim:

> Breach of Duty – whether the defendant's behavior failed to live up to that standard of care [just mentioned]; Causation – whether that … breach of duty caused the plaintiff's harm; and Damages – whether the law recognizes the harm[,] … how we measure it, and how the defendant can compensate for it.[214]

So how does misfeasance vs. nonfeasance fit in considering these concerns?

By way of a quick overview: when one party does something that harms another, that is either malfeasance (intentionally done) or misfeasance (accidentally done). Under what has already been described, such behavior is subject to a legitimate tort claim – in the case of malfeasance, a criminal claim as well.

But if a person does not do something that would prevent harm, he/she is not liable and that is called nonfeasance. The passerby leaving the baby in a puddle or the drive-by witness to a heart attack come to mind. To be clear, to be liable, a person needs to perform an act. The law ascribes different levels of duty among the above types of feasance.

The courts, when considering harm, obviously need to determine which type applies in a given situation. In terms of tort law, one needs a good handle on the meaning and implications of misfeasance and nonfeasance. To attain that handle, a citizen looks at the appropriate cases that provide the relevant precedents. They also tell interesting stories.

---

[214] Cheng, "Torts," *Law School for Everyone*, 256-257.

The case, *Yania v. Bigan*, in 1959, demonstrates how bizarre the determination of whether misfeasance or nonfeasance characterizes an incident can be. John Bigan, the defendant, operated a coal strip-mine. Part of that operation was to dig trenches. In one of his trenches, a pool of water accumulated.

To extract the water, Bigan placed a pump in the trench and someone needed to get into the water to start the pump. Bigan, to encourage Joseph Yania, another mine operator, to jump in for that purpose, started taunting him. Despite his initial reluctance, Yania did eventually jump in and subsequently drowned. His wife, as the dead man's survivor, filed a suit against Bigan for wrongful death.

She, in court, emphasized Bigan's taunting. Yet, the trial court found in favor of the defendant and, upon appeal, the Pennsylvania Supreme Court upheld that finding.[215] The judge held that Yania was a reasonable and prudent adult who could readily see and understand the dangers but chose to jump in the water. The taunting did not undo those factors nor place responsibility – negligence – on the shoulders of Bigan.

Beyond the taunting, did Bigan have a duty to jump in himself and try to save Yania? No, perhaps he had a moral duty, but not a legal one. So, given the above standard, the term "stranger"[216] is broad. If Yania was a child (remembering he was cajoled into jumping in) or an infirm person, then Bigan *might* have had a duty, but Yania was neither; he was a "prudent" adult. As such, in this case, the law draws a line between what is good from what is legal; but why?

Again, as with the question over the shift from strict liability to negligence, there is more than one explanation. In this regard, tort law apparently holds a natural rights view. It states that liberty means a person simply has the right to ignore the cries

---

[215] *"Yania v. Bigan," Case Briefs.*
[216] Referring to the legal tort standard: "no duty to a stranger."

of a flailing baby, a stricken old man, or a drowning fellow coal mine operator. That sense of liberty remains non-committal in terms of what should be done in these types of situations – that's up to the individual.

While this view has a good deal of support in the legal profession, there are other views. Others hold a second explanation in this line of thinking and that other view can be stated as follows: if one places a legal obligation on one citizen to aid another (or at least not to encourage, *a la* taunting, dangerous behavior), where do the obligations end? Can the law demand someone do something or anything that might be needed by another party? Does that not undermine a person's individual integrity by legally forcing him/her to behave morally?

For example, if such legal demands are put in place, does that mean a person needs to bear burdens such as monetary expenses to aid a needy party? Insisting on a duty in nonfeasance cases opens "slippery slope" situations or at least that is what defenders of the existing standard argue. One can argue this claim from a variety of angles, but one needs to keep the focus on legal issues. Does a "slippery slope" concern trump the demand for citizens to help others when it can be demonstrated that the conditions under question are obvious and serious?

Here, the question is asked but not answered. It is proposed as a question for citizens – or students in a civics class – to consider. Further, if the answer is yes, the solution will not be provided by common law, but by statutory law, law that is yet to be devised, much less enacted.

Then there is an extreme – but not legal – case that possibly demonstrates a serious shortcoming with holding nonfeasance as being beyond tort law review. In 1964, in the borough of Queens, 38 ordinary New York residents heard the cries and saw the stabbing of Kitty Genovese. None of those witnesses called the police or provided any assistance to Ms. Genovese; she subsequently died.

This case is so egregious that a quote by a legal scholar seems apt. Edward K. Cheng states something very revealing about the inherent tension between the federated obligations among citizens and what common law has bequeathed this nation, the individualist view of legal obligations:

> And in these cases, duty is not only all-important from a technical sense. Duty also becomes fundamental because it defines the difference between law and morality, and because it implicitly adopts certain values, which can be quite controversial. The no duty to a stranger rule undoubtedly celebrates rugged individualism [a natural rights view] and a desire for personal liberty, but it also sets aside values about community and regard for others, at least from the standpoint of legal obligation.
>
> It is this tension, between individual liberty and collective welfare, that makes the concept of duty interesting. And it is because of this tension that the exceptions to the no affirmative duty rule have historically been a battleground for courts and tort scholars. [217]

This writer would replace the word, "collective," in this quotation with the word "associational," but beyond that, this quote summarizes the main point of presenting this history; that is, should the support for common law be questioned regarding federalist values?

Of course, none of those observers in New York were subject to any tort or criminal action. This case, in its extremity, brings up what many people feel is offensive by the common law's indifference to those in serious need. Is there a compromise between complete indifference and mandated

---

[217] See Cheng, "Torts," *Law School for Everyone*, 264-265.

decrees that insists on affirmative duty to assist those who need help, sometimes to save their lives?

Some states have chosen what might be considered half-steps, i.e., enacting Good Samaritan laws that mostly protect "helpers" from liability when their efforts fail or cause further harm. Other efforts include imposing small fines on those who fail to help someone in jeopardy of physical harm. But there have been no meaningful laws insisting citizens need to help one another.

In addition, there have been legal developments that address what happens if someone provides any assistance to one in need. There are two cases to help one understand this issue: *Erie Railroad v. Stewart*, 1930, and *Zelenko v. Gimbel Bros., Inc.*, 1935. They tell interesting stories – one dealing with railroad crossings and the other with a storied, now defunct, New York department store. Both cases provide one lesson: a person needs to take care in providing help.

In this line of concern, the Zelenko case provides a resulting, relevant legal concept, gratuitous undertaking. It creates a duty. There are various reasons for this duty. Summarily, one can say helping does establish a relationship. And certain relationships do entail duties.

For example, some contractual relationships do identify duties and at times they are not explicit. A lifeguard has a duty to save a drowning person, and a doctor has a duty toward his/her patients, etc.[218] Those are contractual, but some are not, as when a department store salesperson provides initial help to a person suffering chest pains, but then the ailing person is ignored and

---

[218] This reminds one of the *Costa Concordia* cruise ship captain, who abandoned his ship when it ran aground. The accident resulted in deaths and injuries and it also resulted in Captain Francesco Schettino serving a prison sentence. That case was not American – it was Italian – but it does illustrate this contractual obligation and how this captain did not meet it.

dies of a heart attack; that's negligence. Again, one needs to be careful when he/she sets out to provide help.

Factual Causation vs. Legal Causation

While the "indifference" standard ("no duty to a stranger") establishes a legal bias toward indifference, there are exceptions for given relationships. As stated above, a relevant and necessary condition, one that might affect this indifference position in tort claims, is causation. *Kline v. 1500 Massachusetts Avenue Apartment Corporation* helps to define causation.

Here are its relevant facts: some years before 1970, Sarah B. Kline began renting an apartment at the Massachusetts Avenue address. Then, one day of that year, a mugger attacked her, robbed her, and caused her injury. The attack took place in a common hallway of the apartment building.

She sued the owners of the building and the relevant question in this case was whether the owners of the building had a causal duty to Kline and, therefore, were liable? The reader is invited to look up this case in the extended version of this history – there, some relevant facts bearing on its outcome are further explained. But here are its bare facts: Kline balanced her rent amount against the level of protections the building provided, and the owners of the building didn't mug Kline; the mugger did.

The trial court – the federal District Court[219] – found for the defendant. The chain of causation, according to the ruling, ends with the mugger. Kline appealed and the appeals court's decision, while noting this causation argument, stated that a safe common area is basic to this sort of business; similarly, as a landlord is responsible to replace a burned-out hall light, he/she needs to provide reasonable protection. The U.S. Circuit Court

---

[219] Apparently, the apartment building is in the District of Columbia, a federal jurisdiction.

of Appeals, therefore, found the apartment building owners liable for Kline's expenses, to cover mostly her medical care.

The case helps define what related parties (related by contract) have in terms of reasonable duty for a given fault and for a given harm.[220] And this case provides some of the reasoning that goes into determining liable causation. In an obvious way, a question logically follows: what is being reasonable?

When one sets out to answer this question, one quickly can see that everyone is apt to be unreasonable from time to time. A reasonable person – as a defining attribute – is a mythical person. The reasonable person surely is not the average person as one can readily or regularly observe oneself or others acting unreasonably from time to time.

For example, one overpours a liquid ingredient in following a recipe or one's car veers beyond the highway's outer lines are examples of unreasonable behavior. Now, if one does one of these or similar things and it results in harm to someone else, that person can be successfully sued, and the claim would be that the unreasonable behavior resulted in or *caused* the harm and, therefore, he/she performed a negligent behavior.

If the court agrees, then that "unreasonable" person can be held liable to make the victim whole, usually through a monetary award. But one should notice that negligent/unreasonable people are not bad people, immoral people, or hateful people; they are just negligent. Some are negligent more often than others. Some are that way because they are young and impulsive; some because they are old and more apt to be absent-minded.

An insightful quote by Justice Oliver Wendall Holmes is offered: "If … a man is born hasty and awkward, is always

---

[220] "*Kline v. 1500 Massachusetts Avenue Apartment Corporation*," *Case Briefs*.

having accidents and hurting himself or his neighbors, no doubt his congenital defects will be allowed for in the courts of heaven but his slips are no less troublesome to his neighbors than if it sprang from guilty [intentional] neglect."[221] The point is, when it comes to most tort cases, intentions (or a lack of them) do not protect defendants.

Courts instead avoid subjective concerns – e.g., how nice or how absented minded a subject is – by applying the reasonable standard: what a reasonable person would do – to determine the duty of care one person should have for another. This allows jurors or judges a more attainable objective – to consider the external facts and not any subjective feelings.

The courts, though, have made some allowances for individual attributes that steer away from a totally objective view that can be applied to everyone. This leads to some complicated matters. Included in these matters are a person's physical condition (such as suffering from a debilitating condition), an unanticipated medical attack (such as a seizure), limitation due to age (being too young or too old), an occupational or industry custom,[222] or a cost to be reasonable outweighs the cost of not being so.

Here, these deserve only a mention, but the reader should know, as with the other aspects of tort law, that controversy is easily aroused in determining reasonableness. And what these factors indicate is that courts are consistently looking at nuance – i.e., factors that introduce exceptions to what are otherwise established standards as to how to judge reasonableness.

For example, the effects of one extensively influential law, the Civil Rights Act of 1964, were extensive in adjudications involving employment. And mentioning statutory law, *Martin v. Herzog*[223] of 1917, illustrates the potential importance of statutes.[224]

---

[221] Ibid., 268.
[222] See the T.J. Hooper Case. "T. J. Hooper Case," *Case Briefs*.

The famous justice, Benjamin Cardozo, in that case introduced the concept, negligence *per se*; that is, negligence that emanates from disobeying a statutory law and by doing so, causes harm.

With that background – appreciating the role of reasonableness and factors that present nuances in claims of negligence – this history is ready to address, more directly, causation. There are two areas of causation that courts look at: factual causation and legal causation. And two associated concepts that affect whether either is relevant in a case are chain of causation and foreseeability.

Sometimes causation appears to be obvious; other times it is not. There are times, because one tends to associate the sequence of events to indicate causation, that if one event precedes another, the first is the cause of the second. This the reader knows, after reading Chapter 2, can be as illogical as a superstition and does not prove causation.

Causation is just that; one event or factor *causes* another. A saying that helps identify a cause-and-effect relationship is "but for." Y would not have happened *but for* X. In this arrangement, one determines X, by legal standard, to have caused Y. But this is not always easy to determine, and no court case illustrates this issue more than *Daubert v. Merrell Dow Pharmaceuticals*, a 1993 tort case. And the harm in question could not be more serious than that of birth defects.

In the years before this case, there was a noticeable number of birth defects involving babies being born to women

---

[223] *"Martin v. Herzog,"* Case Brief.
[224] One law that has had a profound effect in adjudicating a contentious area of concern, firearms, is the Protection of Lawful Commerce in Arms Act (PLCAA), 2005. That law prohibits the strict liability standard from being applied to gun manufacturers or dealers as a result of a firearm being used in the commission of a crime. This example should be remembered by those who argue for more statutory laws governing tort issues in the belief that said laws will protect common citizens against the interests of big business.

who had taken the drug, Bendectin which Merrell Dow, the defendant, produced and distributed. A review of this case's record reveals the following relevant facts: during those years, some women who consumed the drug did not give birth to babies with defects and, of course, not all birth defects at that time were to babies whose mothers took this drug.

So, in terms of causation, were the incidences of some birth defects and the consumption of the drug happenstance or was there a cause-and-effect relationship? The adversaries in this case argued this question. How to find out? The plaintiff used the testimony of experts to make the link between the drug and the defects. They used what is called epidemiological studies, i.e., observing the incidence and distribution of the phenomena – birth defects and consumption of the drug in question.[225]

Merrill Dow's lawyers attacked this methodology. They argued that that approach was not good enough and they claimed that their view was supported by the scientific community.[226] So, according to the defense, to establish factual causation, a plaintiff must use findings that are arrived at by accepted methods. By whom? By the scientific community. And using this argument, the defense won. In summary, then, factual causation needs to be established by scientific information or findings, and that testimony needs to establish a "but for" relationship.

But one needs to add that when the "but for" formula, even if unchallenged, is used, it doesn't always arrive at liable causation. For some cases, the court looks for *legal* causation. If a person is injured or somehow suffers a harm even if "but for"

---

[225] Ibid.

[226] Before moving on, given the subject matter – birth defects – one should note that optional methodologies are highly limited. It is not as if studies can purposely expose pregnant women to medications to see if birth defects will result as would be called for in an experimentally designed protocol. Whether administering the drug to pregnant animals would suffice is beyond this writer's expertise.

the acts of another party, he/she needs to consider other concerns associated with legal causation. What are those?

By way of introducing this other form of causation, the tension between it and factual causation exists not in determining whether some event or factor caused the harm, but whether the factor or event was approximate enough to the harm. Or stated another way, can one act of negligence be held responsible for all subsequent harm that the act actually causes?

Consider: a person negligently swings a baseball bat and hits another person. Surely, a clear case of liability exists for the injuries incurred by the victim. But suppose that victim was to attend his daughter's marriage that afternoon and since the injury precluded his attendance, the ceremony is delayed at some expense to the injured father and his family.

Surely, "but for" the accident, the father would have attended the wedding ceremony but now cannot. Is the "swinger" liable for those non-medical expenses? This is a question of legal causation and highlights how the role, chain of causation, becomes important. Events, when they happen, can and often do cause many consequences; some result in harm and are immediate and others cause harm down the road from the negligent act.

Courts have held that approximation is a determining, key concern. The *Palsgraf v. Long Island Railroad*[227] case illustrates how approximation works. In that case, a chain of cause and effect occurrences borders on the bizarre. Two men in 1924 run after a train at a railroad station. One gets on but the other struggles to make it. A railroad employee helps by extending his hand. The struggling man grabs the hand and another employee on the platform also helps but what is important is not whether he

---

[227] "*Palsgraf v. Long Island Railroad*," *Case Briefs*. Another case resolved with a Judge Benjamin Cardoza opinion.

makes it, but that in the jostling, he drops a package he was holding.

Unfortunately, the package had explosives in the form of fireworks. Upon hitting the tracks, the fireworks explode. So far, the plaintiff in this case is not involved in these events. She, Helen Palsgraf, happens to be standing some distance away. She was not injured directly from the fireworks; her clothing did not catch fire from a spark, and she was not hit by flying debris. Instead, she stood under decorative scales in front of a store and the explosion caused a shock wave that then loosened the scales causing them to fall on Palsgraf and injuring her.

Was the negligence of the teetering passenger or the railroad employees liable for Palsgraf's injuries? That was Palsgraf's claim in a tort case against the railroad company and the trial court agreed. That decision was further supported by the Appellate Division. But when the case reached New York's highest court, the Court of Appeals, it overturned the lower courts' decisions and found that the harm in this case was too far down the chain of causation.

Yes, one could readily trace a "but for" chain between the explosion and Palsgraf's injuries, but there was a certain aspect missing and, this being the situation, the New York highest court found the link between the explosion and the harm as being too far. The missing factor that subsequently helped establish the standard that today's courts use to determine legal causation is foreseeability; that is, can one determine that there was a foreseeable consequence to a negligent act? If yes, a claim can be successful. If no, as in *Palsgraf*, the chain is broken.[228]

---

[228] Imagine if this principle were not in place, Mrs. O'Leary would have had an unbelievable bill for all the damage her cow caused ("but for" the animal knocking over that lantern, Chicago would not have been destroyed in the ensuing fire). See Cheng, "Torts," *Law School for Everyone*.

Another case, *Madsen v. East Jordan Irrigation*,[229] also illustrates, in 1942, this standard. And it is also, as with *Palsgraf*, a case involving explosives. Without reviewing the facts of that case – having to do with mother minks eating their young – both cases involve ultrahazardous, explosive products – which is usually subject to strict liability – initiating the chain of events. Again, the plaintiff did not prevail and, as with the railroad platform case, what was missing was a foreseeable consequence.

Does that mean that all harm must be foreseeable for it to be actionable in a tort case involving negligence? No. The courts have also adopted an "eggshell-skull" rule. This could be a standard the reader might want to look up; see *Vosburg v. Putney*.[230] It illustrates a limitation to the foreseeable standard. But generally, the foreseeable standard does help courts determine how far a chain of causation can go in terms of determining liability.

That completes this history's review of legal causation and with that, it concludes this truncated history of tort law. The history presented in this chapter summarized three tensions – strict liability vs. negligence, misfeasance vs. nonfeasance, and factual causation vs. legal causation – within the nation's treatment of tort law. These tensions were described and explained, albeit briefly, as products of the nation's common law or case law history.

Lesson Ideas for Teaching about Tort Law

By way of reminding the reader, the elements of the approach advanced here include the application of the HD-to-A instructional approach, i.e., attain relevant historical knowledge concerning the issue/problem at hand, engage in effective dialogue, and harbor a willingness to participate in civic action

---

[229] "*Madsen v. East Jordan Irrigation, 1942,*" *Case Briefs.*
[230] "*Vosburg v. Putney,*" *Case Briefs.*

that is meant to relieve or solve the issue/problem being considered.

In evaluating this nation's efforts in adjudicating torts, citizens can and, perhaps, should question this basic alignment concerning whether negligence should be the central concern of common law. And, in turn, one should understand that to keep a common law system, as opposed to shifting over to civil law,[231] is, as stated above, an active political issue.[232]

Reformers seem to be motivated by their concern over the quality of juries. They argue that juries are too apt to succumb to emotional appeals and render much too generous awards.[233] There have been legislatures that have enacted caps on such awards. Another sore spot is how readily class action suits can be lodged. In effect, class action suits, by aligning plaintiffs together, and, by so doing, lower legal fees for each plaintiff. Cheaper fees encourage more lawsuits.[234]

With these two general concerns, this unit of study, highlighting tort law, can be potentially outlined as follows:

- Lesson 1 can have students grasp and apply the main ideas contained in the above history by participating in a conceptualizing activity (such as filling in a concept wheel). A sample of the ideas or concepts can include misfeasance, negligence, fault, causation, and legal liability.

---

[231] A system based on statutory law as is the case with criminal law.

[232] The reader is reminded of the Stephen D. Sugarman article cited above. See Sugarman, "A New Approach to Tort Doctrine."

[233] A dramatic rendition of this – much to the delight of audiences – is found in the feature film, *The Verdict*. See Lumet (director), *The Verdict*.

[234] From this brief overview, one can surmise "reform" is mostly being advocated by business interests and common law is being defended by consumer groups. Students could investigate whether such biases exist in any current political considerations or debates.

- Lesson 2 can fulfill the obligatory review of the US court system structures both at the federal and state levels.
- Lesson 3 – a two-class period lesson – can have students, individually or in groups, prepare an argument expressing an opinion about how a given case relates to federalist values and how that relationship affects the student's view of how beneficial reliance on common law is.
- Lesson 4 would be dedicated to a unit evaluation choice (described below).

This outline and resulting instruction can be assisted by an exceptionally long history which is provided above in a "shortened" form.

Comparing the above history in its completed form (online), with that of Chapter 3 (and if the reader wants to look forward, Chapter 5), this history is not so short. That is why the above is "truncated" and even at that, one might still find it too long. The length has to do with organizing that history around the three highlighted tensions. A teacher might feel that to assign students to read the online history or some form of it might be asking too much. This developer agrees. That is why the above version is included here and the online version is cited.[235]

With that in mind, he offers some options. In these considerations, teachers should keep in mind the big picture: what do students need to know to be able to evaluate the nation's handling of tort law – especially as it relates to federalist values? And the version of the history provided here might be enough for students to give this question a satisfactory answer. If that is still too long, the teacher can limit the reading to the first tension, strict liability vs. negligence.

One concern in using the online version is that some of that historical account might prove to be too abstract. For

---

[235] The online version provides a richer rendition of the cases identified than the truncated version and, in addition, adds other cases.

example, describing intervening nuances in attributing negligence (under the section "Factual Causation vs. Legal Causation) can be too difficult for many students to appreciate or understand. An option might be to use the online version by either assigning those portions of the history to the more sophisticated students in the class or simply omit it from that history.

A second concern with the online version is the length itself. That can be handled in various ways. One way is for the teacher to divide the class into three groups, assigning each group one of the subsections that corresponds to the three tensions. This can be done several days before the beginning of the unit and, if assigned that way, the teacher can dedicate the first lesson (first class period) to a discussion over the "no duty to a stranger" principle, followed by reviewing a list of organizing concepts.

Initially, the discussion can last about fifteen minutes and then segue into a conceptualizing exercise that can grow out of the discussion. So, as the discussion progresses, the teacher can present organizing concepts: the American court system (its structural elements), its tensions (the three tensions highlighted in the history and which each student has at least read about one of them), common law/case law, civil law, precedent, defendant and plaintiff (the adversaries), cause vs. fault, trial courts, appeal courts, reasonableness, and foreseeability.

During the last half of the lesson (about twenty-five minutes), these concepts or some of them can be reviewed. By reviewing the concepts, the aim is not to impart sophisticated definitions or instill a fluent capacity in their use. Instead, the aim is to introduce the students to these ideas and have them begin using them by reflecting on how they relate to one another. One tool that teachers have used for this type of lesson is a concept wheel.

If chosen, the approach is as follows: a teacher offers the student a central concept – here, that would be tort law – and writes its symbolic representation – "tort law" – in the middle of

176

a large circle. The teacher suggests three or four main sub-ideas. For example: tensions, feasance, cause and fault, and liability standard. If this is a bit too difficult, how about blame, monetary award, duty, and adversaries?

Students, in their notes or on a handout (which can be set up before hand) as the discussion continues, are to fill in the circle with the reviewed concepts as they see them relate to one or more of the sub-ideas.[236] As time allows, the student toward the end of the exercise writes out, to the best of his/her ability, a working definition for three or more of these concepts and, as a homework assignment, a brief paragraph about how one of the concepts relates to the portion of the history they were assigned to read.[237]

The unit can then have lesson two review, in broad terms, the nation's court system. This need not be an overly detailed account of the structure. A working knowledge of the following will do: knowing that there is a federal/national court system and state court systems and within each type of system, there are trial courts (in state systems, county courts; in the federal system, district courts), initial appeal courts, and a supreme court, and that appeals follow that progression (trial-intermediate appeals-supreme court). The teacher can point out federal "specialty" courts, e.g., bankruptcy courts.

The teacher, in explaining what an appeal is, can help students understand this structure and further, that the grounds for appeal can be for various reasons; i.e., (1) a determination of whether a verdict of a trial is reasonable or whether the verdict was supported by the evidence; (2) determination of whether the judge made a mistake in applying the law (either statutory law, common law, or constitutional law), and/or (3) whether an

---

[236] One can readily see what a concept wheel looks like by using an online search engine with the term, "concept wheel," to find it.
[237] If the lesson takes too long, students can finish this assignment overnight and submit it at the beginning of the next lesson – possibly for a quiz grade.

obvious miscarriage of justice was being perpetrated by the verdict or by the trial's process.[238]

Lesson three could have students do an extended exercise (two class periods) in which they analyze their history reading and, using its facts, prepare an argument about how the history relates to federalist values. The teacher begins this by reviewing the federalist moral code – a code presented earlier in this chapter.

The lesson then strives to have students prepare and engage in an argument over the federalist nature – or lack of it – of tort law. This is considered as fulfilling the historical dialogue component, *a la* HD-to-A protocol, in its argument phase. That is, the teacher directs students to pick one of the cases the Great Courses source identifies and that is listed in the accompanying online site[239] and formulate an argument regarding that case.

That is, after pairing students, each pair picks a case. They then read the online material concerning the chosen case, consider the history of tort law, and apply the concepts reviewed in class. They then develop a pro-federalist argument (how the case advances a federalist value) and an anti-federalist (perhaps pro-natural rights) argument. They demonstrate how each either explains how the case challenges a federalist position and/or advances a non-federalist position such as one derived from the natural rights view. Each student adopts one of these positions and writes a supportive argument for their position.

The arguments are written down in a logical format – perhaps utilizing Toulmin's model reviewed and explained in Chapter 2. The aim here is to see to what degree students can manipulate federalist related concepts, demonstrate how well

---

[238] The textbook can be of assistance in this lesson. Most civics textbooks review the structure of the court systems of the nation.

[239] Reminder: The site has the following URL: http://gravitascivics.blogspot.com/ , October 23, 2021.

they understand the meaning of federalist values, and apply logical elements in devising an argument.

The last lesson of this unit would be dedicated to the unit's student evaluation. Here, the students can be tested to see the level of their comprehension of tort law concepts, their comprehension and appreciation of how tort law challenges federalist values, and perhaps their ability to evaluate or, short of that, describe and/or explain an existing critique (either in favor or in opposition) to this nation's tort system or to one of its elements.

Last, in terms of an action component to this unit, if a student has chosen the court system to be the subject of his/her action plan (the course-long assignment), then such activities as writing letters to a congressperson or other official about the student's concern over court reform, he/she might have identified can be written and sent. The letter should express a logical argument and, therefore, be reviewed by the teacher before it is sent.

Teachers could also provide assistance by reviewing any written work product.[240] For example, students could investigate whether the public official, to whom the letter is sent, has a record concerning judicial issues. If so, what does the record reveal? Does he/she have a stand concerning the level of statutory incursion into the law?

A well-written "position" letter[241] from a secondary level student can draw a reaction from a government official. This can

---

[240] See, for example, Ravenscraft, "The Best Ways to Contact Your Congresspeople, from a Former Staffer," *Lifehacker*. This short article reviews various communication outlets, such as tweeting, including writing letters. It contains useful hints as to whom and how such communication should be accomplished.

[241] A "position letter" follows what this writer understands a position paper to be; that is, it is a written report and opinion product in which the writer of the paper first identifies a problem area or other topic, presents various responsible

mushroom into a letter writing campaign. Since engagement is the aim, such developments should be encouraged.

With that "action" idea," the unit of study dedicated to the national judiciary system comes to an end. The book will next turn to an international concern, that of foreign trade.

options a person or group can choose in response to the area of concern, then takes a position as to what option should be chosen and provides a rationale for that choice.

CHAPTER 5: AN INTERANTIONAL ISSUE, FOREIGN

TRADE

Foreign Trade as a Federalist Issue

This chapter develops a third unit of study that, like the previous two chapters, identifies an issue or topic in which federalist values are abused or disregarded. This chapter looks at foreign trade and its effect on job creation and job availability in the US. As with the other chapters, this account only suggests an approach for developing this issue, but it is timely because it had a strong determining effect on the presidential election of 2016, the midterm election of 2018, and promises to remain viable in upcoming elections.

　　This effort relies extensively on a recently published book: *Failure to Adjust: How Americans Got Left Behind in the Global Economy* by Edward Alden.[242] Noting the role of Alden's book, the reader will also detect below that other sources "sneak in." They include journalistic and governmental reports.

　　After some reflection, the writer situates this unit as the last one of the proposed course outlined earlier in this book, the unit slot dedicated to international associations. Much of the unit deals with how US policy should be designed to meet an international challenge. This entails certain burdens on an educator. Through its international content, it is more removed from the students' environment. In turn, this limits the types of action available for students to pursue and its relevant political landscape is foreign and, therefore, potentially obtuse.

　　But as this chapter will point out, there are ample local aspects to this issue. While a teacher might find it more

---

[242] Alden, *Failure to Adjust.*

challenging, the plan below attempts to address this hurdle. Of assistance is that by the end of the course, the unit deals with students who are very familiar with the course's goals and processes; e.g., they would have had the opportunity to practice the skills that HD-to-A – an instructional approach explained in Chapter 2 – identifies.

So, for example, students know that they are to formulate positions regarding political, economic, and/or social conditions. As with the other "unit" chapters, this type of inquiry can be used to satisfy C3 Framework standards. Particularly, this unit as outlined below would address various C3 standards, among them the following: Individually and with others, students

- analyze the impact of constitutions, laws, treaties, and international agreements on the maintenance of national and international order;
- evaluate citizens' and institutions' effectiveness in addressing social and political problems at the local, state, tribal, national, and/or international level;
- distinguish the powers and responsibility of local, state, tribal, national, and international civic and political institutions;
- analyze the impact and the appropriate roles of personal interests and perspectives on the application of civic virtues, democratic principles, constitutional rights, and human rights;
- use appropriate deliberative processes in multiple settings; [and]
- analyze how people use and challenge local, state, national, and international laws to address a variety of public issues. [243]

---

[243] National Council for the Social Studies, *Preparing Students for College, Career, and Civic Life C3*, excerpts from various pages. Other relevant standards are: Individually and with others, students critique relationships among governments, civil societies, and economic markets; ... apply civic

In terms of dialogue, this unit calls on students to engage in a level of dialogue that is quite formal, i.e., a debate. Therefore, a teacher would be well advised to reflect on the sophistication level of his/her students before expecting them to fully implement what follows. Hopefully, they are ready to participate in a formal debate.

Federalism's Link to Foreign Trade

One can, in the use of federation theory as a guide for civics instruction, detect a bias; that is, that theory leans toward equality concerns. As the natural rights construct highlights liberty issues and critical theory highlights equality issues, in advancing societal welfare through communal approaches, federation theory *leans* toward equality. Below, this account delves into the theoretical balancing this "leaning" entails. But for now, the reader should be warned that even with apolitical topics (such as tort law), one can detect an equality angle.[244]

The fact that many Americans have lost their jobs as a result of foreign trade or have been affected by stagnant wages makes this concern a relevant federalist issue because it challenges the federalist value of equality. Summarily, one can make the argument that these Americans who have by and large lived by the obligations of the grand partnership of citizenry, have been treated in an *unequal* fashion by the standards of that federalist value – regulated equality. Below, this chapter explains this claim.

The application of the liberated federalist model calls on an observer or student to highlight a political confrontation. To

---

virtues and democratic principles when working with others; [and] … evaluate public policies in terms of intended and unintended outcomes, and related consequences

[244] As Chapter 4 explained, strict liability was found too expensive to the monied interest groups such as the railroads. This led these monied groups to utilize their resources – according to some – to pressure the judiciary to institute the shift to negligence.

this point, through the issues this account identifies (opioid crisis and tort law), one can detect an ongoing tension between federalist values and natural rights values – between a view promoting communal health and one promoting individual sovereignty. In this chapter, that tension is still pertinent, but there is also the tension between federation theory and critical theory in terms relating to the challenges these affected workers face.

Equality issues are ones that relate to either uneven distribution of societal assets based on economic activity or other bases for unequal treatment such as racism or sexism. As pointed out above, issues that on the surface are unrelated have equality concerns which one can discover upon closer examination. Consider that issues regarding the natural environment – on the surface not a class conflict issue – do reflect how the pursuit of higher profits leads to practices endangering the environment.

In terms of equality, then, federation theory agrees with critical theory that more political challenges emanate from concerns over equality issues than from any other concerns. What follows is a review of how federation theory views equality. By appreciating the federalist view, the reader can more fully apply the instructional elements described below.

Equality –

Overall, equality, in terms of the federalist construct, is a nuanced value. That construct avoids attaching itself to either the natural rights view – equal condition – with its lack of any concern for diverse social/economic conditions in which people find themselves *or* to the critical theory view – equal results – that delegitimizes market determinations in income and wealth distributions.

Equality, according to federation theory, refers to a valued state within a social arrangement in which, despite inequalities in talent, wealth, health or other assets, the entailed value calls for equal consideration of all persons' well-being; that all have an equal right to maintain their dignity and integrity as individuals.

As such, equality has a moral/normative quality since it reflects a respect for being human beyond biological or economic aspects.

Philip Selznick quotes Bernard Williams on this point:

> That all men [and women] are human is, if a tautology, a useful one, serving as a reminder that those who belong anatomically to the species *homo sapiens*, and can speak a language, use tools, live in societies, can interbreed despite racial differences, etc. are also alike in certain other respects more likely to be forgotten. These respects are notably the capacity to feel pain, both from immediate physical causes and from various situations represented in perception and thought; and the capacity to feel affection for others and the consequences of this ...[245]

Factually, Selznick goes on to point out, judgments regarding equality relate to the fact that humans, through their behaviors, are able to equally make moral choices.[246] There exists no elitist standing in this regard; each is humbled by this leveling attribute; each is subject to moral indiscretions; each can fully realize his or her own capacities as a person.[247]

These attributes, assuming the person in question is within normal ranges of human capacity, are what lead to meaningful self-respect and a sense of empathy that allows each to reach out to others.[248] In terms of the formulation of the compact that initiates the existence of a federalist arrangement for a community, an association, or a government, the fact that all entities can equally consent to its creation does allow for them to be federated equally.[249]

---

[245] Selznick, *The Moral Commonwealth*.

[246] This belief was firmly held and expounded upon by Thomas Jefferson and other respected political theorists of his time such as Francis Hutcheson. See Wills, *Inventing America*.

[247] Selznick, *The Moral Commonwealth*.

[248] Ibid.

[249] Lutz, *The Origins of American Constitutionalism*.

In this newer version of federalism, liberated federalism,[250] equality takes on two forms: baseline equality, a term that refers to equal condition, and equality of treatment, a term that describes regulated equality. The distinction between equal condition and regulated equality is made below but summarily, the difference reflects whether equality is basically a legal concern (equal condition) or one that looks after the dignity and integrity of each member of the polity (equality of treatment).

The Second Continental Congress sets equality, in the *Declaration of Independence*, as a requisite to any resulting covenant or compact including any subsequent constitutional agreement.[251] It was so designated because equality has a strong moral component in both religious and secular thinking and its absence has proven highly deleterious to social relations.

If nothing else, experience has shown the evil that flows from its disregard. After all, was that not the main complaint against the British Crown? To state otherwise in this new nation's rationale for independence would be the height of hypocrisy; it would be just an unusual statement by a group of bandits establishing a new structure for exploitation of the people.[252]

---

[250] "Newer" in the sense liberated federalism replaces, in terms of a possible guiding construct for civics educators, the parochial/traditional version of federation theory. If the reader is concerned with how liberated federalism matches up to current political values among the citizenry, this writer can suggest a source that does a commendable job in analyzing this regard along the political spectrum. See Gopnik, *A Thousand Small Sanities*. It is written by a liberal who defends liberalism against the charges lodged by advocates of various political positions. That includes conservatives *and* socialists. What this writer, Gutierrez, sees is that liberated federalism can be considered liberal – many of the attributes ascribed to liberalism by Gopnik match the cited attributes ascribed to the beliefs of liberated federalism; yet, given the core attribute that federalism relies on covenantal or compact-al arrangements, that foundational fact securely gives liberated federalism a conservative standing among political constructs.

[251] Lutz, *The Origins of American Constitutionalism*.

[252] A description of this notion of banditry is offered by Jonah Goldberg. See Goldberg, *Suicide of the West*.

Please note that with federation theory, equality and individualism take on mutually supportive functions. This account below reviews the meaningfulness of this relationship as it describes baseline equality. More ambitiously, equality acts to encourage a community to make decisions from an idealistic frame of mind, to formulate reflected and felt policy, including within any organizing documents such as in constitutions or organizing charters.

That is, the people committed to the initial covenant or compact – the agreement that establishes the commonwealth or community – are strongly encouraged and enabled to formulate a constitutional model that reflects deeply held cultural proclivities. While a federated union does not insist on a singular cultural basis for all social interactions, it does depend on a cultural foundation of support for its basic values.[253] Its claim for equality must be culturally felt if that constitutional framework is to have any chance at success.

Remember, at the constitution forming stage, people are coming together to form a union from a basis of consent, not coercion or tradition. And beyond the formulation of a constitution for governance, the same sense and value motivate the creation and the subsequent maintenance of a commonwealth or society (the community) in question.[254] These constitutional values have a wide berth within a resulting polity. And importantly, they go a long way in defining what is fair.

This account promotes more of an ideal than a legalistic concept. Yes, there are legal aspects to this (e.g., "equal treatment"), but part of the problem with the natural rights perspective is that it likely reduces all political ideas to a transactional, contractual model (*quid pro quo* arrangements). It loses the more generalizable relations and emotions that a healthy union enjoys and values, without becoming indifferent to the

[253] Gutierrez, "A Case for Centered Pluralism" *Curriculum and Teaching Dialogue*, 71-82.

[254] Selznick, *The Moral Commonwealth*.

need for basic reciprocity.

That is, the natural rights view turns away from that sense of relationships – such as formulating a genuine partnership – in which its participants advocate for a federated view. It loses sight of relevant partnerships being necessary to have successful political relationships. It holds another sense – one that looks for more immediate and detached benefits – that can drift into deleterious popular belief systems such as "tribalism" since it ignores naked but real human drives beyond those aimed at advancing self-interests.[255]

Perhaps, when social conditions demand purely legal solutions, as when a person is being arrested or when he/she is suing or being sued, the natural rights view of liberty is proper (as described in Chapter 4). When one is confronted with the power of the state, people are better served by the personal-contractual approach.

But when it comes to normal social interactions – how one deals with a neighbor, how one defines one's role in the community, how one, in everyday life, treats employees or a boss, etc. – federal equality provides a healthier approach. Even when one is dealing with inevitable contractual arrangements, one need not be completely insensitive to the more communal character of federalist ideals, ones that encourage citizens to see each other as partners.

Equality fulfills a central function within the overall conceptual structure of federation theory. By moral equality, Selznick postulates the principle that all persons have the same intrinsic worth by identifying two levels of this attribute: as mentioned, baseline equality and regulated equality.[256] Equality can be a "path to community" in which the members of a

---

[255] Jonah Goldberg points out that a more selfish, self-interest point of view is the natural way to see things, including being unmotivated to maintain any other-directed alliances beyond immediate family and friends. One needs to be taught to be more communal and less tribal. See Goldberg, *Suicide of the West*. This writer, Gutierrez, advances this idea with reservations.
[256] Selznick, *The Moral Commonwealth*.

formulated union are held to be equal in certain important aspects that include moral decision-making, dignity, participation, and consent.

As such, it serves to *undergird*, not define, any societal-contractual arrangement. At that level, these qualities are not contractual (as the term is usually used); they are covenantal or compact-al; they constitute the nature of the entity, be it an individual, an association, or a national union so formulated. So, one can hopefully see that equality deserves a bit of focus.

In the history of America, equality has come in different "flavors." This writer can detect five different views of this value. These five views are genetic elitism (which is really a view supporting inequality), earned elitism, equal condition, regulated equality, and equal results. This account is concerned with the last three views. Here are short definitions of these three:[257]

- Equal condition is the belief that all should stand equally before the law irrespective of other factors and that any advantages are limited to competitive processes in which all are free to participate. This is the dominant, espoused view today and is associated with the natural rights perspective.

- Regulated equality is the belief that, in the main, advantages should be the product of competitive processes, but that given the arbitrary nature of talent and good fortune, all are entitled to minimal living conditions (minimum wage, basic health care, education, etc.). This view is further described below; and

- Equal result is the belief that all are entitled to an equal share of the nation's wealth and the only legitimate terms

[257] Here are the definitions of the other two: Genetic elitism is the belief that some are superior to others due to genetic – innate – factors. This view is alive today through racism and xenophobia. Earned elitism is the belief that some, due to their effort, have attained favored positions in terms of legal, political, and economic concerns. This view is alive today through elitism associated with economic success or "stardom."

of varied rewards would be based on reputational consideration – how much the individual contributes to the general welfare.

(The last two orientations are based on an economy's ability to provide what is distributed, i.e., its wealth.)

Federation theory incorporates a regulated equality view and it describes how individuals who enjoy superior human assets (e.g., intelligence, physical dexterity, humor, etc.) do so because of effort for the most part, but also are advantaged in having been exposed to favorable conditions – according to the concerns expressed by the philosopher John Rawls.[258] Their superiority entitles them to above normal consideration but is limited only to areas associated with their earned accomplishments.

This view can be summarized by the phrase, equal opportunity/limited rewards. Any entitlements (rewards) are time limited as a recipient must continue to demonstrate his or her worthiness and said rewards, other than status, must be purchased. Monetary rewards – compensation or other forms of income – are paid in exchange for the individual's labor and are calculated by reasonable standards to represent that labor's contribution to the welfare of the society. This view also allows for income derived from capital or rents if they are reasonable.

Regulated equality determines reasonableness by the demands of the common good. Rewards rely generally on market forces but can be *regulated* to reflect human, innate qualities and accrued social contribution by the individual in question and by other societal needs. Societies/economies carry out this regulation through mostly taxes, welfare programs, or minimum wage provisions. This orientation allows the

_____

[258] Kukathas and Pettit, *Rawls.* Favorable conditions include genetic factors, loving and caring parents, nurtured years in an environment of ample resources (physical and social), educational opportunities, timing matching skills with the demands of the economy (currently, for example, being a good basketball player), and so on.

individuals to negotiate their compensation, but this process is further regulated in some fashion to advance the common good.

As stated above, this orientation of equality holds that some individuals enjoy superior human assets due to their efforts, but *only in part,* albeit the greater part. Indicated above, Rawls points out that people enjoy various advantages to different degrees and to a meaningful level, they do not totally control who they become or how much they have accumulated.[259] Beyond the role of genetic makeup, this view highlights the role of community and recognizes nurturing forces as having a significant effect on what a person has accomplished.

Note that this view of equality ascribes no innate worth to geographic/demographic accidents such as race, nationality, ethnicity, age, gender, or sexual orientation as contributing (causal factors) to a person's abilities. That is, these attributes should not add to or detract from a person's advantages. Also, to enjoy any special considerations based on income or class, a person purchases them in an open, albeit regulated, market.

As stated above, this version of federation theory identifies two forms of equality: baseline equality and regulated equality. A closer look at each is called for, but baseline equality, the view favored by the natural rights construct, will be reviewed summarily. Again, to remind the reader, Americans hold to a dominant degree a natural rights perspective.

As one reviews these forms, he/she should ask how varying views of equality affect the plight of displaced workers – those who have lost their jobs to foreign competition, automation, and/or have had their wages drastically reduced.

Baseline Equality

One can define baseline equality as a quality related to liberty. One best defines it as a legalistic concept because it refers to the *minimal* level of equality to which each person is legally entitled. If all other concerns regarding equality fall through, as when a person gets arrested, this form of equality

---

[259] Ibid. AND Gladwell, *Outliers.*

holds. Central to it is the belief that all persons are equal before the law.

If two parties, for example, are in a tort dispute, this view of the parties holds that each one does not have a legal advantage over the other due to wealth, income, race, ethnicity, nationality, gender, age, standing in the community, sexual orientation, etc. This nation defines this form of equality as constitutionally based and enshrined in an overall federalist body of law.

How the jurisprudential development of the Fourteenth Amendment has evolved played a central role in the nation's treatment of equality, especially with its provision of equal protection,[260] and to some degree, due process. To guarantee this, one is entitled to basic legal assets – e.g., legal representation in criminal court actions such as the assignment of a public defender. Short of that, though, all are to rely on their own abilities and assets to function within the public, competitive arenas.

Of course, in the US, that competition mostly progresses through markets. Those markets are meant to abide by the "rules of the game" and in turn, the rules that have been established are political determinations. For example, the reader is informed in Chapter 4 that tort law's continued dependence on common law is a political decision.

To understand the role of baseline equality within a federalist construct, one needs important contextual information. Baseline equality adds to the value of liberty. If one can bypass the connection between baseline equality and its attachment to the concept of individual sovereignty, [261] one can hold on to the idea that the individual can act independently in his/her pursuit of self-interest – an essential attribute of the federalist value, federal liberty.

But with the inclusion of a belief in individual

---

[260] Tushnet, "Equal Protection," in *The Oxford Companion to the Supreme Court*, 257-259.
[261] Reiman, "Liberalism and Its Critics," in *The Liberalism-Communitarianism Debate*, 19-38.

sovereignty, the adherents of the natural rights view see liberty as the right to define one's basic goals in life and to pursue associated behaviors if whatever is done does not interfere with others enjoying the same rights. Therefore, to account for this reality, when people have an individual sovereignty bias, they are likely to drift toward anti-communal patterns which effectively degrade the health of the commonwealth.

Once a society holds without substantive moral parameters a view such as the dominant political view, one can expect divergencies to evolve toward radicalized claims and beliefs such as toward tribalism. The claim is that this has been the path the US has taken since World War II.

Therefore, there are two aspects to this reliance on equal condition. One, when the individual faces the demands of the sovereign state, he/she can count on a legal system expecting the authorities to respect that individual's baseline equality and liberty. Two, there is the observable drift one sees in societies that adopt the natural rights view, i.e., a movement toward narcissism and selfishness.

Regulated Equality –

While holding on to the equal treatment before the law provision, federation theory rejects the individual sovereignty view. Instead, federation theory links liberty to a certain reality: that members of a polity are all mutually dependent on a communal existence and that that realization liberates the individual since it allows the individual to appreciate the resources a community offers.[262] As an African proverb puts it: "If you want to go fast, go alone. If you want to go far, go together."[263]

---

[262] Selznick, *The Moral Commonwealth*. Selznick explains the role the maturing process plays as an individual realizes that one attains a truer liberty once he/she realizes that unreasonable satisfaction of immediate desires, at the expense of others' welfare, can be debilitating to them and one's long-term interests. Usually, a person experiences a set of tensions in arriving at a more mature perspective.

[263] Quoted in Crutchfield, *How Change Happens*, 116 (Kindle edition).

In this, the federalist value of constitutional integrity (federal liberty) insists on equal treatment before the law when the law is exercising a negative power (a power that tells a person or a people what they cannot do). But when it comes to public policy decision-making, the two constructs veer in different directions.

The current debate over government-based healthcare provides an apt example. The natural rights advocates see mandated provisions enforcing people to buy health insurance as offending the baseline rights of individuals not to participate in the program. But regulated equality's view holds such a mandate as *potentially* acceptable. For them, such a law possibly establishes, as Social Security establishes, an interdependent system among partners in their attempt to further the common good and meet very real medical needs of most people.

An advocate for regulated equality does not necessarily agree with a national healthcare program, but he/she does not dismiss it because it offends a citizen's liberty. To further explain this nuanced view of liberty and equality, some contextual, definitional issues need to be addressed.

For one thing, pure equality is not possible. One can see this with the simple example that blind people are not allowed to drive. That is a form of unequal treatment or it can also be seen when one considers how the acquisition of sought-after products or services – including essentials – are handled. Not everyone can afford what they need or want, and they are deprived of those things. This is another form of unequal treatment.

In the first case, blind people driving presents an obvious danger even to the blind person. And in the second situation, any product or service is limited – scarce – and needs to be rationed by some method. The pricing system provides a form of rationing. If all are treated equally in either considering what constitutes, for example, safe driving conditions or who can acquire whatever trading assets a given society uses, one can, by any reasonable standard of equality, accept such "inequalities." Even natural rights advocates can concede this point. But the central point here is that one cannot have total equality.

Another contextual issue is how federation theory relates to liberty and equality. Federation theory considers liberty as a person having the right to do what one should do, at least in the ideal. What needs clarification regarding this form of liberty is by what standard does one judge whether something should be done or should not be done. And in addition, how does a commonwealth solicit acceptable exercises of an abiding liberty according to such a determination?

Such inquiries will assist in defining regulated equality. It further helps one place parameters on equality itself since federation theory does not hold it as the trump value; it holds societal welfare as the trump value.[264] In other words, what a citizen should do or should not do are those actions that, when done or not done, bolster the welfare of a society – at least according to federalist values.

How is equality related to the common good? In terms of regulated equality, it adds to what has been pointed out as missing from the baseline form of equality and that is the concern for the dignity and integrity of each member of society. For example, an economy that systematically deprives employment to significant numbers offends the common good. It might be okay for an equal condition sense of equality (the market system doing its thing), but not for a regulated sense of equality.

It is, furthermore, considered immoral by regulated equality standards. A definition of regulated equality might be: a treatment of each entity in which the person or group possesses a baseline equality (equal treatment before the law) *and* the right to equal consideration; that is, consideration of other entitlements related to integrity, respect, and dignity for each citizen. And given the topic of this chapter, a question a student can and should ask is that given these concerns, are the current foreign trade policies concerning job availability immoral?

Such a commitment, in a federated union, can take on

---

[264] The moral code is offered in Chapter 4.

authoritative status as it informs which public policy options should be devised and enacted. The call for laws supporting a living wage exemplifies this view of a policy consideration. Many resulting issues can be complex and there are times when policies might prove ineffective or even counterproductive. That simply reflects human frailties or shortcomings. These should be reviewed and improved upon, but the aim should always be to advance the common good as defined by federalist values.

When this level of respect is honored, it heightens the health of the commonwealth. Unfortunate members of the community (e.g., those who are deprived of employment opportunities and its accompanying dignity) deserve those opportunities to secure their viability. Deprivation among those not able to be viable serves to question the bonds that are essential in a federated arrangement.[265] And this is reciprocal; *anyone is subject to the misfortunes of life.*

When a society holds to regulated equality bias, it categorizes equality as a fundamental right and as such can view equal condition (equal treatment) as a derivative right, derived to accommodate the nature of law in how it is implemented, especially when the individual faces the power of government.

When the society treats people with dissimilar treatment (e.g., blind people not being allowed to drive), it is condoned and even seen as reasonable and necessary because of practical realities in protecting the common welfare. But the authorities must justify dissimilar treatment. Regulated equality proactively seeks and demands those justifications. The dissimilar treatment of blind people in terms of driving is not controversial. But at times, other reasonably discriminatory policies are.

For example, a polity demands justification when, due to some historical developments, policies have posed arbitrary categories that result in unjust conditions for a segment or

---

[265] History provides ample examples of how turning a blind eye to inequality affects societal health, particularly in republics. For example, one can read the accounts of the years leading to the end of the Roman Republic. See Durant, *Caesar and Christ.*

segments of the population and then institutes dissimilar treatment to rectify a former injustice(s). *Such a case would, in the name of equality, call for aiding someone or some group that has been subjected to unequal opportunity, as is the goal with affirmative action.*

Usually, such a policy will be a cost to some – it is, in a limited sense, discriminatory, but it can also be the price for sustaining or advancing the common good. This can meaningfully give substance to a moral equality standard. That is, such a policy extends treatment to people as equals, but within the parameters of a federalist moral code. At least, that would be a federalist justification for such a policy. Citizens would, through their votes and other forms of expression, or perhaps, as in the US, a judicial system of review is needed to indicate if in a given instance such a policy is justified.

Selznick argues that this dissimilar treatment is not meant to downgrade people, but to raise them by helping to create a community in which all are ideally well-born to some reasonable, minimal level.[266] With this possible policy option established, one can "get real" as to what maldistribution of wealth and income means to a federated union; i.e., a union in which the populace is truly federated among themselves.

The inevitable ranking of individuals leads to an uneven distribution of material values. Such a reality, though, threatens the level of moral equality in the commonwealth – especially if the unevenness is extreme or functions to prohibit others from aspiring to improve their level of advantages.[267] In current parlance, the problem is not that there is a top 1% (that's a mathematical certainty), the problem lies in that 1% enjoys inordinate percentage of the national income or the national

---

[266] Ibid.

[267] As the calendar approaches 2020, one can report: "Currently, the richest 1% hold about 38% of all privately held wealth in the United States; while the bottom 90% hold 73% of all debt. According to *The New York Times*, the richest 1 percent in the United States now own more wealth than the bottom 90 percent." "Wealth Inequality in the United States," *Wikipedia*.

wealth.[268]

If that is the case, not only does such a condition threaten the integrity of those not enjoying a reasonable income, but it makes those upper-class individuals have inordinate resources to affect the formulation of public policy. Yes, people have had to face these concerns throughout history; the concerns reflect a ubiquitous human reality and with it, many contingent concerns come into play, e.g., the role of incentives that promote productive behaviors. Many factors ride on getting equality issues correct.

They range from the quality of a democratic republic to the ability of that society to be productive and advance in its social, economic, and political wellbeing. Such biases as honoring and respecting competition, ambition, and a productive disposition play an often-underappreciated role among those most concerned with the plight of the downtrodden. But legitimate entrepreneurial interests, to protect the common good, need to be respected if not advanced.

Therefore, federation theory is not a collectivist perspective or a socialist view; in short, it is not a critical theory view. Selznick writes about this concern:

> The constitutional doctrine of equal protection does not ignore or erase differences of talent, achievement, contribution, or good fortune. It is not a device for leveling gradations or for making society more homogeneous. *It is, however, a path to community.* Equal protection [a provision of the *Fourteenth Amendment*] speaks above all to membership, and membership presumes that all who belong share a core identity. This identity is wholly compatible with rich diversity so long as

---

[268]In 2015, the *average* gross income of people in the top 1% was $480,930; for the top .01% it was $35.1 million, and for the top .001% it was $152 million. The top 1% paid 39% of the federal income tax. The gap between the top groups and the rest is growing. See Picchi, "How Much Do the 1, .01 and .001 Percent Earn?" *CBS News*.

that diversity does not undermine equality of membership. The most serious threat to such equality is division based on moral stigma ... [T]he effect of moral stigma is to rank some people as intrinsically less worthy than others.[269]

With such a view of equality, the individual is free – he or she has liberty – to do what he or she should do, which is beyond baseline concerns.

Social institutions, chief among them being public schools, have a duty to promote this more communal view. This is, in terms of policy, often a balancing act between and among parties in legitimate competing arenas. Thus, students should be introduced to nuance in the consideration of polities and their policies.

Short History of Foreign Trade

The history this account offers begins roughly one hundred years ago. And it begins somewhat in a disruptive way with the punitive policies that the victorious countries of World War I imposed on the defeated ones. To punish Germany and Austria-Hungary, the Allies (led by Great Britain and France) assigned heavy war reparation charges on the defeated nations that, in turn, hampered the economies of those losing countries and caused deep-seated resentment. There are analysts who see this earlier policy as being one of several causes of World War II.

The lesson learned was that victorious nations should not be so punitive. Of course, this lesson was not absorbed until the earlier mistakes became obvious with the lead up and the destruction of the Second World War. But there were other developments that are part of this history. They are actions by the industrial nations in the interim years between the two global wars that have little to do with war, at least not directly.

---

[269] Selznick, *The Moral Commonwealth*, 489. Emphasis in the original.

For example, in the US, there was the passage of the Smoot-Hawley Tariff in 1930. That tariff acted to restrict foreign trade in the hope of keeping jobs in the US, especially at a time when many were losing their employment due to the ensuing depression. The tariff, instead of meeting its goals, backfired and hastened the disastrous unemployment figures associated with that depression. Historically known as the Great Depression, it lasted for more than a decade.

Tariffs, taxes on imports, increase the effective prices on those imports and lower their demand, resulting in lower levels of trade. The role of tariffs can be further seen when other countries, as they retaliate, increased their tariffs and decreased the demand for American products in their countries. Of course, that meant higher unemployment figures globally.

Due in part to the depression and the effects of the tariff law, one can begin to understand US policy in the years after World War II. Beginning with the Marshall Plan and the thinking supporting that program, "Marshall Plan thinking," certain dispositions were reflected in the ensuing American policy. And that is where the story of this unit begins in earnest.

Looking back, foreign trade was not so much a dominant area of concern in the US as the nation approached World War II. Its economy in those years was only involved in foreign trade at a rate of less than 10 percent of GDP.[270] Yes, if one looks back to the early 1800s, one finds that up to the beginning of the Civil War – both in terms of imports and cotton exports – the American economy did depend on foreign trade a great deal.[271] But the Civil War and the rise of industrialization profoundly changed this nation's economy.

---

[270] GDP refers to Gross Domestic Product; it is the dollar amount of what is produced in a country for a given year for domestic and foreign consumption minus what is imported from other countries.
[271] Beckert, *Empire of Cotton.*

By the end of the 19th century until about the end of the 1930s, the US had become an autarky. An autarky is an economy that is totally or almost totally self-reliant. The American people provided just about all the natural resources the nation's economy used, produced just about all they consumed, and provided almost all the labor to produce what they needed or wanted.

As will be shortly explained, World War II caused certain processes and developments to take place and, as a result, the nation shed its autarky status. As early as 1944 (before World War II ended), there was the Bretton Woods Conference conducted to establish international agreements that had profound effects on foreign trade and on the US participation in it. The conference was meant to address those lessons alluded to above.

Furthermore, the US was the only leading industrial nation not suffering from extensive damage due to the war. The US had to take the lead in reestablishing the industrial capacities of those other nations if the world economy was to become viable again and if lasting peace was to have a chance. This led to a general trend toward liberalization of trade polices among nations.

After World War II, that included and was led by the US and a change of thinking about foreign trade took hold. One can, as just mentioned, attach the phrase, Marshall Plan thinking, to this change. It led to various developments such as in 1947 the General Agreement on Trade and Tariffs (GATT), in 1994 the North American Foreign Trade Agreement (NAFTA), in 1995 the World Trade Organization (WTO), and in 2018 the Trans-Pacific Partnership (TPP).

Generally, nations lowered tariffs, loosened trade restrictions and in subsequent years, eventually instituted floating currencies – that is, market forces (demand and supply) were to set the value of any currency. Summarily, one can consider these moves as aspects of a liberal trade policy bias, a bias aimed at avoiding the mistakes instituted after World War I.

A word on the currency aspect – its evaluation – is helpful. It is a very important factor since all trade between and among nations is conducted in the currency of a selling nation – either directly or through some clearing mechanism. To illustrate: If someone in Japan, for example, wants to buy a Chevy (something rarely done), US dollars are needed to pull off the sale.

Therefore, the exchange rate of US dollars affects what the buyer pays for a Chevy or any other export from the US. That is the case for any purchase made between a seller in one country and a buyer in another country; a buyer needs the currency of the seller or of a reserve currency (as part of a clearing mechanism) and the US currency is the world's most dominant and most used reserved currency (further explained below).

To return to liberalization, what the national players set up was a global system in which buyers and sellers of goods, services, and labor could be bought, leased, or hired across borders with increasing ease. Technological advancements such as the use of computers also affected this trend. So, one can say that a new set of policies – international agreements – and changes in technology paved the way to create a global marketplace for goods, services, and labor.

In terms of technology, the role of the computer – introduced to business processes since World War II – is central. For example, businesses could make deals halfway around the world with a few clicks and suddenly a nation's workforce was susceptible to international competition. Someone who gives a good accounting of this is Thomas Friedman.[272]

Things, given the conditions of the postwar period and the advantaged position of the US, were going along swimmingly for Americans for about two decades (1945-1965). Then things

---

[272] Friedman, *The World Is Flat.*

began to go in the wrong direction for the US – at least for segments of the US economy. Chief among those segments were men (some women) who worked in manufacturing jobs.

With the rise of what used to be called third world countries or lesser developed countries and/or countries heavily damaged by the war (e.g., China and Japan), American workers began competing against low-wage workers of those and other foreign countries. Suddenly, changing economic relationships brought about the introduction of several negative conditions in the late 1960s that interfered with US interests. A turning point (or year) was 1971 when, among other developments, the US got off the gold standard.

Relatively expensive domestic labor costs presented the first negative condition that affected America's position in international markets. This factor did not hurt the US when the nation was an autarky, but times changed. Just to give the reader an idea, average wages in the US, according to Edward Alden,[273] rose 75% between 1947 and 1973.

Many factors led to this, but the rise of labor unions headed the list. Those were great for workers if they competed only against other highly paid workers. But with the moves toward more global markets for products and labor, Americans began competing with cheap labor from foreign lands, especially in terms of manufacturing jobs.

The fact that the US before 1971 valued its currency on the gold standard – at $35 per ounce of gold – served as a second factor. It made the US dollar a very expensive currency (and made US gold very cheap). This helped lead to horrific trade imbalances – further explanation below. For now, it should be noted that this expensive currency – one of the results of the Bretton Woods accords – made American products expensive in other countries.

---

[273] Alden, *Failure to Adjust.*

So, with cheaper currencies abroad, this set up the third condition, increasing imports into the US. In the 1970s, imports more than doubled. By the end of that decade, foreign goods and services accounted for about 20% of the US economy. Why? Because products abroad were being produced at much lower costs for many reasons, chief among them cheaper labor costs. Adding to that factor, one can add expensive currency here and cheap currencies elsewhere.

And to boot, foreign markets did not find US products very popular; they were judged to be expensive and not of the best quality – a by-product of lacking effective competition in the previous autarky economy. Of course, a more thoroughly global market made these realities more acute, a market Americans had to face beginning with the 1970s.

One number that stands out is that 20% of US steel consumption by the end of the 1970s came from foreign producers. Yet, steel produced in the US accounted for small consumption levels in other countries. The same can be said for textiles, clothing, radios, and TVs. Subsequent years, as a further example, would see a deluge of foreign cars in the US while American cars were judged to be inferior and expensive abroad.

And American interests overseas also included the escape of investment capital – expenditures in production facilities – from the US to other countries. US investment abroad in the 1960s was less than $34 billion; by 1980 it had ballooned to $216 billion. Cheaper production costs in foreign lands motivated a lot of that investment.[274]

But apparently, since then, American business activity has changed further. Here is a 2017 summary issued by the Congressional Research Service of these later changes:

---

[274] Jackson, U. S. Direct Investment Abroad. Given the other research reported here, this citation is a bit controversial; but there is reference to other factors such as automation.

The United States is the largest direct investor abroad and the largest recipient of foreign direct investment in the world. For some Americans, the national gains attributed to investing overseas are offset by such perceived losses as offshoring facilities, displacing U.S. workers, and lowering wages. Some observers believe U.S. firms invest abroad to avoid U.S. labor unions or high U.S. wages, but 74% of the accumulated U.S. foreign direct investment is concentrated in high-income developed countries. In recent years, the share of investment going to developing countries has fallen. Most economists argue that there is no conclusive evidence that direct investment abroad as a whole leads to fewer jobs or lower incomes overall for Americans. Instead, they argue that the majority of jobs lost among U.S. manufacturing firms *over the past decade* reflect a broad restructuring of U.S. manufacturing industries responding primarily to domestic economic forces.[275]

This quote indicates a more recent turn, but certain conditions from previous policies have already had their effects, resulting in the trends which this overall history describes. And in addition, there is the role of automation. That role is a bit unclear. Susan N. Houseman writes of the controversy over whether automation is playing a central role in determining the current economic state.[276]

While the victims of lost jobs are many former factory workers and one can attribute to some degree the effects of competition of foreign, cheap labor countries in creating those unfortunate conditions, the US still relies mostly on its own labor and resources to run its economy. Foreign trade even today still

---

[275] Ibid. (emphasis added).
[276] Houseman, "Is Automation Really to Blame for Lost Manufacturing Jobs? What the Conventional Wisdom Gets Wrong," *Foreign Affairs*.

accounts for a small percentage of the nation's economy.[277] The US is almost an autarky. This fact tends to be overlooked when one sees how certain pockets are being negatively affected.

Beyond the conditions facing American producers, Americans saw a significant shift in national income away from workers and toward the more successful segments of the entrepreneur class or to those with high levels of capital accumulation.[278] In addition, that trend has accelerated; in 2013, the median wealth of the upper-income families ($639,400) was seven times greater than that of middle-income families ($96,500) – the largest gap in the 30 years the FED kept such statistics.[279] While these numbers refer to wealth, the gap reflects the shifting of income toward the upper-class.

Another factor affecting this trade is the value of the American currency. Since, as stated above, a foreign purchaser of American products needs US dollars to purchase those goods and services, the relative cost of attaining the dollar affects how expensive American products are abroad.

But the American dollar, as also mentioned, is the primary exchange currency known as a reserve currency. Abandoning the gold standard in 1971 highly encouraged the use of a reserve currency. Buyers and sellers in international markets drifted toward accepting the US dollar as being reliable and, therefore, a "strong" currency.

This is one way to handle the need for the seller's currency; just about every business engaged in foreign trade does it using US dollars, and those institutions who service these

---

[277] Banerjee and Duflo, *Good Economics for Hard Times*.

[278] Piketty, *Capital in the Twenty-First Century*. Capital accumulation (investments) can be in stocks and bonds or real estate.

[279] Fry and Kochhar, "America's Wealth Gap between Middle-Income and Upper-Income Is Widest on Record," *Fact Tank*. The FED refers to the Federal Reserve System.

exchanges sell and buy currencies to even out any imbalances – the clearing mechanism mentioned above.

These mechanisms also affect America's balance of trade. That is, usually a country that sees its products not in high demand abroad will also find its currency losing value since the currency is not being sought after to buy that country's exports. Therefore, that country's cheaper currency will lower the prices of that country's products in other countries.

Cheaper products have, in turn, the effect of increasing their demand. That is, the value of a nation's currency acts to automatically assist in getting what are otherwise less popular products sold in other countries. But the US does not benefit from this automatic mechanism because the US dollar is the reserve currency and therefore, others want to hold it or acquire it and so it maintains its relatively high demand, and in turn, keeps prices for American products high in other countries.

This leads to the US having trade deficits year after year. There are benefits in having the reserve currency, but this is a disadvantage.[280] If the US currency did not serve in this role, then America's imbalance of trade would naturally get "fixed" or not be so large. And it turns out that no products are more susceptible to this factor than manufactured goods.[281]

All this was taking place while real wages in the US first stopped growing and then began to fall, especially among – the reader can guess – male, manufacturing workers. It also negatively affected the communities that lost the manufacturing facilities that had, up to that point, pumped sustaining amounts of money into their local economies.

---

[280] Bunker, "Being the Reserve Currency Has Its Privileges and Costs," *Washington Center for Equitable Growth*.
[281] For an overview of reserve currency, see Amadeo, "Why the Dollar Is the Global Currency," *The Balance*. Here is a factoid: US imbalance of trade is regularly over $400 billion dollars a year.

There used to be a complaint regarding the existence of a "company town" situation in which one producer hired so many local workers that the company enjoyed inordinate amounts of political and economic power in the community where the company's facility existed. But this changed. Overall, several developments were taking place.

The pressures from foreign trade prompted the following: American manufacturers lowered costs in the US (including wages); capital flight (significant investments abroad[282]) relative to prior levels; and the resulting shaky economic conditions that encouraged enormous rise in personal debt that would later contribute to the start of the Great Recession of 2008.

This, therefore, begs a question: given the advantages the US enjoyed at the beginning of the 1960s, how did it let things get so bad that not only did the Great Recession take place, but it also led to the civic turmoil the nation is currently (2020) facing? And more important, the deliberative question is what should be done?

In order to answer such questions, one needs a general explanation for what is/was happening. The just cited financial crisis provides a reference in which to couch an explanation; it threatened America and the world economic system. That crisis inspired William K. Tabb[283] to share a meaningful observation.

He points out that economic growth depends a great deal on economic players having a predictive capacity and this in turn relies on people sharing what that author calls a social structure of accumulation (SSA) perspective or a general view of how the

---

[282] In 2017 that investment amounted to $6.01 trillion dollars (compared to $259.6 billion in foreign investments in the US). See "Direct Investment Position of the United States Abroad from 2000- 2017(in Trillion of Dollars, on a Historical-Cost Basis)," *Statista* AND DePillis, "Foreign Investment in the United States Plunged 32% in 2017," CNN Business.
[283] Tabb, *The Restructuring of Capitalism in Our Time.*

economy functionally works. According to Tabb, the US economy in its history has gone through a series of these SSAs.

He explains how, because of the Great Depression of the 1930s, the Keynesian SSA became prominent. That mental construct provided for a strong government presence within the economy and led to such federal programs as Social Security, Federal Deposit Insurance Corporation, and an array of regulatory agencies to oversee the economy. It held prominence in the perspectives of American entrepreneurs and policy makers from the 1930s through the 1960s.

For most of those years, it enjoyed a healthy reputation as the economy experienced unprecedented growth. But during the 1970s, with its rampant inflation and the perceived ineffectiveness of the Jimmy Carter Administration, the Keynesian view fell into disfavor. Then there was the rise of Ronald Reagan with his highly conservative agenda. His view has been called neoliberal and that designation has been given to the SSA that Reagan's policies introduced.

It instituted a general libertarian view that government should have a highly limited role in the economy. Historically, it replaced the Keynesian SSA. Through Reagan's leadership, the nation's economy opted for this neoliberal SSA[284] to guide its economic activities until the financial debacle of 2008. This writer likes to add that the political construct, the natural rights perspective, enabled the adoption of the neoliberal view.

That span of years saw a high degree of deregulation. Whether the Great Recession has been enough to dislodge it is still an open question, but one is tempted to see the upsurge of both Donald Trump (a nationalist) and Bernie Sanders (a socialist) during the presidential election cycle of 2016 as

---

[284] The term "liberal" can be misleading. The use of it here does not refer to left-of-center politics, but to classical liberal philosophy that is more akin to libertarian, extreme right-wing politics.

reflecting a higher sense of anger and anxiety among the American people – their collective discontent. Those voices can still be seen and heard as the nation approaches the 2020 election. They reflect the very emotions that led to shifting SSAs in the past in the 1930s and 1980s.

Perhaps one can view the year, 1971, as pivotal. In that year, Americans abandoned the gold standard and the American public started to question the Keynesian SSA. It would take another ten years for Reaganomics and its neoliberal SSA to become dominant. Currently, in the time leading to the 2020 elections, many factors seem to be unsettled and perhaps the economy is looking for a new SSA.

Yes, the economy as of this writing has seemingly put the Great Recession in its rearview mirror, but not all is well. With Tabb's treatment of SSAs, this short history ends. Other elements of the history of post-World War II foreign trade – including the role of an important memo – are highlighted in the following lesson ideas.

A Set of Lesson Ideas: A Suggested Progression

By the time students approach this unit as the last one of the course, they should be aware of what the course is generally trying to accomplish. They know, for example, that students have been preparing to engage in a formal debate. As visualized by this writer, this unit should take two weeks to be implemented; that is a total of ten, one-hour (50 to 60 minutes) class periods.

Here is an overview of this unit in the form of an outline:

- Lesson 1: Students define the problem area as containing various attributes. These include historical developments such as the loss of jobs to "cheap labor" nations and automation, how such a development affects the US' commitment to federalist value, particularly that of equality, and an accounting of the benefits and costs liberal trade policies have on the American economy.

- Lesson 2: Students will formulate definitions for the following concepts: productivity, comparative advantage, balance of trade/payments, trade deficit, intellectual property, and product "dumping."

- Lesson 3: Students, through their activity in a suitable simulation, will demonstrate a working understanding of how currency valuations affect trade behaviors by businesses that wish to export and consumers regarding their demand for the goods produced in foreign nations.

- Lesson 4: Students apply the two opposing approaches to foreign trade – "beggar thy neighbor" strategy and nurturing strategy – to describe various national foreign trade policies. This plan calls for students to formulate an argument that takes a position regarding the prudence of implementing a policy addressing the detrimental effects of post-World War II trade policies as described below. In doing so, they trace historical developments associated with these effects.

- Lesson 5: Students, over a three-class period lesson, participate in a debate over what their home state should do regarding foreign trade policies. For example, should the state institute, strengthen, or abolish "right-to-work" laws?

Initially, in the first lesson, the student is going to define the problem under study by identifying (in broad strokes) what caused the loss of manufacturing jobs in the US economy after the 1960s and how that relates to federalist values. Familiarity with the above history should assist in this broad objective as that history identifies results of foreign trade decisions in the years since World War II. To assist this, students should be given a version of the above history, have time to review it, and be given a class period to discuss it.

The teacher should prepare suitable questions focusing student attention on the overall policy biases that made up what is known as Marshall Plan thinking. They might include such questions as: what was the general aim of American foreign policy in the years following World War II; how did nations around the world fare because of the war; did the US have moral responsibilities to address the conditions that those nations faced in the years following 1945, and did the US have self-interests that led to certain foreign relation/trade policies?

Other possible questions might include: *A la* a federalist concern, what should national policy be regarding the effects trade policy has had on factory workers and their ability to viably engage in the nation's and in their own affairs? Are they less than equal among American citizens because of these developments? On another front, how have technology and the internet affected foreign trade and related policies?

Additionally, if time allows, the teacher can ask which factors have been more influential in job availability: foreign trade, automation, or restructuring American manufacturing businesses.[285] How has America pursued equality since Reagan's neoliberal policies have been in effect?

The aim of the overall unit is to have students gain a working knowledge of the various trade issues World War II created for the US and other nations. Generally, students can have an appreciation of the major challenges the nations of the world faced because of that war's destruction. But that did not

---

[285] Houseman, "Is Automation Really to Blame for Lost Manufacturing Jobs? What the Conventional Wisdom Gets Wrong" AND Yueh, *What Would the Great Economists Do?* Yueh points out many post-industrial nations are looking at ways to reindustrialize their economies.

necessarily necessitate, some would argue, the policies that one can associate with Marshall Plan thinking. Students can have various opinions including favoring Marshall Plan thinking but believing it held sway for too long a time.

On the other side of the ledger, students can cite the positive effects of the post-World War II foreign policy. That includes advancement in technologies, broader markets for US products, exporting or outsourcing of US manufacturing jobs, and the eventual introduction of cheaper and more diverse consumer products into the American market from redeveloped countries with their renewed industrial capacities.[286] Often, accounts of this trade have ignored the advantages that liberal trade policies have provided such as new opportunities and cheaper products.

Note: These are a lot of questions and, obviously, a teacher can choose which ones to ask. In turn, those can be based on what a teacher wants to emphasize and more closely reflect the relevant conditions that his/her school's locality reflects or experiences.

Next, a second lesson can focus on key concepts. This unit has students pay special attention to six concepts: productivity, comparative advantage, balance of trade/payments, trade deficit, intellectual property, and product "dumping."[287]

---

[286] This lesson will not completely provide all the instruction needed to meet this lesson's objective. It will partially provide that instruction. For example, subsequent instruction will define "Marshall Plan thinking."

[287] Here are some definitions: **Comparative advantage** occurs when, in using resources, an economic actor will choose that resource or asset that accrues higher profit even when that actor has access to another resource in which there is a higher productivity advantage from what is offered by another resource or actor. **Productivity** is a measure of the value of a production process relative to the costs or depletion of assets used to produce a good or service in question. It can also include the same measure for collective production, e.g., the productivity level of a nation's economy. Labor, due to its high cost, is usually what is most responsible for productivity levels. **Balance of trade/payments** is the difference in value – money amounts – of goods and/or services that are exported (a positive amount) and imported (a

213

These concepts (for definitions see cited footnote/endnote) can be a bit sophisticated for seniors – much less for middle schoolers – but perhaps they are not. If the teacher can share short analogous stories or narratives demonstrating the meanings of these concepts, that can be helpful.

Example: in terms of comparative advantage, the teacher can compare the comparative advantage of a typist who types 70 words a minute and a highly skilled physician who, on the side, types 130 words a minute. Even though the physician has an absolute advantage over the typist in terms of typing, the typist has a comparative advantage over the physician. By hiring the typist, the physician can spend his/her time seeing patients and earning much more money. Therefore, the physician should hire the typist. This same principle applies to countries.

As for the rest of the planned activities of this unit, they center on students utilizing factoids and insights concerning foreign trade. If the teacher relies on the above C3 Framework standards, he/she will use the factoids and insights to design inquiry lessons by which students will discover related information. Here is a sample of related information (factoids) relevant to the issue under study:

---

negative amount). **Trade deficit** occurs when a nation sustains a negative balance of trade/payments. Further, a trade deficit has a negative numerical amount when calculating Gross Domestic Product (GDP). **Intellectual property** is the ownership and the related rights of ownership of ideas, written representations of ideas, plans, descriptions and the like, usually having to do with inventions or improvements of products or processes. A source of problems is that the US has claimed the theft of such property by foreign countries. China is one country so charged. Consequently, this has been a disincentive to export to those countries. Product **Dumping**, in terms of international trade, occurs when a company or a country sells a product in another country at a lower price than what it is sold domestically. Naturally, these concepts reflect complex economic interests and processes. For example, the illustration of comparative advantage here is offered as suitable for secondary students. For a more academic presentation of this and other foreign trade factors, see Banerjee and Duflo, *Good Economics for Hard Times.*

Factoids related to post World War II, US foreign trade and employment –

- There was a famous memorandum issued in the 1970s. The "Peterson memo," during the Nixon Administration, brought into question the elements of Marshall Plan thinking. It called for, one, a change in trade policy that recognized the diminished status of the US in global markets during those years and, two, suggested extensive changes in policy aimed at rehabilitating the economic health of other nations (see insights below).

- The federal government's structural bureaucracy that is involved with applying federal foreign trade policy includes the State Department, advisory personnel to the President, and other trade officials. These might include officials from the Department of the Treasury, Department of Commerce, etc.

And foreign trade and employment insights can include –

- The Peterson memo suggested increased support for education initiatives to prepare Americans to compete; adjustments to currency valuations of the US and other countries to improve America's balance of trade/payments; improvements in American products, and for Americans to become more competitive to meet the demands of the global markets both in terms of labor and product innovations. These should improve US position in foreign trade relations.

- The US did not adhere to the suggestions of the Peterson memo because not all departments of the Nixon administration supported it; chief among them was the State Department. That department considered the memo antagonistic to other countries.

The teacher is directed to an online site for a more complete listing of relevant factoids and insights. That list not only contains information in the form of the above examples, but also includes the sources (footnotes) for further information. The URL for that site is: http://gravitascivics.blogspot.com/ , October 23, 2021.

With that context, lesson three, the next one, instructs students to describe the function of currency valuations on foreign trade. More specifically, he/she will be able to list the instrumental elements of currency's role in heightening or depressing demand levels for the products that a trading nation produces and wishes to export. Students will already be familiar with this function by reviewing the history in lesson one.

As an aside, this lesson might be assisted by development of a simulation or simulation game in which students can be divided into national groups and asked to not only "trade" goods but also to "purchase" either foreign currencies or a reserve currency. A creative teacher or material developer can design such a simulation/simulation game to be administered during one class period (or perhaps two class periods).[288]

And how other nations see these factors is a topic for lesson four; it can ask what their strategies have been. In terms of the actions and policies of other nations, they can be classified as using one of two approaches in dealing with foreign trade. One approach can be summarized as "beggar thy neighbor" and is implemented by mostly Asian countries such as China. The other approach is followed by European countries and reflects a

---

[288] As a way of seeing such a simulation, a teacher or lesson developer can consider an outline of a simulation this writer has roughly developed. See the online site this chapter uses to list factoids and insights. It has, toward the end of its text, a rough outline of a suitable simulation entitled, "Simulating Currency Trade." It is a step-by-step description of a simulation game and is presented, as a potential way to organize such a simulation. See the URL site http://gravitascivics.blogspot.com/ , October 23, 2021.

nurturing strategy that keeps its actions, domestically and in terms of foreign trade, within market mechanisms and protocols.

In simple language, the "beggar" strategy takes on the general view that foreign trade is a zero-sum affair – what is good for one party is bad for another. Therefore, that strategy includes high tariff policies (taxes on imports), stealing intellectual property (plans, patented inventions, copyrighted processes, and the like), insisting on forced technology transfer provisions before allowing trade in an industry,[289] blocking access by foreign competition to natural resources, and other similar policies advancing this approach.

On the other hand, a nurturing strategy sees foreign trade as the possibility for win-win interactions. Hence, such a posture supports liberal trading policies; it respects intellectual properties, looks for joint development of resources and seeks means

---

[289] This strategy, especially ascribed to China, insists that to pursue certain business opportunities there, this needs to be done through joint ventures with Chinese firms and that consequently allows the Chinese firms to access all technological innovations – their designs and other sensitive, protected information. This exposes those innovations and makes them subject to being stolen by the Chinese. Lee Branstetter explains how this takes place:

> The foreign direct investment regime in China is still partly closed. In order to operate in some industries in the country, foreign companies have to operate through joint ventures with local firms in which the multinational partner is not allowed to retain a controlling stake. This is the case in the auto industry, for example, where the combination of foreign ownership restrictions and high tariffs force foreign automakers to serve the Chinese auto market — the world's largest — through joint ventures. Operating under these conditions, European carmakers have complained that they are being pressured to turn over sensitive technology for electric vehicles to joint venture partners who may later compete with them in China and other markets.

See Lee Branstetter, "What Is the Problem of Forced Technology Transfer in China?," *Econofact.*

between or among nations for the joint defense of resources. The nurturing approach seems more akin to Marshall Plan thinking.

Of importance here is to have students correctly identify, from an appropriate description of a nation's trade policy, whether the elements represent a "nurturing" policy or a "beggar thy neighbor" policy. This objective is especially timely these days and the political rhetoric relating to the consequences of these two options is likely to be part of the national debate in the years ahead.

As for lesson five, students can begin preparing for their role in a formal debate. This debate phase will last three class periods and will take the unit to its penultimate lesson day. It will have students prepare and conduct a debate (deliberation) over what a local jurisdiction (the students' home state, e.g. Florida) and its citizens should do to reverse or enhance that jurisdiction's position regarding foreign trade.

The following debate issues identify specific courses of action by state governments to improve a state's economy and by doing so, enhance the interests of a state's businesses and its workers. The lesson has students identify and apply appropriate information regarding their state's ability to solicit foreign investments and/or to transfer manufacturing facilities into that state.

The objective will primarily be evaluated through their roles in the debate and their role in devising their action strategy (more on this below). Taking time restraints into account, the class, involving different sets of students, can debate one or two (from a choice of three) different questions. Each question or issue is designed to consider two options. The questions suggested are:

- Should a state government pursue a policy orientation that supports a "beggar thy neighbor" strategy or a nurturing strategy?

- Or should their state rely or not rely on a "right-to-work" legislation that it either currently has or should begin the process to attain (by changing its laws to acquire the sought-after status)?

- Or should their state engage in an aggressive tax incentive strategy – yes, or no?

As for the debate itself, each debate format can include at least three groups. Two of the groups will argue the chosen question. Each of those groups will argue one of the following: the "beggar" option, the right-to-work option, or the "yes" option according to which of the above questions is chosen. The other debater group will argue the nurturing option, the anti-right-to-work option, or the "no" option. The third group will be a panel of interrogators/judges. This activity, if arranged appropriately with added roles, can afford enough different roles so that each student in the class has a role to play.

And through that role, the student, individually or in a group, can express his/her understanding of the issues involved in the question under debate. He/she can also incorporate relevant information available from the factoids and insights provided for in the accompanying online site.

In the first of the class periods of this lesson, students can discuss which topic they will research and debate and what roles each of them will take. The roles can be debater for one of the sides just identified (e.g., in favor of the beggar thy neighbor option), debater for the opposite side (e.g., the nurturer option), debate judge, (if separated from interrogator), an interrogator, and if more roles are needed, journalist/reporter, an editorialist, and a TV pundit or two.

Generally, the time before the debate can be taken up by students preparing for the debate chosen. The roles of debaters are straightforward: one side argues for the proposal or an option and the other argues against the proposal or for the other option. The judges determine the winner and provide a rationale for their decision. That rationale not only provides the decision and the reasons for that decision, but it also passes judgement on the performance by pointing out the *positive* aspects of each side's presentation.

The interrogators (whether they are the judges or separated from the judges' role) fulfill a reflective function. They ask questions of the debaters during predetermined pauses in the debate. Such questions can ask for clarifications and perhaps introduce nuances to the deliberations. That is, questions that might take the form of pointing out that suggested courses of action might not progress as one side of the debate is suggesting.

Finally, if needed, the teacher can have students take on journalistic roles. They can be reporters, editorialists, TV or radio commentators (pundits). They either report what has happened, or they express their opinion about what should be the preferred policy option. This role opens the assignment to generate various imaginative work products (for example, video reports, "radio" reports, or other imaginative presentations).

In whatever role, the teacher evaluates the student by his/her ability to synthesize and logically apply the information that the unit presented and relates to the proposal under debate. This will be evaluated by student performance in the debate or any written or video work product. Of course, the debates take place during the last or the last two periods, first one and then the other.

Again, in all of this, certain concerns need to be emphasized: how does the information reflect on federalist values; how logical and true to Selznick's pillars of reason[290] (see Chapter 2) are student work products, and how geared toward action by citizens are students' recommendations? Also, of assistance is Toulmin's[291] elements of a sound argument that are also reviewed in Chapter 2.

---

[290] Selznick, *The Moral Commonwealth*.

[291] Toulmin, *The Uses of Argument*.

Beyond the aims mentioned here are the elements of a good debate. For teachers unfamiliar with debating as a formal activity, the reader is referred to Jarrod Atchison's work, *The Art of Debate – A Transcript Book.*[292] And there is, as already mentioned more than once, the online site listing factoids and insights to assist students and teachers in gaining further understanding of the developments that have transpired since World War II.

If a civics teacher follows this progression and students perform as outlined to this point, they should be ready for the unit's evaluation and for an action component. As for an action component, one needs to consider that this is the last unit of the course. To accommodate time constraints, an action could be to develop an individual or group action *strategy* that addresses the challenge of foreign trade on the local economic conditions.

And in turn, this strategy can be written in conjunction with the topic the class chose to debate. In other words, there can be an overlap among three-unit elements: the debate, the action component, and the unit's evaluation. But if any students choose to combine their efforts in this way, they would need to know what the debate choices will be earlier in the course.

As for the debate, nothing more needs to be added to what is identified above. And for the action component, once the class selects the topic, students can choose one side of the debate and research how a citizen can help advance that side's policy choice and devise the strategy of how to implement what that choice suggests. During the test period, using their researched notes, the student can write out that strategy. If needed, students might be given extra time – homework – to finish their strategy plan.

By actively inquiring into the various elements of this unit's topic, students can better be informed as to how foreign trade not only affects millions of their fellow citizens, but also

---

[292] Atchison, *The Art of Debate.*

gives them a realistic sense of what the world of work looks like today. And that ends this account's presentation of a unit dedicated to the effects of foreign trade on job availability.

CHAPTER 6: CONCLUSION

Beginning in Chapter 2, this account describes and explains federation theory – more specifically, the liberated federalism construct. Early on, this book made a distinction between two versions of federation theory. They are the parochial/traditional version and the liberated federalism version. This account promotes the latter version that steers federation theory to be proactively inclusive of a diversified population and therefore, more apt to be valued in a liberalized society which characterizes current day America.

The effort here makes the case that this construct can serve as a guiding view of governance and politics applicable in developing a civics curriculum. Each curriculum has two elements: a scope and a sequence. This book makes the case that the scope – the content – should be the driving force of a curriculum.

Beyond that aim, this book strives to demonstrate how a guiding construct can be accommodated in a procedural approach currently being promulgated by a professional organization. The procedural approach – the sequence – is provided by a branch of the educational establishment, the National Council for the Social Studies (NCSS).

That organization, in cooperation with the US Department of Education and its Common Core Standards project, issued a set of standards – available for states, if they so choose to implement them in their civics curricula. The publication containing the standards is *College, Career, and Civic Life (C3) Framework for Social Studies Standards: Guidance for Enhancing the Rigor of K-12 Civics, Economic, Geography, and History*[293] – referred to here as the C3 Framework.

---

[293] National Council for the Social Studies, *Preparing Students for College, Career, and Civic Life C3*. The standards themselves are accessible through this site. The actual document containing the standards is downloadable once

So, for example in Chapter 3, this account, by choosing to address the opioid crisis, describes that portion of federation theory most applicable to that topic. In addition, the chapter presents a set of instructional ideas demonstrating how the NCSS's standards could be achieved in an American secondary classroom. Similarly, Chapters 4 and 5 apply federation theory and the NCSS standards to the issues associated with tort law and foreign trade, respectively.

As this account approaches its final pages and by way of summary, Chapter 6 provides an overall model, federation theory, that aims to provide guidance to civics curriculum developers. With its use, those developers can design lessons and units that place in context those problems and issues that a polity experiences as defined by federalist values. To this point, the reader has been encouraged to view those topics, issues, or political problems as offenses against a federalist moral code (presented in Chapter 4). What remains is a theoretical overview of how these situations fit within a polity and the study of that polity.

But how does one accomplish that aim? The reader is reminded that much of what is described and explained is in the language of the ideal; that is, any of the highlighted political wrangling one can devise will expose a type of tension. It will be a tension between a "real" claim and that of an "ideal" aspiration. Any resulting model, at its basis, needs to identify and reflect that tension.

As one analyzes federalist values, federalist goals reflect a duality. That is, there exists inherently bi-level points of concern between the forces that focus political studies on either local communal levels or on a national level that deals with either a national or an international issue.

The aim in using federation theory is to revitalize the ideals of the founding fathers, but in such a way as to be *realistic*. In addition, educators should aim to extend student attention

---

one logs on to this online site and clicks on the option, the PDF document.

beyond the parochial but not to ignore them either. Can an "ideal" model, "handle" such a tension or bi-level concern? Consider that while the tension includes recognizing several national and international forces that impinge on political and economic realities – and in some cases, social realities – the construct is not willing to give up on the power of local participation.

This localism is usually referred to as "grass roots" politics and can be considered a basic federalist tenet as both an aspiration for ideal politics and a reality in which many are able to engage.[294] Since they have the necessary resources, average citizens can get involved in addressing these realities. This does not downplay the challenge this duality poses but recognizes the tension the challenge represents. And in thinking of this and other tensions in this fashion, federalism offers a responsible way to bridge the gap between the real and the ideal.

The argument in considering this and other issues is not to *reestablish* the parochial/traditional federalist view of governance and politics – the political construct that was dominant in this nation from its colonial days to World War II. Instead, it is for federalism to accommodate the factual conditions that characterize the world as it is.

With the presence of transnational corporations, global markets (including labor markets), global communication capabilities, and the resulting global conflicts, local politics with its challenges get easily lost in the shuffle. This occurs to the detriment of engaging the common citizen.

And further, a concern is for federalism to be true to its espoused commitment for inclusion; to treat all equally. These political conditions cannot be ignored and a political theory, to be viable, demands a synthesis between the concerns of federalism, as originally defined in the US with its calls for duty and obligation with a parochial sense and the natural rights' view of

---

[294] To see an application of these sentiments, see Crutchfield, *How Change Happens*. While this cited book relies on systems language (a behavioral based perspective), a closer look betrays a federalist bias.

liberty as expressed through its notion of "individual sovereignty."

It is *that* synthesis – or compromise – that provides a context for what follows: a review of an ideal model by which to analyze, for instructional purposes, a political confrontation – deciding who gets what – even in a local community, a courtroom, or in a roomful of negotiators ironing out a trade agreement.

This model is meant to provide a starting point and a source of ideas and questions that would be suitable for designing curricular content regarding the study of government and politics at the secondary level of American schools – not to initiate or guide political science research. It does what it attempts to do by first presenting an ideal, one that is mindful of what is.

The Model

The model is made up of three main components: the community, participating entities, and the association. As one goes through the components, one should keep in mind that this is an ideal model by which students can gauge and judge reality – a reality that includes a concern for how beneficial or harmful a political confrontation or a legal action can be.

A review of the elements is as follows:

- The **community**, the social, contextual reality within which an arrangement or association exists, is an ideally open environment which is accessible to outside entities such as individuals, arrangements, associations, or other communities. An ideal community is characterized as functioning with a cultural commitment to federalist values, a set of functioning and interacting institutions, and a general disposition among its members to uphold a moral primacy.

- The community's participating **entities**, comprised of those persons, arrangements, or associations, are the individual parties. These entities can be individuals who hold federalist values as being viable and worth pursuing. They can also be groups that uphold federalist values in

226

their dealings. If the entity is an individual, he/she can belong or be part of an arrangement (any organization) or of an association (an organization that operates under federalist values) which is characterized by several attributes or qualities.

- The **values or attributes** exhibited by an association are:
  - bonds of partnership among its participants, with respected responsibilities by its entities to the association which includes extending it loyalty, trust, skills, and knowledge relevant to the issues eliciting the association's concern and dealings,
  - expectations by its entities of equal standing within the association as a right and,
  - if needed, allowances so that any entity can viably participate in its processes not as an allotment, but as being inherent (a condition of birth or existence).

- The **characteristics** among an association's entities include status, conscience, and practical attributes, and the harboring of three transcending provisions within its boundaries: a fraternal ethos (genuine emotional commitment for upholding the legitimate interests of the members of the association and the association's aims), sense of partnership (a general belief that what benefits one member benefits all members), and a proclivity to support the elements of a communal democracy (a disposition to uphold and support the common institutions and norms of the association).

In addition, associations have the following structural characteristics:

- a founding agreement in the form of a compact or covenant,
- two political structural qualities, a qualified majority rule and minority rights, and
- a deliberative and open process by which decisions are made.

The final elements of the model refer to the specific conditions under study, i.e., the conditions that comprise the political confrontation being highlighted in an instructional lesson. In this book, the examples of the opioid crisis, tort law, and foreign trade and its effect on employment are described. It is with such issues that dialogue – discussions, arguments, and/or debates – between entities would be studied and practiced.

By focusing on a political confrontation, the model sheds light through the resulting study about how related events or conditions affect the structural, procedural, functional, and contextual factors of the association, the entities, and/or the community in question. They initiate the political actions that get the model into "operation." Or stated another way, they are the starting point.

In general, the model attempts to highlight a procedural event, much as the systems model offered by David Easton.[295] A difference, though, is that instead of analyzing how a political system processes supports and demands, the liberated federalist model focuses on the quality the components exhibit – how federated they are – as they interact or on how they *should* interact as the political confrontation plays out. Here, the effort is to be, as phenomenologists prescribe, comprehensive or holistic, not reductionist as is common in systems' approaches.[296]

Political confrontations are events or a set of related events that offend a federalist value(s). The model illustrates what should occur ideally – as a normative standard by which real life situations can be compared by analyzing, synthesizing, and evaluating the real events and situations the confrontation includes. The use of this model begins in an ideal realm and ends in evaluating a reality. Last, the model can pertain to any level of political behavior from local politics – as local as the home – to

---

[295] Easton, *The Political System.*

[296] A reductionist study aims to identify a set of factors in the form of hypothesis, e.g., they ask whether factor A happening correlates with factor B happening.

international confrontations.

Yes, this is a limited explanation, but if interest is generated, a more complete explanation can be provided in another venue. This model is offered to judge reality – through idealistic lenses – and identify how current governance and politics exemplify or fall short of federalist ideals.

Next, to give the reader a sense of how the components are developed in this model, one of its elements is chosen and further described and explained. That element, the association, in its description, most inclusively demonstrates the central essence of the entire model, i.e., to communicate how a federated populace goes about its business. To give the association context and to assist the reader, an overall image of the model is provided by the graphic representation in Figure 2.

The Association

The liberated federalist model identifies as a third component the association and, for the purposes of this conclusion, it deserves further attention. Associations are a type of social arrangements or stated another way, groups of people who may function in various levels of formality toward common goal(s). They can be inclusive of the whole community but in terms of instruction, the reference is of a grouping within the community.

Not all arrangements or collectives are associations. The term association, as used by Philip Selznick,[297] refers to those arrangements that are formal in that they are initiated by a compact or a covenant (in writing or at least verbally) and operate significantly within federalist ideals.

---

[297] Selznick, *The Moral Commonwealth.*

Figure 2:   Graphic Representation of the Liberated Federalism Model

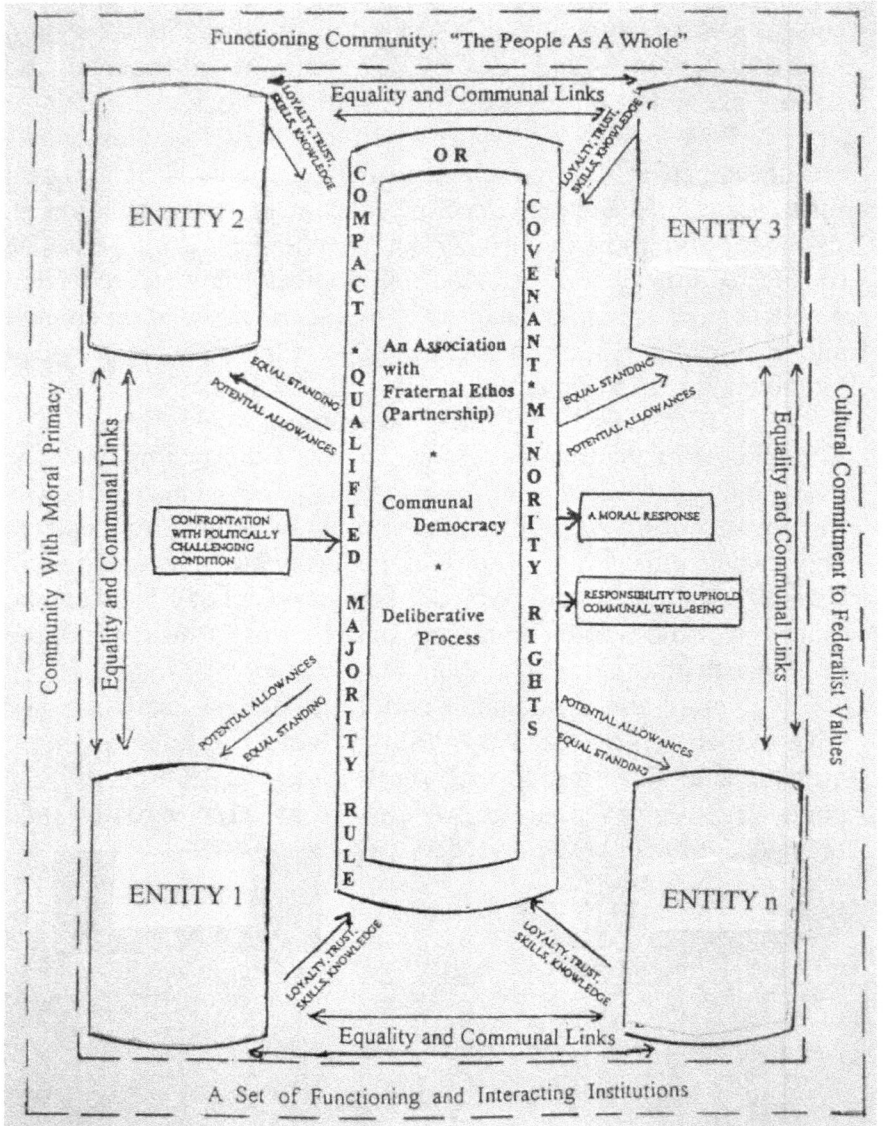

Of course, the national, all embracing association is the federal union of the people and the states of the United States of America as designated by the *United States Constitution*, its compact. Ideally, an association as well as those that make up the state and local governments are, in the ideal, communal democracies as defined by Selznick.

That is, any collection of entities, public or private, can be an association if it meets, to a significant degree, the following:

- One, an association is an arrangement formulated under the auspices of a compact or covenant that lays out its various provisions. Ideally, that agreement should be in writing, but a verbal, binding agreement can meet this requirement. That agreement, at a minimum, contains certain provisions: the aims of the association, certain structural requirements (being a qualified majority rule with a strong provision for guaranteeing the rights of minorities and individuals), countervailing power arrangements,[298] and a clear purpose or set of purposes for its existence that is publicly stated.

- Two, an association is characterized by having a fraternal ethos that respects the dignity and integrity of each of the entities that comprises it and an emotionally felt commitment of inclusion for those entities.

- Three, an association has a covenant of reason upon which its moral standing rests. The covenant of reason includes a deliberative process of decision-making, a provision of critical review of its decisions and actions, and a set of communal interests that reflects its purposes as well as its

---

[298] Referred to in common discourse as "checks and balances." The US government also meets this provision by allotting certain powers to the central government and others to the states.

standing as an association as opposed to a non-federated arrangement.

- And four, the association has an overarching responsibility to uphold the communal well-being of the greater community in which it resides.

To partially review these attributes, the following is offered:

The compact or covenant refers to the formal agreement among the entities. The agreement contains the characteristics identified by Daniel J. Elazar. To review his characterization of a compact/covenant, here is a definitional account of a covenant and another quote that further describes the common structure of covenants:

> Covenantal foundings emphasize the deliberate coming together of humans as equals to establish politics in such a way that all reaffirm their fundamental equality and retain their basic rights ... Polities whose origins are covenantal reflect the exercise of constitutional choice and broad-based participation in constitutional design. Polities founded by covenant are essentially federal in character, in the original meaning of the term (from foedus, Latin for covenant) ... [299]

And:

> [The old covenants followed a recurring format or model which was] ... an historical prologue indicating the parties involved, a preamble stating the general purposes of the covenant and the principles behind it, a body of conditions and operative clauses, a stipulation of the agreed-upon sanctions to be applied if the covenant were violated, and an oath to make the covenant morally binding.[300]

---

[299] Elazar, "Federal Models of (Civil) Authority," *Journal of Church and State*, 233-234.

Donald S. Lutz points out that the distinction between a covenant and a compact is that a covenant calls upon God to be a witness to the agreement and a compact does not.[301]   So, for example, the *Declaration of Independence* is a covenant, and the *US Constitution* is a compact. In any event, the formulation of either calls for soul searching.

It demands that the entities involved seriously consider the consequences of such an act due to the nature of the commitment involved. In addition, there should be at least some minimum level of emotional commitment among the entities for the agreement and each other since the union will most likely last for a significant amount of time – they have mostly been designed to last in perpetuity. In other words, those involved agree to be federated among themselves and that agreement stands regardless of the behavior of any entity.

Therefore, compacts and covenants should not be drawn up for frivolous reasons. As Elazar describes these unions, the commitment is for the duration of the concern(s) involved. In terms of a national union and such institutional arrangements as marriages, the commitments, as just alluded to, are in perpetuity.

As stated, the purpose or purposes need to be of sufficient importance. Importance can, at a minimum, be measured by the number of people affected by the activities of the association and the importance ascribed to that effect. For example, a school staff with its responsibilities makes it a suitable arrangement for such a commitment by those who work at a school site but seldom is – instead, those relationships are defined by personal contractual agreements, not covenants or compacts.[302]

The next attribute is qualified majority rule. While an association has a general commitment for democracy, it holds

---

[300] Ibid., 244.

[301] Lutz, *The Origins of American Constitutionalism.*

[302] Staff relationships are defined by formal, employment contracts issued between a school district and the individual teacher, not a compact or covenant. As such, they reflect a *quid pro quo* relationship.

that a raw majority rule arrangement in group decision-making should be avoided. One problem is that raw majority rule involves a lack of concern for minorities. Majority rule should be limited by constitutional (structural) parameters, such as insisting on a 60-vote majority[303] in the US Senate to pass a legislative bill or that the Senate consists of equal representation – two per state – regardless of a state's population.

Each minority and each person are entitled to protection from the majority and its potential abuses. Basic rights, as identified by the *Bill of Rights*, serve as an appropriate starting point. But on a more human level, this concern should be emotionally felt among all entities of the association. Minus that, there is still the reciprocal, practical concern that a majority today can be a minority tomorrow.

Then there is the attribute, fraternal ethos. It can best be considered as a "partnership" among the entities, a partnership that emotes a sense of solidarity on some meaningful level; that is, fellow participants are genuinely held in high regard and a mutual concern for each other's well-being and success is felt. Under a partnership, a benefit for one, under the experiences of the union, is a benefit for all, at least in the long run. Or, as Tocqueville is often quoted: "self-interest rightly understood."[304]

This quality does not do away with self-interests, but it does ideally place it within the concerns of the common good. This longer-term perspective is not a natural proclivity among human beings. To reach this emotional state, one needs to engage in focused, supportive emotional commitments and cognitive reasoning and reflection.[305] By such reflection (when one places the "head" before the "heart" when considering such matters), the emotions can hopefully be eventually "hooked" to

---

[303] For most legislative bills, the Senate, to avoid a filibuster, needs at least 60 senators to agree to consider the bill.

[304] See Steenbergen, "Enlightened Self-Interest.," *Learning to Give*.

[305] Sapolsky, *Behave*. Jonah Goldberg offers a harsher description of this disinclination among humans. See Goldberg, *Suicide of the West*.

take in the interests of others and/or the interests of the common condition – at least, that is the aim.

This can be described, if achieved, as an appropriately federated political union. It also reflects a significant level of maturity within the citizenry.[306] One can question whether a given citizen or polity can achieve a general level of such commitment. The role of civics education seems obvious here: to encourage an understanding of the benefits of such a view.

Hence, so guided, such a goal can be considered as the essential role that civics education plays in supporting this type of arrangement. That responsibility does not belong solely to schools and their civics programs, but they should meaningfully support and be vital factors in this socialization. While a people's challenge to generally be so disposed is a real concern, it being abandoned, with its consequences, is just as real – one need only look around.

Formulating a general association calls on active policies among the various institutions of society, including education. For example, for the established educational bureaucracy to issue the C3 Framework – assuming one views those standards and its definition of civic virtue through a federation theory perspective – these bureaucrats are engaging in such an effort.

The final attribute of an association is a covenant of reason. This attribute is the foundation for making possible the actualization of planned moral actions by the association as a matter of course. Entities engage or operationalize this foundation by anchoring their efforts in a deliberative process by which decisions are made by the association.

Educators so motivated do the following: perceive the entailed challenges, identify the affected self-interests, (logically simultaneously) review related ideals, review relevant knowledge, reflect and devise a moral mission, formulate from options and an open debate process an action strategy, devise and select an evaluation component (including formative and

---

[306] Selznick, *The Moral Commonwealth.*

summative phases), decide and commence to act, and evaluate, against federalist and practical values, the action that has been taken.

These activities are presented here in a logical sequence, but they do not have to be carried out in that order except for the last three steps which would naturally be at the end of the process. This is how this construct views ideal politics. In addition, the process by which to study associational politics utilizes historical and social science literature (along with other sources such as literary works – novels, short stories, poems, etc. – and other artistic materials) as information sources.

Those implementing this attribute operate, as much as possible, in a transparent fashion. That presupposes an association that has communal interests and, whenever possible, is open and forthcoming with information regarding these elements. Of course, they must consider competitive considerations, as with proprietary information of a business or by a concern for national security facing the defense establishment; these can restrict this attribute.

Those, then, are the attributes of an association. Implementors of this approach utilize similar reasoning when applying the other elements of the federalist model. While recognizing the inherent competitive nature of politics, according to this model, politics need not sacrifice the communal benefits that a federated populace can secure.

An educator who uses it aims to impart an appreciation, i.e., to work toward "going far" in meeting an association's aims by being federated. And through the efforts of such teachers, school administrators, district officials, and all other educators who work to present a responsible civics program, an application of the C3 Framework through the guidance of federation theory offers a way to arrive at that aim.

At least, that is the argument presented here. To be federated, arrangements need to secure these characteristics on meaningful levels. Civics education should prepare students to become useful members of associational arrangements. If so, they can contribute to the health of their social/political environments.

Goals of a Federalist Civics

So, in a summary review, here is what this book is encouraging: there are four main elements upon which a federalist guided course should be constructed.

- One, the course should highlight political topics, problems, or issues suitable for students to participate with politically relevant action. Areas of concern should start with issues close to the student toward issues encompassing larger and larger areas – from the individual and his/her immediate surroundings to international issues. At each level, the student becomes knowledgeable about corresponding, American governmental institutions.
- Two, the course, in a progressive way, should have students develop dialogue skills from discussion to formal debate. As the course provides appropriate instruction, the students should be expected to participate in more sophisticated modes of deliberative dialogue.
- Three, the course should introduce students to action, i.e., to participate in more proactive political engagements which include reviewing local "action" resources, participating in action strategies (from development to implementation), and evaluating local governmental efforts. The course can accomplish this aim on two fronts: a course-wide assignment in which students individually or in groups can tackle a meaningful strategy, and unit segments that address meaningful portions of such a strategy.
- Four, the course should tackle political topics/issues/societal problem areas – usually one per unit – that offend federalist values and therefore, pursue achieving the C3 Framework standards by seeking civic virtue and a federated citizenry.

This account has made the case for a civics curriculum to take seriously the aim of attaining an American citizenry being federated among themselves – to move toward the ideal of a federated nation.

To remind the reader, previous pages have outlined the central concept of federation theory (be it of the parochial/traditional variety or what this book has favored, liberated federalism). A federal union is one in which a group of people come together and inviolably promise to do something. At times, this takes the form of a covenant or it might be a compact. If one reviews the oath that aspiring citizens take at a naturalization ceremony, one can see those hopeful people voluntarily committing to a compact.[307]

Some might argue that this oath should not be limited to immigrants who are seeking citizenship but one in which a natural born citizen be called upon to take; perhaps when they initially register to vote, hopefully when they are eighteen. As it is, just being born within the borders of the nation ascribes to a person the status of citizen. Of course, such a person, if he/she does not want to be part of the union compact, can renounce his/her citizenry. That person can seek citizenship in another country. The assumption here – both culturally and legally – is

---

[307] By taking the oath, the person makes a set of promises and those promises have been part of the ceremony since the 1700s. The promises are duties that include to:

- Support and defend the Constitution of the United States and its laws, particularly those formulated to protect the nation from its enemies;
- Forego any allegiance to other nations or sovereigns;
- Renounce any hereditary – such as those of nobility – titles;
- Submit to military and civilian service when the government calls for such service.

This oath is taken voluntarily – he/she chooses to take it; there is no coercion involved.

that if a citizen resides here, he/she voluntarily agrees to that promise or oath.

But beyond the legality, one can endow that oath with a spirit. The promises are a minimum, but the spirit of allegiance calls for more; it calls for a proactive disposition to live in accordance with the values of a federated union. And a citizen abides by them not because he/she is forced, but because he/she loves that union.

To describe this spirit, in earlier pages, this book shared an extended quote by the political writer, Alexis de Tocqueville. Elsewhere in the book, it reminds the reader of its content. Here is another reminder of an America of the 1830s with an excerpt:

> ... [T]he political activity which pervades the United States must be *seen* in order to be understood ... Everything is in motion around you; here, the people of one quarter of a town are met to decide upon the building of a church; there, the election of a representative is going on; a little further, the delegates of a district are traveling in a hurry to the town in order to consult upon some local improvements; or in another place the labourers of a village quit their ploughs to deliberate upon the project of a road or a public school ... Societies are formed which regard drunkenness as the principal cause of the evils under which the State labours, and which solemnly bind themselves to give a constant example of temperance ... [308]

This, according to Tocqueville, represented common scenes of those years.

---

[308] de Tocqueville, "Political Activities in America," in *Alexis de Tocqueville*, 78-101, 78-79.

America has changed. One would be hard pressed to describe this nation in this fashion today. This book has referenced the general reluctance Americans have in becoming politically engaged. Yet structurally, Americans are still a federalist union. This writer has written this book to inform and encourage a more general understanding of what a commitment to a federal union looks like; what should be the dispositions among students and citizens in general. Is there, in the nation's current state of affairs, any evidence indicating a move toward a more involved citizenry can be realized?

This book, in Chapter 3, provides a general description – as a topic for students to investigate – of the opioid crisis. To use a more concrete issue to describe what is happening in terms of citizen involvement, this crisis is helpful. In that light, these final pages will describe a more current instance of how this issue of non-involvement has played a role in this crisis with a ray of hope from the state of Ohio.

One aspect of the opioid nightmare is the role Mexican heroin dealers have played.[309] This account has been reluctant to report on this aspect because of a generally perceived prejudice some Americans have voiced against Mexican immigrants. But to be complete, this description of the epidemic should report on the role that a small percentage of Mexicans has played

As it turns out, this drug trade originates from a small town, Xalisco, Nayarit, in Mexico. The town's name is pronounced as another Mexican city, Jalisco, but is spelled with an "X." Near that town, the opium poppy plant grew extensively. It was harvested and its milky fluid was extracted and cooked into a substance resembling black tar.

This, in turn, was molded into small round shapes – marble type balls – and were smuggled into the US. In the US, Xalisco dealers set up across the nation effective and extensive

---

[309] Quinones, *Dreamland.*

distribution systems using non-descript cars and a pool of drivers with cell phones. One aspect of the distribution was its efficient delivery service.

All that a user or addict had to do was make a call and a driver showed up with the requested drug. These deliveries were cheap and convenient. They were particularly attractive to people – many of them young – who were hooked on pain pills such as OxyContin that were usually more expensive and harder to get. Chapter 3 describes this "medical" aspect of the opioid crisis.[310] The point here is that the victims were hooked on pills and shifted to heroin via these Xalisco distributors.

While the epidemic has affected most regions of the country, one state has been among the hardest hit; that was/is Ohio. One town in Ohio, Portsmouth, is highlighted by the journalist, Sam Quinones, in his book, *Dreamland*.[311] He begins the book by describing a recreational area in Portsmouth that apparently was the center of the town back in the 1960s. It had a large pool and adjacent recreation area called Dreamland where the town "hung out" during the warmer days of the year.

In those years, the town was doing relatively well with a strong manufacturing base. But, as with many manufacturing towns since those earlier days, Portsmouth lost those factories to mostly foreign competitors. The results of such a development was obviously devastating. But that is only the backdrop to the tragedy. Then, the selling of opioids in the form of pain pills took hold. Many otherwise average Americans became victims to the opioid epidemic.

They – the Mexicans – devised effective, on-demand distribution arrangements in numerous communities around the US including Portsmouth. Their customers are not inner-city

---

[310] And see Gutierrez, "And Then There Is Law-Abiding Behavior, Part II," *Gravitas.*
[311] Quinones, *Dreamland.*

junkies as the heroin trade of old was and in major urban centers, but among, in many cases, middle class whites who have gotten themselves hooked on opioids.

Often, these middle-class customers became addicted after they were exposed to a chronic pain management protocol under the supervision of legitimate doctors. A lot of this, in turn, was based on an underestimation of the addictive quality of the drugs prescribed and the aggressive drug company strategies in marketing opiates. Once hooked, these people became desperate to find cheaper and unlimited supplies of a substitute drug – heroin, a type of opioid – to satisfy their cravings.[312]

But time moved on and many aspects of the story have changed since the early years of this century. One, the cartels of Mexico, earlier not interested in cheap drug sells, eventually moved in and disrupted the Xalisco system. Also, the general reaction to opioids in the US is taking a toll on the trade and there seems to be some improvement in meeting the crisis. In this, Portsmouth has gone through some positive changes. These changes remind this writer of the above cited Tocqueville quote.

Here is another quote offered by Quinones:

> Angie Thuma, the veteran Walmart shoplifter [to pay for her addiction] … told me the last time we spoke, "when I think about all the things I went through and I'm still alive, it gives you courage to keep bettering yourself."

> That seemed to be Portsmouth's attitude. The town still looked as scarred and beaten as an addict's arm. Wild-eyed hookers strolled the East End railroad tracks, and too many jobs paid minimum wage and led nowhere. Portsmouth still had hundreds of drug addicts and dealers. But it

---

[312] Ibid. All of this was described in Chapter 3.

also now had a confident, muscular culture of recovery that competed with the culture of getting high – a community slowly pitching itself.

Proof to that was that addicts from all over Ohio were now migrating south to get *clean* in Portsmouth. No place in Ohio had Portsmouth's recovery infrastructure.

On my last trip to Portsmouth, I met a young woman from Johnstown, a rural town northeast of Columbus that from her description sounded a lot like the 740 that RWR rapped about. She had been buying heroin from the Xalisco Boys in Columbus for a couple of years. When she tried to quit, a driver who spoke English called her for a week straight.

"But, senorita, we have really good stuff. It just came in."

Finally, she threw away her phone. There wasn't much on it but dope contacts anyway. She was twenty-three, alone with a ten-month-old son, and – seeking to get clean with nowhere else to turn – she found refuge in Portsmouth.

"I love it here. I'm really afraid to go back," she told me in the lilting drawl of rural Ohio, when we met at a party for a woman celebrating her first year clean.

So the battered old town had hung on. It was, somehow, a beacon embracing shivering and hollow-eyed junkies, letting them know that all was not lost. That at the bottom of the rubble was a place just like them, kicked and buried but surviving. A place that had, like them, shredded and lost so much that was precious but was

243

nurturing it again. Though they were adrift, they, too, could begin to find their way back.

Back to that place called Dreamland.[313]

Is there a silver-lining? Perhaps. Maybe the bottom of a nightmare offers enough motivation to rekindle the communal base of a spirited federal union. Sadly, if so, what a price to pay. Perhaps a more proactive civics program can help avoid such a price. Of course, neither the nightmare nor a proactive educational program can make the total difference, but they can be used toward putting solutions in place.

So, to those who belittle idealism, even when it attempts to account for reality, one can mention Portsmouth or an America of the 1830s. But such idealism calls for the utilization of various attributes that can be found in the human experience. This includes an attribute of true maturity in that it bridges the gap between one's views of oneself and one's social environment, of seeking a false sense of liberty – of a narcissistic type – but instead understanding the truly liberating sense one experiences when one can tap into the resources of a community.

If successful, a civics curriculum guided by such an idealism serves to find equilibrium between one's emotions and one's intellect so that he/she can be empowered and enriched by the warm relationships that federation accrues and gain access to those resources the greater citizenry harbors. By doing so, the nation can feel secure in knowing it is being faithful to the founders' wishes for their posterity.

---

[313] Ibid., 344-345. For another general description of various community-based efforts to address the opioid crisis, see Macy, *Dopesick*. Macy's account covers non-Mexican dealings in opioid.

Bibliography

"Addiction Rare in Patients Treated with Narcotics." *The New England Journal of Medicine*, January 10, 1980. Accessed June 21, 2018, https://www.nejm.org/doi/full/10.1056/NEJM198001103020221 .

Anderson, Leigh. "Heroin." Drugs.com., May 18,2014. Accessed June 25, 2018, https://www.drugs.com/illicit/heroin.html .

Alden, Edward. *Failure to Adjust: How Americans Got Left Behind in the Global Economy*. Rowman and Littlefield, 2017.

Amadeo, Kimberly. "Why the Dollar Is the Global Currency." *The Balance*, n. d. Accessed July 17, 2018, https://www.thebalance.com/world-currency-3305931 .

Argyris, Chris and Donald A. Shon. "Evaluating Theories in Action." In *The Planning of Change*, Fourth Edition. Edited by Warren G. Bennis, Kenneth D. Benne, and Robert Chin. New York, NY: Holt, Rinehart and Winston, 1985, 108-117.

Aristotle, "Aristotle: The Politics." In *The Great Political Theories*. Edited by Michael Curtis, New York, NY: Avon, 1961, 64-101.

Atchison, Jarrod. *The Art of Debate* – A Transcript Book. Chantilly, VA: The Great Courses, 2017.

Banerjee, Abhijit V. and Esther Duflo. *Good Economics for Hard Times*. New York, NY: PublicAffairs, 2019.

Beckert, Sven. *Empire of Cotton: A Global History*. New York, NY: Alfred A. Knopf, 2014.

Benne, Kenneth D. "The Current State of Planned Changing in Persons, Groups, Communities, and Societies." In *The Planning of Change*,

Edited by Warren G. Bennis, Kenneth D. Benne, and Robert Chin, New York, NY: Holt, Rinehart and Winston, 1985.

Bishop, Molly. "Legal and Legal Practice." *Law School for Everyone* – A transcript book (Chantilly, VA: The Teaching Company, 2017).

"*Blyth v. Birmingham Waterworks Co.*, 11 Exch. 781 (1856), *Case Briefs*, n. d. Accessed September 16, 2018, http://www.casebriefs.com/blog/law/torts-keyed-to-prosser/negligence/blyth-v-birmingham-waterworks-co/ .

Bow, James. "Logic." In Mathematics: *An Illustration History of Numbers*. Edited by Tom Jenkins. New York, NY: Shelter Harbor, n.d., 19.

Branstetter, Lee. "What Is the Problem of Forced Technology Transfer in China?" *Econofact*, August 3, 2018. Accessed December 18, 2018, https://econofact.org/what-is-the-problem-of-forced-technology-transfer-in-china .

"Briefing Guide for First Responders." U. S. Department of Justice/Drug Enforcement Administration. Accessed July 2, 2018, https://www.dea.gov/druginfo/Fentanyl_BriefingGuideforFirstRespond ers_June2017.pdf.

Briggs, Saga. "How to Make Learning Relevant to Your Students (and Why It's Crucial to Their Success)." *Inform Ed*, October 4, 2014. Accessed November 7, 2019, https://www.opencolleges.edu.au/informed/features/how-to-make-learning-relevant/ .

Bunker, Nick. "Being the Reserve Currency Has Its Privileges and Costs." Washington Center for Equitable Growth, n. d. Accessed July

22, 2018, https://equitablegrowth.org/reserve-currency-privileges-costs/
.

Caldwell, Christopher. "American Carnage: The Landscape of Opioid Addiction." *First Things*, April 2017. Accessed June 18, 2018, https://www.firstthings.com/article/2017/04/american-carnage .

"The Categorical Imperative: An Ethics of Duty." City University of New York, n. d. Accessed January 27, 2019, http://www.qcc.cuny.edu/socialsciences/ppecorino/MEDICAL_ETHIC S_TEXT/Chapter_2_Ethical_Traditions/Categorical_Imperative.htm .

Cheng, Edward K. "Torts," *Law School for Everyone* – a transcript book. Chantilly, VA: The Teaching Company/The Great Courses, 2017.

Cherryholmes, Cleo H. "Critical Pedagogy and Social Education." In *Handbook on Teaching Social Issues: NCSS Bulletin 93.* Edited by Ronald W. Evans and David Warren Saxe, 75-80, Washington, DC: National Council of the Social Studies, 1996.

"Civic Education." Stanford Encyclopedia of Philosophy, (2013/2007), https://plato.stanford.edu/entries/civic-education/ .

"Civics Education Testing Only Required in 9 States for High School Graduation: CIRCLE Study." *Huff Post* October 12, 2012. Accessed November 4, 2018. https://www.huffingtonpost.com/2012/10/12/circle-study-finds-most-s_n_1959522.html .

Clear, James. "How Vietnam War Veterans Broke Their Heroin Addictions," *Behavioral Psychology (Habits).* No date. Accessed August 7, 2018, https://jamesclear.com/heroin-habits .

Conover, Pamela J. and Donald D. Searing. "A Political Socialization Perspective." In *Rediscovering the Democratic Purposes of Education.*

Edited by Lorraine M. McDonnell, P. Michael Timpane, and Roger Benjamin. Lawrence, KS: University of Kansas Press, 2000.

Crutchfield, Leslie R. *How Change Happens: Why Some Social Movements Succeed While Others Don't*. Hoboken, NJ: John Wiley & Sons, Inc., 2018.

Cutway, Adrienne. "Orlando Man Pleads Guilty to Selling Heroin Mixed with Fentanyl." Orlando.com, March 20, 2017. Accessed July 2, 2018, https://www.clickorlando.com/news/orlando-man-pleads-guilty-to-selling-heroin-mixed-with-fentanyl .

Dan-Cohen, Meir. *Harmful Thoughts: Essays on Law, Self, and Morality*. Princeton, NJ: Princeton University Press, 2002.

DePillis, Lydia. "Foreign Investment in the United States Plunged 32% in 2017." *CNN Business*, July 11,2018. Accessed February 2, 2019, https://money.cnn.com/2018/07/11/news/economy/foreign-direct-investment-2017/index.html .

de Tocqueville, Alexis. "Political Activities in America." In *Alexis de Tocqueville: On Democracy, Revolution, and Society*. Edited by John Stone and Stephen Mennell, Chicago, IL: Chicago University Press, 1980/1835.

Dewey, John. "John Dewey on Liberalism and Civil Liberties, 1936." In *Major Problems in American Constitutional History, Volume II: From 1870 to the Present*. Edited by Kermit L. Hall. Lexington, MA: D. C. Heath and Company, 1992.

"Direct Investment Position of the United States Abroad from 2000 to 2017(in Trillion of Dollars, on a Historical-Cost Basis). *Statista: The Statistic Portal*. No date. Accessed February 2, 2019, https://www.statista.com/statistics/188571/united-states-direct-investments-abroad-since-2000/ .

Doherty, Neil, Scott Gottlieb, Elinore McCane-Katz, Anne Schuchat, and Nora Volkow. "Federal Efforts to Combat the Opioid Crisis: A Status Update on CARA and Other Initiatives." National Institute on Drug Abuse, October 25, 2017. Accessed June 21, 2018, https://www.drugabuse.gov/about-nida/legislative-activities/testimony-to-congress/2017/federal-efforts-to-combat-opioid-crisis-status-update-cara-other-initiatives.

Dowell, Deborah, Rita K. Noonan, Debra Houry. "Underlying Factors in Drug Overdose Deaths." *Journal of the American Medical Association.* 318, 23 (December 19, 2017). Abstract accessed December 18, 2019, https://www.ncbi.nlm.nih.gov/pmc/articles/PMC6007807/ .

"Drug Scheduling," DEA, no date. Accessed December 12, 2018, https://www.dea.gov/drug-scheduling .

Durant, Will. *Caesar and Christ: A History of Roman Civilization and of Christianity from Their Beginnings to A. D. 325.* New York, NY: Simon and Schuster, 1944.

Dvorak, Petula. "The Epic Fail of the American Electorate." *The Washington Post*, November 3, 2016. Accessed December 25, 2018, https://www.washingtonpost.com/local/the-epic-fail-of-the-american-electorate/2016/11/03/fa734a0c-a1ca-11e6-a44d-cc2898cfab06_story.html?noredirect=on&utm_term=.37f4247a2a92 .

Easton, David. *The Political System.* New York, NY: Alfred A. Knopf, 1953.

"Edwin Fenton Papers," Carnegie Mellon University, http://digitalcollections.library.cmu.edu/awweb/awarchive?type=file&item=726112 .

Elazar, Daniel J. *American Federalism: A View from the States.* New York, NY: Thomas Y. Crowell Company, 1966.

---. *Exploring Federalism*. Tuscaloosa, AL: The University of Alabama Press, 1987.

---. "Federal Models of (Civil) Authority." *Journal of Church and State*, 33, 2 (March 1, 1991), 231-254.

---. "How Federal Is the Constitution? Thoroughly." Readings for Classes Taught by Professor Elazar. National Endowment for the Humanities Institute, Steamboat Springs, Colorado, 1994.

Ellis, Charles M. "Roger B. Taney and the Leviathan of Slavery. *The Atlantic* (February 1865). Accessed December 10, 2017, https://www.theatlantic.com/magazine/archive/1865/02/roger-b-taney-the-leviathan-of-slavery/387241/ .

Euchner, Charles. *Extraordinary Politics: How Protest and Dissent Are Changing American Democracy*. Boulder, CO: Westview, 1996.

Eyler, Janet. "The Power of Experiential Education." Association of American Colleges and Universities, n. d. Accessed December 11, 2018, https://www.aacu.org/publications-research/periodicals/power-experiential-education .

Fenton, Edwin, David Fow, and Irving Bartlett. *A New History of the United States: An Inquiry Approach*. Pittsburg, PA: Carnegie Mellon University Press, 1975.

"The First 'On Liberty.'" Intercollegiate Studies Institute: Educating for Liberty, October 28, 2011. Accessed on July 1, 2018, https://faculty.isi.org/blog/post/view/id/686/ .

Follet, Ken. *A Column of Fire*. New York, NY: Viking, 2017.

Freire, Paulo. *Pedagogy of the Oppressed*. New York, NY: Continuum, 1999.

Friedman, Thomas. *The World Is Flat: A Brief History of the Twenty-first Century*. New York, NY: Farrar, Straus and Giroux, 2005.

French, Jr., John R. P. and Bertram Raven. "The Bases of Power." In *Current Perspectives in Social Psychology*. Edited by Edwin P. Hollander and Raymond G. Hunt, New York, NY: Oxford University Press, 1967, 504-512.

Fry, Richard and Rakesh Kochhar. "America's Wealth Gap between Middle-Income and Upper-Income Is Widest on Record." *Fact Tank*, December 17, 2014. Accessed August 31, 2017, http://www.pewresearch.org/fact-tank/2014/12/17/wealth-gap-upper-middle-income/ .

Gaarder, Jostein. *Sophie's World: A Novel about the History of Philosophy*. New York, NY: Farrar, Straus, Giroux, 1996.

Gladwell, Malcolm. *Outliers*. New York, NY: Little, Brown and Company, 2008.

Goldberg, Jonah. *Suicide of the West: How the Rebirth of Tribalism, Populism, Nationalism, and Identity Politics Is Destroying American Democracy*. New York, NY: Crown Forum, 2018.

Goodnough, Abby. "Debating the Use of Drugs to Curb the Abuse of Drugs." *The New York Times*. 168, 58 (December 30, 2018), 1 & 19.

Gopnik, Adam. *A Thousand Small Sanities: The Moral Adventure of Liberalism*. New York, NY: Basic, 2019.

Guelzo, Allen C. *The American Mind* – a transcript book. Chantilly, VA: The Teaching Company/Great Courses, 2005.

Gutierrez, Robert. "And Then There Is Law-Abiding Behavior, Part II." *Gravitas: A Voice for Civics*, a blog, May 21, 2019. Accessed July 1, 2019, https://gravitascivics.blogspot.com/2019/05/and-then-there-is-law-abiding-behavior_21.html .

---. "A Case for Centered Pluralism." *Curriculum and Teaching Dialogue*, Volume 5, number 1: 71-82.

---. "Fallacy Types." *Gravitas: A Voice for Civics* – a blog, August 29, 2017. Accessed December 31, 2018, http://gravitascivics.blogspot.com/2017_08_27_archive.html .

---. *Gravitas: A Voice for Civics* – a blog, https://gravitascivics.blogspot.com/ . A review of posting regarding a review of the Magruder textbook can be retrieved from https://onedrive.live.com/view.aspx?resid=CED163627385DD3C!1531 1&ithint=file%2cdocx&app=Word&authkey=!AH6RD7ctTgqkX4I .

---. "How to Define and Evaluate Theories," *Gravitas: A Voice for Civics* – a blog – July 17, 2018. Accessed July 17, 2018, https://gravitascivics.blogspot.com/ .

---. "Our Federalist Roots: A Neglected Past?" *Theory and Research in Social Education*, vol. 31, no. 2 (2003), 218-242.

---. "Moral Code for the Current Secular State of Affairs." *Education*, Volume 125, number 3, 2005, 353-372.

---. "The Predisposition of High School Students to Engage in Collective Strategies of Problem-Solving." *Theory and Research in Social Education*, 33, 3 (2005), 404-428.

---. "The Prevailing Construct in Civic[s] Education and Its Problems." *Action in Teacher Education*, 32, 2 (2010), 24-41.

---. "Rekindling Concerns over Moral Politics in the Classroom." *The Social Studies*, 92, 3 (2001), 113-119.

---. "What Can Happen to Auspicious Beginnings: Historical Barriers to Ideal Citizenship." *The Social Studies*, 93, 5 (2002), 202-208.

Haidt, Jonathan. *The Righteous Mind: Why Good People Are Divided by Politics and Religion*. New York, NY: Pantheon, 2012.

Hall, Kermit L. "Laissez-Faire Constitutionalism and Liberty in the Late Nineteenth Century" (introductory remarks to Chapter 2). In *Major Problems in American Constitutional History, Volume II: The Colonial Era Through Reconstruction*. Editor Kermit L. Hall. Lexington, MA: D. C. Heath and Company, 1992.

Hampton, Ryan. "What Americans Don't Know about the Purdue Pharma Bankruptcy Hurts All of Us." *Time* (October 6, 2021).

Heisig, Eric. "How OxyContin Maker Purdue Pharma's Potential Bankruptcy Filing Would Stall Thousands of Lawsuits before Federal Judge in Cleveland." *Cleveland.com*, March 4, 2019. Accessed March 7, 2019, https://www.cleveland.com/court-justice/2019/03/how-oxycontin-maker-purdue-pharmas-potential-bankruptcy-filing-would-stall-thousands-of-lawsuits-before-federal-judge-in-cleveland.html .

Houseman, Susan N. "Is Automation Really to Blame for Lost Manufacturing Jobs? What the Conventional Wisdom Gets Wrong." *Foreign Affairs*, September 7, 2018. Accessed November 10, 2019, https://www.foreignaffairs.com/articles/2018-09-07/automation-really-blame-lost-manufacturing-jobs .

Howard, Jacqueline. "Why Opioid Overdose Deaths Seem to Happen in Spurts." *CNN*, February 8, 2017. Accessed July 2, 2018, https://www.cnn.com/2017/02/08/health/opioids-overdose-deaths-epidemic-explainer/ .

Hwang, Catherine S., Hsien-Yen Chang, and G Caleb Alexander. "Impact of Abuse-Deterrent OxyContin on Prescription Opioid Utilization." *Pharmacoepidemiology and Drug Safety*, 24, 2 (2015).

"Information Sheet on Opioid Overdose." World Health Organization (UN), November 2014. Accessed June 14, 2018, http://www.who.int/substance_abuse/information-sheet/en/.

"Interview: Dr. Robert DuPont." *Frontline*, 2014 (estimated). Accessed June 18, 2018, https://www.pbs.org/wgbh/pages/frontline/shows/drugs/interviews/dupont.html .

"Is Marijuana a Gateway Drug?" *National Institute on Drug Abuse.* Accessed on August 21, 2017, https://www.drugabuse.gov/publications/research-reports/marijuana/marijuana-gateway-drug .

Jackson, James K. "U. S. Direct Investment Abroad: Trends and Current Conditions." Congressional Research Service, June 29, 2017. Accessed January 14, 2019, https://fas.org/sgp/crs/misc/RS21118.pdf .

Kaczorowski, Robert J. "The Common-Law Background of Nineteenth-Century Tort Law," Fordham Law School, 1990. Accessed September 17, 2018, https://pdfs.semanticscholar.org/74ba/0630b8c59bb5fcef22fbffaf96e56b91282f.pdf .

Kingston, Jeff. "Why Did Japan Surrender in World War II?" *The Japan Times*, August 6, 2016. Accessed July 17, 2019, https://www.japantimes.co.jp/opinion/2016/08/06/commentary/japan-surrender-world-war-ii/#.XS_QkehKjIU .

"*Kline v. 1500 Massachusetts Avenue Apartment Corporation*." *Case Briefs.* 439 F.2d 477, 1970 U.S. App. LEXIS 7831, 141 U.S. App. D.C.

370, 43 A.L.R. 3d 311 (D.C. Cir. Aug. 6, 1970). No date. Accessed
October 3, 2018, https://www.casebriefs.com/blog/law/torts/torts-
keyed-to-prosser/owners-and-occupiers-of-land/kline-v-1500-
massachusetts-ave-apartment-corp/ .

Kolodny, Andrew, David T. Courtwright, Catherine S. Hwang, Peter
Kreiner, John L. Eadie, Thomas W. Clark, and G. Caleb Alexander.
"The Prescription Opioid and Heroin Crisis: A Public Health Approach
to an Epidemic of Addiction." *Annual Review of Public Health*, 36
(2015). Accessed June 25, 2018,
https://www.annualreviews.org/doi/abs/10.1146/annurev-publhealth-
031914-122957 .

Kramnick, Isaac. "John Locke and Liberal Constitutionalism." In
*Major Problems in American Constitutional History, Volume I: The
Colonial Era Through Reconstruction.* Edited by Kermit L. Hall.
Lexington, MA: D. C. Heath and Company, 1992, 97-114.

Kukathas, Chandran and Philip Pettit. *Rawls: A Theory of Justice and
Its Critics.* Stanford, CA: Stanford University Press, 1990.

Lanham, Richard A. *A Handlist of Rhetorical Terms: A Guide for
Students of English Literature.* Berkeley, CA: University of California
Press, 1969.

Leung, Pamela T. M., Erin M. MacDonald, Matthew B. Stanbrook,
Irfan A. Dhalla, and David N. Juurlink. "A 1980 Letter on the Risk of
Opioid Addiction." *New England Journal of Medicine*, 376, 22
(August 26, 2016). Accessed June 21, 2018,
https://www.nejm.org/doi/full/10.1056/NEJMc1700150 .

Lumet, Sidney (director). *The Verdict.* 20th Century Fox, 1982.

Lutz, Donald S. "The Articles of Confederation, 1781." In *Roots of
the Republic: American Founding Documents Interpreted.* Edited by

Stephen L. Schechter. Madison, WI: Madison House, 1990, 227-248.

---. "The Declaration of Independence, 1776." In *Roots of the Republic: American Founding Documents Interpreted.* Edited by Stephen L. Schechter. Madison, WI: Madison House, 1990, 138-145.

---. "The Fundamental Orders of Connecticut, 1639." In *Roots of the Republic: American Founding Documents Interpreted.* Edited by Stephen L. Schechter. Madison, WI: Madison House, 1990, 24-35.

---. "The Mayflower Compact, 1620." In *Roots of the Republic: American Founding Documents Interpreted.* Edited by Stephen L. Schechter. Madison, WI: Madison House, 1990, 17-23.

---. *The Origins of American Constitutionalism.* Lawrence, KS: University of Kansas, 1992.

---. "The Virginia Declaration of Rights and Constitution, 1776." In *Roots of the Republic: American Founding Documents Interpreted.* Edited by Stephen L. Schechter. Madison, WI: Madison House, 1990, 150-165.

MacLaren, Erik. "Cocaine History and Statistics." *DrugAbuse.com.* No date. Accessed June 21, 2018, https://drugabuse.com/library/cocaine-history-and-statistics/ .

Macy, Beth. *Dopesick, Dealers, Doctors, and the Drug Company That Addicted America.* New York, NY: Little, Brown and Company, 2018.

"*Madsen v. East Jordan Irrigation, 1942.*" *Case Briefs.* No date. Accessed October 18, 2018, https://www.casebriefs.com/blog/law/torts/outline-torts-law/strict-liability-outline-torts-law/case-overviews-66/22/ .

"*Martin v. Herzog.*" *Case Brief.* No date. Accessed October 11, 2018, 176 A.D. 614, 163 N.Y.S. 189, 1917 N.Y. App. Div. LEXIS 5114 (N.Y. App. Div. Feb. 2, 1917), https://www.quimbee.com/cases/martin-v-herzog .

McClenaghan, William A. *Magruder's American Government* (Florida Teacher's Edition). Boston, MA: Prentice Hall/Pearson, 2013.

McDonald, Forrest. "The Power of Ideas in the Convention." In *Major Problems in American Constitutional History*, Volume I: The Colonial Era through Reconstruction. Edited by Kermit Hall. Lexington, MA: D. C. Heath and Company, 1992.

McGinty, Emma E., Elizabeth A. Stuart, G. Caleb Alexander, Colleen L. Barry, Mark C. Bicket, and Lainie Rutkow. "Protocol: Mixed-Methods Study to Evaluate Implementation, Enforcement, and Outcomes of U. S. State Laws Intended to Curb High-Risk Opioid Prescribing." *Implementation Science*, 13, 1. Accessed August 6, 2018, https://www.ncbi.nlm.nih.gov/pmc/articles/PMC5828404/ .

Meier, Barry. "In Guilty Plea, OxyContin Maker to Pay $600 Million." *The New York Times*, May 10, 2007. Accessed June 29, 2018, https://www.nytimes.com/2007/05/10/business/11drug-web.html?mtrref=www.google.com&gwh=5EB54309CD06FBA62024 8E850CC5CC0B&gwt=pay .

Moghe, Sonia. "Opioid History: From 'Wonder Drug' to Abuse Epidemic." *CNN*, October 14, 2016. Accessed June 18, 2018, https://www.cnn.com/2016/05/12/health/opioid-addiction-history/ .

Myrdal, Gunnar. *An American Dilemma: The Negro Problem and Modern Democracy.* New York, NY: Harper and Brothers, 1944.

National Council for the Social Studies. *Preparing Students for College, Career, and Civic Life (C3)*. Washington, D. C.: NCSS, 2013. Accessed April 16, 2018, https://www.socialstudies.org/c3 .

NBC Nightly News with Lester Holt, broadcast. *NBC News*. December 12, 2018.

"New York Urbanized Area: Population & Density from 1800 (Provisional)." *Demographia*, n. d. Accessed September 16, 2018, http://demographia.com/db-nyuza1800.htm .

Newmann, Fred M. and Donald W. Oliver. *Clarifying Public Controversy: An Approach to Teaching Social Studies*. Boston, MA: Little, Brown, and Company, 1970.

NIH: National Institute on Drug Abuse, June 2016. Accessed August 1, 2018, https://www.drugabuse.gov/publications/drugfacts/fentanyl .

Oliver, Donald W. and James P. Shaver. *Teaching Public Issues in the High School*. Boston, MA: Houghton Mifflin, 1966.

Oliver, John. "Opioids." *Last Week Tonight* (HBO, TV cable production). May 21, 2018. Accessed August 27, 2018, (available on YouTube) https://www.youtube.com/watch?v=5pdPrQFjo2o .

"Opiate Withdrawal Timelines, Symptoms and Treatment." *American Addiction Centers*. No date. Accessed November 26, 2018, https://americanaddictioncenters.org/withdrawal-timelines-treatments/opiate .

"Opioid Crisis Fast Facts." *CNN Library*. June 16, 2018. Accessed June 25, 2018, https://www.cnn.com/2017/09/18/health/opioid-crisis-fast-facts/index.html .

"Opioid Crisis: The Letter That Started It All." *BBC*. June 3, 2017. Accessed June 21, 2018, https://www.bbc.com/news/world-us-canada-40136881.

"The Opioid Crisis Response Act of 2018." U. S. Senate. No date. Accessed November 16, 2018, https://www.help.senate.gov/imo/media/doc/The%20Opioid%20Crisis%20Response%20Act%20of%202018%20summary.pdf .

"Opioid Data Analysis." Centers for Disease Control and Prevention. No date. Accessed July 2, 2018, https://www.cdc.gov/drugoverdose/data/analysis.html .

"Opioid Overdose Crisis." National Institute on Drug Abuse, revised March 2018. Accessed September 3, 2018, https://www.drugabuse.gov/drugs-abuse/opioids/opioid-overdose-crisis .

Pakula, Alan J. (director). *All the President's Men*. Warner Brothers, Wildwood, Wildwood Enterprises, 1976.

"*Palsgraf v. Long Island Railroad*." *Case Briefs*. No date. Palsgraf v. Long Island R. Co., 248 N.Y. 339 (N.Y. 1928). Accessed October 17, 2018, https://www.casebriefs.com/blog/law/torts/torts-keyed-to-dobbs/negligence-the-scope-of-risk-or-proximate-cause-requirement/palsgraf-v-long-island-r-co/ .

Picchi, Aimee. "How Much Do the 1, .01 and .001 Percent Earn?" *CBS News*, February 27, 2018. Accessed March 28, 2019, https://www.cbsnews.com/news/how-much-do-the-1-01-and-001-percent-really-earn/ .

Piketty, Thomas. *Capital in the Twenty-First Century*. Cambridge, MA: Harvard University Press, 2014.

Pinker, Steven. *How the Mind Works*. New York, NY: W. W. Norton, 1997.

Porter, Jane and Hershel Jick, M.D. "Addiction Rare in Patients Treated with Narcotics." *The New England Journal of Medicine*, January 10, 1980. Accessed June 21, 2018, https://www.nejm.org/doi/full/10.1056/NEJM198001103020221 .

Postman, Neil. *Amusing Ourselves to Death: Public Discourse in the Age of Show Business*. New York, NY: Penguin, 1986.

"Purdue Pharma Lawsuit: Sackler Family Sued over Toll of Opioid." *CBS News*, updated October 24, 2018. Accessed January 24, 2019, https://www.cbsnews.com/news/purdue-pharma-lawsuit-sackler-family-sued-over-toll-of-opioids/ .

Putnam, Robert D. "Bowling Alone: America's Declining Social Capital." *Journal of Democracy*, January 1995. Accessed December 18, 2019, https://www.directory-online.com/Rotary/Accounts/6970/Downloads/4381/Bowling%20Alone%20Article.pdf .

Putnam, Robert D. *Bowling Alone: The Collapse and Revival of American Community*. New York, NY: Simon & Schuster, 2000.

Quinones, Sam. *Dreamland: The True Tale of America's Opiate Epidemic*. New York, NY: Bloomsbury, 2015.

Ravenscraft, Eric. "The Best Ways to Contact Your Congresspeople, from a Former Staffer." *Lifehacker*, November 15, 2016. Accessed

December 16, 2018, https://lifehacker.com/the-best-ways-to-contact-your-congress-people-from-a-f-1788990839 .

Reiman, Jeffrey. "Liberalism and Its Critics." In *The Liberalism-Communitarianism Debate*. Edited by C. F. Delaney. Lanhan, MD: Rowman and Litttlefield, 1994.

Santayana, George. "The Genteel Tradition in American Philosophy." In *The Annals of America*, vol. 13. Chicago, IL: Encyclopaedia Britannica, 1968/1911, 277-288.

Sapolsky, Robert M. *Behave: The Biology of Humans at Our Best and Worst*. New York, NY: Penguin, 2017.

"Saving Your Child from an Opioid Overdose." *60 Minutes, CBS News*, November 18, 2018. Accessed November 18, 2018, https://www.cbsnews.com/news/naloxone-saving-your-child-from-an-opioid-overdose-60-minutes/ .

Schwartz, Bryan. "My View: New Approach Needed for Opioid Epidemic." *Portland Tribune*, July 25, 2017. Accessed August 23, 2018, https://pamplinmedia.com/pt/10-opinion/367132-248727-my-view-new-approach-needed-for-opioid-epidemic- .

Scott, Peter Dale and Jonathan Marshall. *Cocaine Politics: Drugs, Armies, and the CIA in Central America*. Berkeley, CA: University of California Press, 1991.

Selznick, Philip. *The Moral Commonwealth: Social Theory and the Promise of Community*. Berkeley, CA: University of California Press, 1992.

"Senate Passes the Opioid Crisis Response Act of 2018." *Revenue Cycle Advisor*, September 18, 2018. Accessed November 21, 2018, https://revenuecycleadvisor.com/news-analysis/senate-passes-opioid-crisis-response-act-2018 .

Sizer, Theodore R. *Horace's Compromise: The Dilemma of the American High School.* Boston, MA: Houghton Mifflin, 1984.

Steenbergen, James B. "Enlightened Self-Interest." *Learning to Give*, n. d. Accessed February 23, 2020, https://www.learningtogive.org/resources/enlightened-self-interest .

Sugarman, Stephen D. "A New Approach to Tort Doctrine: Taking the Best from Civil Law and Common Law of Canada." No Date. A downloadable document.

"T. J. Hooper Case." *Case Briefs*. No date. Accessed October 11, 2018, https://www.casebriefs.com/blog/law/torts/torts-keyed-to-epstein/the-negligence-issue/the-t-j-hooper-3/ .

Tabb, William K. *The Restructuring of Capitalism in Our Time.* New York, NY: Columbia University Press, 2012.

Thomas, Evan. *Robert Kennedy: His Life.* New York, NY: Simon and Schuster Paperbacks: 2000.

Timmons, Mark. Significance and Systems: Essays on Kant's Ethics (New York, NY: Oxford University Press, 2017.

Toulmin, Stephen. *The Uses of Argument.* London, England: Cambridge University Press, 1969.

Tushnet, Mark V. "Equal Protection." In *The Oxford Companion to the Supreme Court*. Edited by Kermit L. Hall. New York NY: Oxford University Press, 1992, 257-259.

Twain, Mark. *The Adventures of Huckleberry Finn*. Westminster/London, GB: Penguin Classics, 2003/1885.

Tyler, Ralph W. *Basic Principles of Curriculum and Instruction*. Chicago, IL: University of Chicago Press, 1969/1949.

Urofsky, Melvin I. *Louis D. Brandeis: A Life*. New York, NY: Pantheon, 2009.

"U. S. City Sues OxyContin Maker for Contribution to Opioid Crisis." *NPR*. Accessed January 6, 2019, https://www.npr.org/2017/02/03/513196772/u-s-city-sues-oxycontin-maker-for-contributing-to-opiod-crisis .

"U. S. City Sues OxyContin Maker for Contribution to Opioid Crisis." *NPR*, February 3, 2017. Accessed January 6, 2019, https://www.npr.org/2017/02/03/513196772/u-s-city-sues-oxycontin-maker-for-contributing-to-opiod-crisis .

Van Zee, Art. "The Promotion and Marketing of OxyContin: Commercial Triumph, Public Health Tragedy." *American Journal of Public Health*, 99, 2, (February 2009). Abstract accessed December 18, 2019, https://www.ncbi.nlm.nih.gov/pmc/articles/PMC2622774/ .

Veilleux, Jennifer C., Peter J. Colvin, Jennifer Anderson, Catherine York, and Adrienne J. Heinz. "A Review of Opioid Dependence Treatment: Pharmacological and Psychosocial Intervention to Treat Opioid Addiction." *Clinical Psychology Review*, 30, 2 (March 2010).

Abstract accessed August 23, 2018,
https://www.sciencedirect.com/science/article/pii/S0272735809001421.

"*Vosburg v. Putney.*" *Case Briefs.* 86 Wis. 278, 56 N>W> 480, 1893
Wisc. LEXIS 133 (Wis. 1893). No date. Accessed October 18, 2018,
https://www.casebriefs.com/blog/law/torts/torts-keyed-to-
epstein/intentionally-inflicted-harm-the-prima-facie-case-and-
defenses/vosburg-v-putney/ .

Waismann, Clare. "The Devastating Effect of Opioids on Our
Society." *The Hill*, August 26, 2016. Accessed June 18, 2018,
http://thehill.com/blogs/pundits-blog/healthcare/293473-the-
devastating-effect-of-opioids-on-our-society .

"Wealth Inequality in the United States." *Wikipedia.* Accessed on
December 15, 2017,
https://en.wikipedia.org/wiki/Wealth_inequality_in_the_United_States
.

"What Science Tells Us About Opioid Abuse and Addiction." Abuse,
National Institute on Drug, January 27, 2016, Drugabuse.gov. This site
no longer posted.

"Why It Matters," *CBS Sunday Morning Show, CBS News.* November
5, 2018.

Wilde, Marian. "Global Grade: How Do U.S. Students Compare?"
Great Schools, April 2, 2015. Accessed May 12, 2018,
https://www.greatschools.org/gk/articles/u-s-students-compare/ .

Wills, Gary. *Inventing America: Jefferson's Declaration of
Independence.* New York, NY: Vintage, 1978/2018.

"*Yania v. Bigan.*" *Case Briefs. Yania v. Bigan*, 397 Pa. 316, 155 A. 2d 343, 1959 Pa. Lexis 457 (Pa. 1959). No date. Accessed September 26, 2018, https://www.casebriefs.com/blog/law/evidence/evidence-keyed-to-waltz/nonfeasance/yania-v-bigan/ .

Yueh, Linda. W*hat Would the Great Economists Do?: How Twelve Brilliant Minds Would Solve Today's Biggest Problems*. London, UK: Penguin, 2019 (Kindle edition).

www.ingramcontent.com/pod-product-compliance
Lightning Source LLC
Chambersburg PA
CBHW022103280326
41933CB00007B/235